A TIME TO JUMP

A TIME TO JUMP

JONATHAN EDWARDS

THE AUTHORIZED BIOGRAPHY
OF AN OLYMPIC CHAMPION

Malcolm Folley

HarperCollins*Publishers*

HarperCollins*Publishers*
77–85 Fulham Palace Road, London W6 8JB
www.fireandwater.com

First published in Great Britain in 2000
by HarperCollins*Publishers*
This edition 2001

1 3 5 7 9 10 8 6 4 2

Scripture quotations are taken from the HOLY BIBLE,
NEW INTERNATIONAL VERSION. Copyright © 1973,
1978, 1984 by International Bible Society

Malcolm Folley asserts the moral right to be identified
as the author of this work

A catalogue record for this book is available from the
British Library

ISBN 0 00 274072 9

Printed and bound in Great Britain by
Omnia Books Ltd, Glasgow

There is a time for everything,
and a season for every activity under heaven:
a time to be born and a time to die,
a time to plant and a time to uproot,
a time to kill and a time to heal,
a time to tear down and a time to build,
a time to weep and a time to laugh,
a time to mourn and a time to dance,
a time to scatter stones and a time to gather them,
a time to embrace and a time to refrain,
a time to search and a time to give up,
a time to keep and a time to throw away,
a time to tear and a time to mend,
a time to be silent and a time to speak,
a time to love and a time to hate,
a time for war and a time for peace.

I know that everything God does will endure for ever;
nothing can be added to it and nothing taken from it.
God does it so that men will revere him.

ECCLESIASTES 3:1–8, 14

Contents

Acknowledgements

I am indebted to Jonathan Edwards and his wife Alison, without whose co-operation, understanding and enormous assistance this book could not have been written. They embraced this project with open minds and open hearts. When we began working together we had an acquaintance; now we are friends.

Thanks, in no particular order, to all those who shared time and valuable experiences: Reverend Andy Edwards and his wife Jill, Tim and Anna Edwards, Rachel Edwards, Ralph and Anne Biggs, Brendan Foster, Roger Black, Kriss Akabusi, Norman Anderson, John Hedley, Jonathan Marks, Andy Norman, Phil Wall, Carl Johnson, Brian Wellman, Dick Booth, Rogel Nahum, Jo Svarovsky, Michael Downward, Lawrence Whittal-Williams, Graham Rainey, Martin Robbie, Steve Ojomoh, Chris Ponder, David Clark, Tony Davis, Steve Backley, Jan Pospisil, Val Davison, John Crotty, Patrick Collins, Colin Hart, Willie Banks and all those connected with Christians in Sport. Thanks also to Sheila Elliott, Linda, Pam and Jennie who so painstakingly transcribed hours of taped interviews.

I am grateful to the *Mail on Sunday* Sports Editor Dan Evans and his deputy David Walker for their support and patience.

Last, but definitely not least, I wish to thank my in-laws Vyvyenne and Peter Kingman for materializing from Wilt-shire at the sound of a telephone call; and thanks most of all to Rachel, and our daughters Sian and Megan, for inspiration, encouragement and for letting me make believe I was invisible.

Malcolm Folley
West Horsley
January 2001

Foreword

'Daddy, when I grow up I want to be…' Parents are used to hearing their children articulate such desires. Whether it be their favourite footballer or the latest pop sensation, youngsters seem instinctively to look for role models; it is part of growing up and we only hope that they choose well.

Early in 1996, my two-and-a-half-year-old son Sam came up to me and said, 'Daddy, when I grow up I want to be Jonathan Edwards.' I took him on my lap and replied, 'But Sam, *I* am Jonathan Edwards.'

Needless to say, the television in our household had been tuned to all the major athletics events during the summer of 1995 and Sam had watched most of them. 'On the runway now, world record holder Jonathan Edwards … it's a massive jump; Jonathan Edwards has broken the record again … and in first place, and the new world champion [you've guessed it] – Jonathan Edwards!'

At such a tender age Sam inevitably had difficulty in grasping that this man he kept seeing on the television screen was also the man who changed his nappy. He was not the only Edwards to fall victim to this crisis of identity; but I did not have the excuse of age.

Most of us know the joke about the man who was standing behind the door when the brains were being handed out. Conversely, I have this nagging doubt that I was mistakenly ushered to the rear of the queue that included the likes of Carl Lewis and Michael Johnson. Only, it is my judgement that God does not play dice. Which is just as well. Because without the belief that it was God who gave me both an ability to triple jump and the sense of vocation to foster that talent, it is unlikely that I would be sitting here today composing the foreword to my biography – the biography of a triple jump world record holder.

And this faith has continued to be the mainspring of my athletic endeavours. A substantial minority considers that this commitment has proved more hindrance than help to my progression: initially through my refusal to jump on Sundays, latterly for want of ruthless ambition. I am content to receive such criticism, if indeed it is meant that way. It is more important to me to be a faithful follower of Christ than an all-conquering sportsman. If there has been no clear witness to that, then I have uttered many empty words regarding the heartbeat of my life.

My aspiration is to have 'walked the walk' and I invite you to judge whether it is a hope that is able to bear the scrutiny of biography. It has not always been easy. It is a path that has at once offered clarity and confusion, love and hatred, triumph and humiliation; a path that has furnished untold fulfilment alongside excruciating conflict; a path that has taught me you cannot have all the answers.

Mercifully, the regrets are few and far between, and they mostly involve cars! I have been the semi-willing victim of great self-deception in the transport sector as I have pursued its twin vanities of status and speed; and I have paid for it – literally. More seriously, I trust that this book will not itself become a cause for self-reproach. Alison and I still vividly recall the response that Kriss Akabusi's wife, Monika, gave us in reply to a question about Kriss's own book. 'With hindsight, would you do it again?' we asked. With little hesitation, she said, 'No.'

I am sure, however, this will not be the case. Indeed, as I pen these words, I can only say that the effects have been beneficial, notwithstanding the late-night editing sessions. In rehearsing the past, the future has become more transparent.

I have represented my country at three Olympic Games, and a fourth beckons. I am under no illusions. The evaluation of my career as an athlete will be tied inextricably to my performance in Sydney. I possess the physical ability to have dominated the triple jump event since my breakthrough in 1995. This book will tell you that I have not done so.

Moreover, although it is extremely difficult to judge oneself with objectivity, I am willing to speculate that winning the Olympics is more important to me than I care to admit. And here, perhaps, we arrive at the root of my inner conflicts – the tension between the reality of the person I am and the one I would like to be. Success and its attendant bedfellows have uncovered vistas of temptation which have struck more than a few nerves.

So I stand at the beginning of the final chapter with a greater awareness of both my spiritual frailties and the magnitude of the athletic challenge ahead. The former's resolution is of the utmost importance, but is not mutually exclusive to the pursuit of the latter. Indeed, they are inseparably coupled. It has ever been so.

Sydney, here I come. So much for the identity crisis.

Sydney has now famously come and gone. The British Olympic Team performed better that anyone could have forecasted, and even I managed to win one of those global titles that, apparently, have been mine for the taking in the post-Gothenburg era!

I am penning these few lines in the lead up to Christmas, and already the Olympics are a distant memory, as if the events surrounding the Games happened in another lifetime, and to another person. Seems to be a familiar theme … though this is probably the best way for it to be. If it were otherwise, I would be in grave danger of believing my own propaganda.

This past year has been an intensely personal and private affair for Alison and I as we have tried to meet the challenge of her mum's death, and my quest to win the Olympics. We both now feel some of the exhaustion and detachment that often follow the cessation of prolonged and concentrated activity. We also moved house on my return from Sydney, so I am sure that you can empathize with our frequent desire to simply close the door on the outside world, catch our breath, and do some decorating!

One of the questions most often asked of me since the Games has been: 'What are you going to do now?' It is a question that has irritated me from the start. The wise king Solomon suggested this: 'Everyone should eat, drink, and enjoy the good of his labour – it is the gift of God.' And I intend to do just that, albeit in moderation as I would like to vaguely resemble an Olympic Champion when I compete in 2001! In our achievement-oriented culture, it is all too easy to forgot to celebrate what we have achieved, before moving on to the next challenge.

In reality, though, being Olympic Champion changes nothing for me. As much as I love it, athletics is only the context in which I work out my commitment to Christ. And when these legs will no longer propel me towards, and even beyond, 18 metres, that devotion will be worked out in a different arena.

Thirteen years ago I boarded a train bound for Newcastle, unprepared for real life, armed 'only' with a child-like trust in my God. He has not let me down, and I hope I will not let him down.

Thanks

To Alison and the boys, for more than I could ever express in words.

To my Dad and Mum, for giving me the kind of upbringing that all children deserve and having the courage to support my attempt to become a triple jumper after all the sacrifices they made to educate me.

To West Buckland School for that education.

To Carl Johnson, Norman Anderson, Peter Stanley, Mark Byron, John Hedley, Andy Norman, John Crotty, Lawrence Whittal-Williams, Brendan Foster, all the guys at Gateshead International Stadium and the many others who have enabled me to develop my athletic ability.

To all my friends, who have given more to me than I to them.

To the Christian community, who have supported and encouraged me tremendously.

Finally, to Malcolm, who wrote this book. For his belief in and commitment to the project; for his sensitivity and insight; for his grace in the face of extreme provocation – the interference of a sportsman on points of grammar and style! But above all, for his friendship; there would have been no book without this.

Jonathan Edwards
January 2001

Chapter 1

Spanish Inquisition

---

*Life breaks us all … but some of us are made
stronger at the broken places.*

ERNEST HEMINGWAY

He looked like a man who had walked from the wreck-
age of a train crash, not climbed out of a sandpit.
Instinctively, the director responsible for television coverage on that airless, stinking hot summer's night in the
Estadio Olimpico in Seville kept his cameras trained on
Jonathan Edwards. As Edwards trekked slowly down the
track, a camera pierced his face and probed him like a
searchlight. What we saw in those long, penetrative, close-
up images was a man ghostly pale; a man haunted by his
past, ridiculed by the present and fearful of the future.

Out of shot, a young woman could watch his anguish
no more. Down on the track, Edwards was seen beckoning
her with his open palm. She ran to position herself
behind the advertising hoarding separating the sandpit
from the public. She held her arms open and Edwards fell
into them, his tears dampening her reddish hair. For
moments, for an eternity, Edwards clung to her like a man

1

clinging to a life belt in rough seas. As photographers surrounded them, he sobbed an apology into the woman's ear. 'I'm sorry,' he said repeatedly, but Alison Edwards was already reassuring her husband that the result was unimportant.

She had flown into the Spanish city the day before with her parents-in-law Reverend Andy Edwards and his wife Jill, and they had travelled with optimism and belief. It was not the reunion Edwards had planned for Alison or his watching parents. For the previous 12 months he had dedicated his life obsessively, selfishly, to winning a gold medal in the triple jump at the seventh IAAF World Championships, Athletics Sevilla '99; and now he was coming to terms with his failure.

He was crying not entirely through self-pity. His tears were also for Alison. For months she had known that her mother Anne was dying from a brain tumour and Edwards had wanted a gold medal in Seville for his wife. 'I did not want her to have to deal with any more disappointment,' he said when we met the next evening for dinner at the Bar Gonzalo, an unpretentious restaurant with tables spilling onto the pavement in the ancient walled quarter of the city.

Edwards had seen a gold medal at the World Championships as tangible vindication for his commitment to his profession. Now that he owned a bronze medal, the hours, days and weeks he had spent away from Alison and their two young sons, Sam and Nathan, seemed to all real purpose a pointless and wasted exercise. 'Alison is devastated about her Mum and I have been worried about the World Championships. Is that right?' he asked.

For Edwards, the answer was abundantly clear. 'I've not really been supporting Alison, yet when I needed her she was here for me. We have been a little bit in our own corners; she's been concerned about her Mum and I've been preoccupied with my athletics. I was wrapped in myself. Yet I had this sense of peace beforehand, a feeling that I was going to win. I felt how I did when I broke the world record and won the World Championships in Gothenburg in 1995; it was going to be my night, *my* night. Being beaten like I was is a shock. I liken it to when York Minster was hit by lightning when there wasn't a cloud in the sky. I was hit, bang, out of the blue.'

The analogy was chosen with care. His faith is the heartbeat of his life and he has always interpreted his athletic prowess as a gift from God. In the immediate aftermath of his professionally dispiriting evening in Seville, Edwards felt a profound and unexpected calm. 'I feel God has spoken to me very clearly through this and I believe it's probably the best thing that could have happened,' he explained. He acted swiftly and in accordance with the message he heard.

His carefully organized training schedule for the Olympic Games in Sydney in September 2000 – effectively the final meaningful competition of his life – was instantly shredded. He had been intending to spend three weeks in November 1999 in a training camp in Sierra Nevada, Spain; he had a further two weeks' training in winter sunshine pencilled in for Lanzarote in December, with additional fly-away camps proposed in South Africa and Morocco in the early months of 2000. Instead, Edwards committed to remaining at home in the Northeast of England for the winter to train at Gateshead Stadium, just a 15-minute drive from his home in Gosforth. He would not bemoan the isolation, nor complain about the biting wind that at times seems to arrive from the Arctic. 'I have been challenged and I have to be here for Alison. It's not like we've been fighting, but emotionally there has been a detachment. We love each other deeply and we're very close and rely on each other a lot. To the outside world, there would not seem to be anything wrong, but it has been a big issue.'

On that night in Seville, and in the days afterwards, Edwards came to understand much about himself and the spiritual path he has set. Unlike most athletes, the accumulation of wealth and fame were never Edwards' primary motives for being a sportsman. As the son of an Anglican vicar, he felt he was answering a calling to be an evangelist, a witness to God in running spikes. As a young, unknown athlete, Edwards first attracted headlines not for his jumping, but for his non-jumping. He would not compete on a Sunday and many people, tired of the self-aggrandizement of footballers earning thousands of pounds a week, tired of the tantrums of tennis players who become millionaires before their twenty-first birthdays, applauded this man of rare principle. Even though over seven years have elapsed since Edwards re-evaluated his position and found it possible, in his own mind, to jump on a Sunday without compromising his faith, he is still remembered wherever he travels for the stance he adopted. 'It still amazes me,' he says. 'It's a subject that is always brought up, no matter where I am in the world.'

Never in those long-ago days, when he said 'Never on a Sunday', did he suspect for a moment that he would hold the world record with a phenomenal leap of 18.29 metres. Even now that feat, accomplished in Gothenburg in 1995, might be interpreted as a flight of fantasy. He could never have supposed in his wildest dreams that he would be named BBC Sports Personality of the Year.

Yet he had flown – and the word is not inappropriate when Edwards leaves the take-off board – and performed with such grace, charm, humility and old-fashioned decency that he sprang into the consciousness of a nation until then blissfully ignorant about the science of the triple jump. Suddenly, retired footballer Gary Lineker and Rob Andrew, late of the England Rugby Union team, were being challenged for the title of the sportsman most mothers would like their daughters to bring home.

While Edwards enjoyed the initial acclaim – and who would not have done? – he could never have anticipated the conflict his success would introduce into his daily life. 'Alison has said she feels we have created this monster that we cannot control any more,' he says. 'It's grown out of all proportion. I mean, it was a zero to hero scenario; I never envisaged it was going to be anything like this. Not for me, a triple jumper.'

Edwards had mesmerized maiden aunts in the Cotswolds and won the approval of working men in the Northeast, hard-living men accustomed to confining their sporting idols to those who wear the black-and-white stripes of Newcastle United. Here was a man who was a Christian by faith and a Corinthian by attitude, but here, also, was a man and his family totally unprepared for stardom. There is no known degree course and Edwards has had to learn about the pitfalls and try to side-step them as he has gone along. He has made some mistakes, but through the trials and tribulations of his career Edwards has retained his reputation as a man of honour, courteous and incorruptible. At 33 years old, he felt he had some perspective on his career and life. Then his mother-in-law was diagnosed as terminally ill and he realized he had not.

For Edwards the defeat in Spain in August 1999, and his wife's fears for her sick mother, left him to contemplate more than his jumping technique and training programme. As we dined at one of the pavement tables at Bar Gonzalo, Edwards sipped a glass of Rioja and let his mind wander through time. He recalled how in the afterglow of his world-record-breaking triumph, when he redefined the parameters of triple jumping, he had pledged that his ambition was to be a good husband and father. 'Perhaps,' he said, 'I have failed those ideals and aspirations. Possibly, the realization that I am get-ting to the end of my career has made me more obsessive, made me think only of the World Championships and the Olympics.'

He no longer recognized, or especially liked, the man he had unwittingly become. 'Obviously I want to win the gold medal at the Olympics in Sydney. What happened in Seville showed me I have to work on my technique, but it has also shown me I don't want to be this hard-hearted, selfish athlete disregarding all other things. I will train as hard as I can, but if I can't win the Olympics without being selfish, then I can't win. If I'm using my athletic gift as part of my service to God, I can't be selfish because that would be completely contradictory.' For Edwards this amounted to an extraordinary change of philosophy. Only months before he had been talking earnestly about having to become so focused as an athlete that his family would have to grow accustomed to his absences until after the Sydney Olympics were over.

Edwards was required that evening in Seville, and through long conversations with Alison and close friends over the following week, to pose some hard questions of himself, to try to fathom where God was in all of this. Others from outside his circle were more simplistic. At 33,

Edwards was deemed by the majority of the newspaper critics in Seville to be an athlete past his best, something of which he was bluntly informed by one journalist. 'A well-meaning Japanese sportswriter said to me as I left the arena, "You're just too old." I know there will be many who think that.' Earlier in the summer Colin Hart, a veteran and much respected reporter of the old school, whose values have never been diluted by the crash-bang-wallop demands of the *Sun*, had observed, 'Very few people can defy nature. I hope I am wrong – I'd love him to win gold in Sydney – but I think Jonathan, a thoroughly good, honest man, has had his time. He isn't going to get better at 33 than he was at his peak four years earlier in 1995.'

The argument has a validity Edwards understands, but does not accept. 'Age is not a factor,' he said, smiling engagingly as he signed an autograph for an English-woman who had come to our table to tell him how much her 11-year-old son admired him. Edwards' hair is splashed grey, but he is lean and supple; and he had shown 24 hours before that he was still astonishingly fast down the runway, visibly faster than any of his competitors. 'Of course, what I achieved in Gothenburg gets a more distant memory, but in the end that doesn't matter. All that matters is what shape I'm in now, how mentally sharp I feel. I know how close I was to landing a big, big jump, but the fact that I didn't had nothing to do with my age. This is a fickle event. Everything is on a knife edge.'

Not least Edwards himself. 'I probably give the impression of being quite independently capable, but in reality I'm more vulnerable than I'd like to think.' His vulnerability is transparent to Roger Black, an Olympic silver medallist turned broadcaster. For years Black travelled with

Edwards, often sharing a room with him in the British team's quarters and frequently engaging in cerebral combat across a chessboard. 'Jonathan became very good–so quickly, but he was still Jonathan,' says Black. 'He was still a devout Christian and his principles, his morals, didn't revolve around being very rich, didn't revolve around being famous. They revolved about his wife, his kids, his church and his friends. Jonathan never looked like a superstar, never thought he would be one, like say Daley Thompson and Linford Christie did. But then he started making a lot of money. He was incredibly famous and all he did was jump into a sandpit. It just didn't weigh up.' Black repeats the sentiment for emphasis: 'It just didn't weigh up. He wasn't built for that sort of fame. I think it put him under a lot of pressure and I think the question he needed to ask was this: "Why do I need to succeed?"'

Black remains to be convinced that Edwards knows the answer to that. Is his faith, the idea that he is jumping for the Lord, an invisible barrier preventing him from making the most of his genuine athletic abilities? Has he entrusted in God at the expense of developing his technique? Is he inwardly disturbed by his wealth? While he is unembarrassed to strike a hard bargain for his appearance at an event, while he studies the small print before he places his signature on a contract, there is evidence to suggest that he is uncomfortable with having more money than he ever imagined. Edwards will argue that he has addressed all these factors and he will confess there has been spiritual conflict, a conflict that on occasions has confounded him. 'Maybe I have underachieved these past few years, but there are many reasons for that,' he says.

Unquestionably, he has been troubled by a catalogue of injuries. By the pounding nature of the event, all triple jumpers are susceptible to those. 'How hard is the event on the body?' I ask Brian Wellman, an athlete from Bermuda who won the silver medal behind Edwards in Gothenburg. 'It feels like going to the second storey of your apartment and jumping off the porch,' he says. 'And you do that six times in a competition, without taking into account the times you do it in practice. So, yes, it's like mini car wrecks, I would say.'

Even so, Edwards would not excuse his record in the prestigious championships solely on the grounds of the succession of injuries which have plagued him down the years. The harsh facts are that in the years since Edwards broke the world record in 1995, since he threatened to dominate his event for Britain like Steve Ovett and Sebastian Coe once dominated middle-distance running, he has failed to win gold at the three most important championships. He won a courageous silver medal at the Atlanta Olympic Games in 1996, an unsatisfactory silver medal at the World Championships in Athens a year later, and a disappointing bronze in Seville. 'It crossed my mind to throw the bronze away; certainly it was in my pocket before I left the podium. If I consider my potential superiority over my rivals, then the years since 1995 have not brought me the success we might all have expected.'

Athletically, all that counts for him now, really counts, is his performance at the Olympic Games in Sydney in September 2000. Everything else is a rehearsal. But his mind was opened to a stark realization on that sultry evening in Seville, when he felt compelled to delve deep within himself. 'Perhaps I'm not some specially anointed messenger of God after all,' he said then. 'Maybe I've harboured illusions of the importance of what I'm doing. I always believed God chose me to be an athlete, that with all the ups and downs that occur, it was still going to be onwards and upwards. I'm starting to wonder if that is necessarily the case. Perhaps in the past that belief has even been the inspiration to carry on, the belief that there is likely to be something better around the corner. But there are no guarantees, no assurances about the Olympics. I know I can win the gold medal, but I no longer feel it's my destiny. It may not be. A verse of Proverbs talks of the horse being prepared for the day of battle, but victory belongs to the Lord.'

Nonetheless, those words, raw and sharp-edged in the hours after a disappointing defeat, should not confuse or be taken in isolation from the broad context of Edwards' faith. He willingly confesses that for a period he found a futility in what he was doing, sensing that the vital connection between being an athlete and being a Christian had been severed. The low point occurred in 1997. 'I saw where I'd gone wrong. I became an athlete because I thought that was what God wanted me to do and I felt I'd lost sight of that.' He searched for a solution. After much deliberation he changed church, and by the end of that troublesome year he felt he had rediscovered the link between jumping and sharing his faith. 'One of the specific decisions I made was to be involved in more evangelistic work. That has made a real difference. When I use the opportunities my fame has afforded me to share the gospel, I know I'm fulfilling God's will. It's a fundamental Christian responsibility to proclaim the truth that God loves the world and Jesus Christ died for our sins and rose again. I do think that's a good reason to believe that God has allowed me to be successful. He has given me the ability to be a good athlete, but with the ability is a big responsibility.'

Edwards' faith is entrenched, then; but his challenge is to establish a balance between that and the triple jump. 'I am sure that some part of Alison wishes I wasn't an athlete,' he acknowledges. 'Some sacrifices are easy; some are a decision of will. For Alison, they are mostly a decision of will. I would say it gets harder every year. That night in Seville, as we lay in bed I can remember saying, "What was that all about?" I desperately wanted to win for Alison; I was in fantastic shape and ready to jump miles. With Alison's mother dying from a brain tumour, what further motivation did I need? We were just trying to make some sense of all this. It's easy to talk in general terms, but when it applies to you, it takes on a whole new meaning. You think, "God loves me, so why can't I win the World Championships for Alison? Why can't her Mum be healed?" Of course, if all Christians were to win, if all sick people were cured, you would live a life of constant victory over daily circumstances, which is not what the Bible teaches us to expect. Perhaps I'm just a good athlete and there's nothing more or less miraculous about my story. I think God has given me a profound gift, an amazing opportunity to share my faith through that gift, but I'm not sure I still feel that same sense of destiny that I had before.'

His wife's presence in Seville was critically important to Edwards, widening his vision beyond the runway. In public, Alison Edwards is a resilient, unaffected woman, a pillar for the family, as all their friends will tell you, and as she heartrendingly illustrated in the stadium as she hugged her husband and smothered him with consoling words while he fought in vain to stem his tears. She is not remotely interested in reflected glory. In private, she confesses to being disillusioned at times; not ungrateful for the rewards of the track, but resentful of Edwards' self-absorption. 'I get annoyed sometimes when he is very focused on his athletics. Sometimes it's all him, him, him, and we do take a back seat,' she says. 'But sometimes, I suppose it has to be like that.'

Alison is a pragmatic woman, practical and caring. This is no less than you would expect of a girl brought up with two sisters on the Isle of Lewis in the Hebrides, in a household where her father Ralph was a port missionary. Her faith is fundamental to her life, too. Her challenge in the summer of 1999 was daunting and unenviable; she was dealing with the terrible agony of watching her mother die, while trying not to burden her husband with her grief.

'I think everything else is slightly meaningless at the moment,' Alison said, as we sat in the lounge of the family's large, semi-detached home a few weeks before the World Championships. Her mother had undergone surgery on the tumour in November 1998 and she was sufficiently fit to share a Mediterranean cruise with her husband in June 1999. Yet the family were soon confronted with the awful news that Anne was experiencing a relapse and the symptoms were ominous. A scan in early August brought confirmation that the tumour had recurred. Three days later, Jonathan left Alison in Gosforth to go to a prearranged, week-long training camp in Nymburk in the Czech Republic. 'As a husband I should be looking after my wife; as an athlete I have to prepare for the World Championships,' he would say, encapsulating his dilemma.

If Alison was upset, she successfully disguised her emotions. 'I know it's hard for Jonathan too,' she said with predictable loyalty when we were alone two months before she came to Seville. 'He's got to support me through this and, at the same time, try to compete. It's a nightmare really. I would love to see him do well. He works hard and takes his preparation all very seriously. Ultimately, though, Jonathan can walk away and know that whether he jumps 18.99 metres or 16.98 metres, it isn't going to fundamentally change who he is, or what he believes in. But that's the foundation upon which he does everything and it does affect him on a day-to-day basis. So much is asked of him: he's being a father, he's being a husband, he's being an athlete, he's being a star, he's being a Christian, and I think he does remarkably well. But sometimes, I can't help thinking that since Gothenburg, when that wonderful thing happened to us, it has been all too much to bear. It's the standard by which he is judged and nothing comes up to that.'

Certainly the World Championships in Seville did not. For Alison, the business of being in the stadium when her husband is competing is never an experience she relishes. In Spain, her torment was hard to witness. She sat with her husband's parents, some 10 rows back from the track and almost parallel to where the organizers had placed the letters 'WR' beyond the 18 metre mark alongside the sandpit. The marker showed the current world record, the record held by her husband. Reverend Andy Edwards, in baggy polo shirt and shorts, an unrecognizable figure to his parishioners at home in Cumbria, had a small camera strung round his neck. His wife Jill wore a pink and blue checked summer dress as though ready to attend a garden fête.

In front of the main grandstand on the other side of the track Haile Gebreselassie was collecting his gold medal for winning the 10,000 metres, but the Edwards family were not watching the ceremony. Their eyes were focused on

Jonathan, loosening up near the start of the triple jump runway. He was wearing No 525 on his bib and if you looked through binoculars you could see he was moistening his lips with his tongue. He was drawn to compete second, behind Australian Andrew Murphy and before the men he considered his principal rivals, Yoelbi Quesada from Cuba and the Russian Denis Kapustin. Alison tried to make light conversation. 'At least this is better than Barcelona; at least we've got to see him,' she smiled. Seven years earlier, she had arrived in Barcelona a few hours after her husband had been unexpectedly eliminated from the Olympic Games in the qualifying round. She had not returned to a major championships until now.

Her unease was evident, and when Edwards ran through his first jump, aborting after over-rotating as he attempted the first phase, the hop, Alison's frayed nerves were stretched to near breaking point. Edwards, you could see, was not much calmer. As he planned his next jump, he was pacing backwards and forwards over the same two metres of ground beside the runway as though he was testing an Axminster for wear. Across the track, Colin Jackson went to his blocks for the 110 metre hurdles. Swoooosh, and Jackson breasted the line to reclaim the World Championship gold he last held in 1993. Edwards and Jackson had spoken a couple of days earlier in the British team hotel, speculating which one of them might become the first British athlete to regain a world title. Edwards knew he had to jump big in the first round if he was going to pip Jackson, still to go to his blocks. That proved a forlorn hope and Jackson would soon pass him on his lap of honour. The Welshman stopped for long enough within earshot of Edwards to yell some encouragement.

14

Edwards appreciated the gesture, though his facial expression never changed. He wore the look of a man awaiting sentence at the Old Bailey. He finds it galling to be told that he might jump better if he was to smile more often, as he had on that fabled night in Gothenburg. 'I've always been uptight when I jump,' he would insist later. 'But all people can remember is that I smiled on the runway at the beginning of my second jump in Gothenburg. I'd already jumped a world record, I'd won the competition – is it a surprise I had a smile on my face? But normally I'm uptight and nervous; to think I could be anything else is utter nonsense.'

For Edwards on this night in Seville, the target had been established by the first-round jump of Rostislav Dimitrov. The Bulgarian leapt 17.49 metres, which was 18 centimetres further than he had ever jumped before. To an athlete of the calibre of Edwards, the distance was hardly exceptional. He removed his tracksuit trousers and began thrusting his arms backwards and forwards in violent-looking semaphore. He went to his starting position and slapped his hands above his head, demanding that the crowd join him. Edwards rocked on his heels in unison to the rhythmic clapping, once, twice, three, four times and then exploded down the runway to a huge roar. He took off and this time there was a synchronization to his movement and when he landed in the pit Edwards knew he was in contention.

Over the public address system came the information that he had jumped 17.48 metres and in the grandstand Reverend Edwards released a slow smile, although it was apparent that neither Alison nor Jill were feeling any more comfortable. When Edwards aborted his third-round jump, the two women vanished into the bowels of the stadium to go for a walk to an undisclosed destination. Anywhere without a view of the track was fine with them. Alison could not erase from her mind the words her six-year-old son Sam had said on the telephone to her that morning. 'I'm so nervous about the competition,' he had declared. His prescience was uncanny.

Although Quesada, the defending champion, and Kapustin, the only man to have beaten Edwards in 1999, were eliminated at this halfway stage of the competition, the Englishman was looking far from convincing. His position deteriorated in the fourth round when Germany's Charles Michael Friedek catapulted from the pit to celebrate a jump of 17.59 metres. Ironically, when asked before the event to name his three most feared rivals, Friedek had replied, 'Edwards, Edwards and Edwards.' Now the German was fearing no one.

Reverend Edwards made a request for his bag to be policed as he too left the stadium. Out of sight, he joined hands with Jill and Alison in prayer. Down on the track, Edwards was saying prayers of his own. 'It's a normal part of competition for me.' His fourth-round jump was a poor 16.84 metres and in the seats near the start of the runway various delegates had gathered to impart advice, with the best of intentions. Linford Christie and Fatima Whitbread, past Olympic medallists, showered him with encouragement; Israeli triple jumper Rogel Nahum, a friend who had not qualified for the final, tried to pacify him; Andy Norman, the former overlord of British athletics, now an independent promoter and agent responsible for Edwards' calendar, told him that the only person who could beat him was himself. It is a conviction Norman has always held and when he heard later that Edwards was not entirely comfortable with the new shoes his Japanese manufacturers Asics had provided, he said gruffly, 'Jonathan is good enough to have beaten that lot wearing the box the shoes came in.' Edwards is used to such homilies from Norman and does not take offence. Indeed, he would endorse the view over dinner 24 hours later. 'I should have won hands down.'

On the track when it mattered, however, Edwards could not find any rhythm in his approach to the board. He had been preparing all winter, all summer for this night and now he was reduced to two jumps. Two jumps to make some sense of his dedication, to provide some small compensation for all the hours and days when Alison had been left through professional necessity to deal with her own inner suffering. His body language was overtly aggressive; before his penultimate jump, Edwards most uncharacteristically threw his T-shirt at the bench where the athletes store their clothes. Sadly, his technique could not equal his raging ambition and his fifth attempt was what triple jumpers call a run-through. He ran rather than jumped into the sand and when he came out he cast a disconsolate glance at his father. By now, Alison and Jill were encamped in the dark tunnel that led from the grandstand to the stadium exit. They were looking for a miracle, and on this night they were in short supply.

As can happen in athletic arenas when so many events occur at the same time, we were soon distracted by loud cheering from the British contingent of fans around the stadium. Dean Macey, a 21-year-old from Canvey Island, had just run a superbly disciplined 1500 metres to win the silver medal in the decathlon, the event once the dominion of Daley Thompson. Macey jogged past the sandpit draped in a Union flag as the photographers demand. Here before us was a young man for whom a silver medal at the World Championships was the stuff of fairy tales; and not 10 metres away from Macey was Edwards, staring at the probability of winning bronze and feeling he was the victim of his own worst athletic nightmare.

Edwards had one, final jump in reserve. He waited impatiently for the pit to be raked clean, then clapped his hands and clenched his fist. Alison was unable to look. His speed down the runway was impressive, as it had been all competition, but his positioning at take-off left him with little chance of executing the kind of jump that we know he is capable of producing. He would discover a week later that his run-up had been affected by the size of his latest shoes, smaller by one centimetre, causing the measurement of his 18-pace run-up to be around one metre short. This meant his body position was too far forward on take-off, hence the debacle that followed. On the night he was oblivious to such detail and was simply overwrought by his performance.

As Edwards excavated himself from the pit that final time – officially the jump was measured at 16.94 metres, though he had only gone through the motions – Reverend Edwards looked lovingly down on his son. He shrugged his shoulders and summoned a smile. His son walked away, hands on his hips, a confused, bewildered and despondent man. Then Edwards thought of Alison, he thought of her anguish and came walking back down the runway where moments before he had been sprinting. Seconds later, husband and wife were entwined beside the track and the cameramen came running. They knew, as we all knew, that the image of Jonathan and Alison weeping and expressing their heartfelt love for each other was one that would endure long after Friedek's winning jump had been forgotten.

Later that evening, Edwards visited his parents' hotel room and broke down again. 'I still couldn't believe what had happened. Like Alison, Mum and Dad had been forced to watch me have my guts ripped out, my abject failure. I was so aware how difficult it must have been to watch their boy go through such agony. I knew it would break my heart if I had to watch my children, Sam or Nathan, go through the same ordeal.'

The next morning Edwards breakfasted with his wife and parents, then arrived to meet the British media at an Asics-hosted press conference in a marquee erected in a children's nursery across the road from the Estadio Olimpico. The setting was surreal, the conference bordering on the amateurish. Edwards was asked if retirement was an option, and once he had reassured the athletics correspondents that he would remain on the road to Sydney they ceased questioning him. They had their story for the day and he was called Dean Macey, the unlikely hero from Canvey Island.

Edwards broke quietly away to wish Alison, a nervous flier, and his parents a safe journey back to England, before returning to the city to meet Andy Norman. Business had to go on as normal. A few hours later, Edwards visited the Estadio Olimpico again to fulfil a promise to appear live on the Italian national television station Rai. On the roadside, a sign told us that the temperature was 41 °C. The heat Edwards felt could not be measured in Celsius or Fahrenheit, but astonishingly his mood was light and he would not let the Italian broadcasters down. The previous evening, as he trudged forlornly from the track, he had given interrogators from BBC Television, Eurosport and BBC Radio Five Live barely audible, monosyllabic responses. He had been on autopilot. Now, he sat in Rai's beautifully understated makeshift studio in the roof of the stadium, chatted gamely and waited for his answers to be translated, even though there seemed neither rhyme nor reason for his appearance. Can you imagine Des Lynam interviewing an Italian jumper 24 hours after he had won a bronze medal? Perhaps Edwards' image was the reason for his appearance; perhaps being a nice guy, a man of easy disposition, was attraction enough. There seemed no other logical answer.

As we left the stadium to go for dinner, he was soon surrounded by people arriving for the evening's programme. 'Meester Edwaaards, Meester Edwaaards! Sign pleees!' Of course, he stopped to give autographs and pose for photographs and he could not resist saying, 'Imagine if I'd won...' The reality was, however, that Edwards had never looked remotely like winning and as we washed down some prosciutto and cheese with our Rioja, he disclosed that he had discussed his defeat with his room-mate Steve Backley, a friend and javelin thrower of distinction. 'I agree with Steve when he says that we have this idea that we can control our destiny when, in truth, we are as vulnerable as egg shells. We are subject to all sorts of emotion swings, subject to time and to chance. Steve also expressed the feeling that, though consciously you think you want something, your subconscious is telling you it's better not to have it now. In other words, Steve was saying that by not winning the World Championships you would go to the Olympics more determined. What might seem bad now is actually good. To be honest, I don't buy that!'

Yet Edwards admitted that there was no adrenaline surge in the stadium, no passion about his performance after the third round, and that mystified him. 'On the night something in my heart was not touched by what I was doing. In my head, I wanted to be world champion. But in my heart, I don't know. I knew the sense of emptiness I would feel if I didn't win – I've experienced that before – and I know what it's like to be fêted as a champion. I had that in Gothenburg with bells on. It's great. Yet if I didn't want to win, why did I react as I did after I lost?'

During dinner Edwards feasted on beef casserole and wished, just once, he could rebel against his trait for self-analysis. 'Maybe it would be better if I swore, head-butted the wall and got drunk.' He is more likely of course, to dine with the devil.

On returning to his hotel for a last night in Seville, Edwards met Rogel Nahum, the Israeli triple jumper, and Tudor Bidder, the technical director for jumps on the British team. Nahum asked how Edwards was, and was told that everyone had been nice to him. 'I am not here to be nice,' Nahum said. 'Look, Jonathan, you are the best by a mile, you are just not looking like you are. Everyone is trying to jump like you, except you. It's crazy.' Nahum has been a houseguest of the Edwards and he has also hosted his friend in Israel. 'You are not the same person; something has changed,' observed Nahum. 'You are anxious, confused, you are striving too hard. It is not right.' As Edwards reflected later, 'Wounds from a friend can be trusted!' (Proverbs 27:6) Bidder made a similar statement. When he first met Edwards, he said, he presented himself as a man who did not want to travel. 'Now when I speak to you, you're always going somewhere or other.'

The essence of the message Edwards heard in Seville, and in the days after he got home was this: 'You've thrown away a World Championship, which you should have won any way you chose, and we do not want to see you do the same again at the Olympics.'

Edwards could appreciate such sentiments, yet he also felt a strong sense of wellbeing. One door had shut, but another had truly opened and there was a shaft of light where there had been darkness. 'I would have expected weeks, if not months, of soul-searching after Seville, but I don't feel any real scars; in my mind I can see a purpose in what happened. I know I have to be there for Alison.' The dawning of this truth came in time to spare Edwards seriously hard words from another friend, Phil Wall. Like Andy Norman, another man who supports Edwards but does not spare his blushes, Wall was once in the Metropolitan Police Force. It was Edwards' good fortune that Wall came to stay with him on the weekend he came home from Seville.

'I wasn't looking forward to the weekend,' admits Wall. 'Firstly, because Jonathan had lost, I sensed I'd have to pull him out of the depths of despair. Secondly, I knew I was going to have a serious word in his ear about the direction I felt he was going. It needed changing dramatically. It needed changing urgently.' Wall these days is a mission leader in the Salvation Army; his skills are in communication and training. As a man who knows the streets – he was born and brought up in the East End of London and later was a member of the Met's Riot Squad – he is sharp and direct. He is unafraid to tell Edwards what he might not wish to hear.

'One thing I enjoy about my friendship with Jonathan is that it's brutally honest,' he explains. 'Our friendship is not just about his life as an athlete. He's a mate, a buddy, he's a Christian co-worker; and he's a husband and the father of two kids. During what is a very challenging time for his wife I was concerned that he had lost perspective. In conversations we had prior to the World Championships, he was talking about the distractions he was having to deal with that were having an effect on his jumping. What he was not grasping was that Alison couldn't give a toss about a man jumping into a sandpit, because her Mum was battling with a brain tumour. I wanted to share with him the thought that he was losing the perspective. There are some things in life you have to dig deep for, like athletics, and that's fine because as someone who did sport [Wall once boxed for the British Police] I can understand that. Yet on the other hand there are deep covenants and commitments like a marriage and that should take pre-eminence. I felt he'd lost perspective.'

The words were timely and they were confirmation of what Edwards had sensed the moment he fell into his wife's arms at the Estadio Olimpico. Mostly, however, they had impact because they had come from Wall, whose forthright opinions Edwards has respected since the day they met as fellow speakers at an evangelistic, open-air meeting in South Shields in 1992. 'I wake up every day believing we can change the world and I want to give my life to doing that,' says Wall. He is a zestful man, dedicated to social justice, and Edwards finds him attractive and inspirational company. 'In 1995 when Jonathan's world went ballistic with the gold medal, the awards, the MBE, I felt he needed someone who would ask him tough questions.' Wall, 36, has never deviated from that role.

'I think at times Jonathan has gone through waves of insecurity about what he does, asking himself what significance there is in running down a rubber track and jumping into a sandpit, for heaven's sake. Now, I happen to think there is significance, in terms of the fun and hope that he provides for others. But there is more: Jonathan's success, his personality, opens doors.'

During the weekend they spent together on Edwards' return from Seville, Wall spoke sincerely about arranging his timetable to be able to be at the Olympic Games in Sydney in September 2000. 'Sport is so cynical. When you're up people are with you; when you're down no one wants to know you,' argues Wall, and it is not a statement to invite much debate. 'It's just such a negative, insecure culture and part of the British psyche. I said to Jonathan right from the beginning that I wanted to authenticate our friendship. Whether he was a hero on the runway or a dad struggling to be a good father at home with the kids, I was going to be his mate. If we were going to express our genuine Christian faith through our friendship, it needed to be something that wasn't conditional on the fact that he was the man bringing home the gold.

'I think I can play a certain role in Jonathan's life. I do a lot of teaching on leadership and I talked to him over the weekend about what I would call a mentoring network. He has a number of mentors, people to help him with his jumping, people to help with the physical stuff, and I want to help him with his confidence and self-belief – just to be there, come hell or high water, for you, pal. If I can make it happen, practically and financially, I'm going to do my best to be in Sydney for him when he jumps. Put it this way, if he wins the gold, which he is more than capable of doing, he's going to need some mates around him to keep his feet on the ground. If he doesn't, he's going to need some mates to pick him up off the floor. Friendship is about both of those.'

Edwards is gratified by the offer and would welcome Wall's presence in Sydney. He will not expect Alison to be in Australia, though. 'I have no wish to put her through that ordeal again!' he says, and laughs. 'And after previous experience Alison has no intention of going.'

He took a sucker punch in Seville and that opens the door for Edwards to join a club with a long and distinguished membership. From Muhammad Ali to George Best, from Carl Lewis to Ian Botham, from John McEnroe to Michael Schumacher, great champions have had the capacity to fall over their feet once in a while. But Edwards is no longer 25 years old; he no longer possesses the energy or the desire of a young fighter to circumnavigate the globe to restore his pride. His professional focus is to be in the peak of condition, the absolute right frame of mind, for just one more day of his life – the day they stage the triple jump final at the Olympic Games in Sydney.

He will receive an avalanche of advice between now and embarking on the plane for Australia, but he might hear no more sound words than those belonging to Brendan Foster. 'Go and enjoy it, that would be my advice to Jonathan,' suggests Foster, woven into the legend of Northeast athletic circles as an Olympic bronze medallist, television analyst, businessman and, coincidentally, one-time benefactor for Edwards. 'You have been through the turmoil of an Olympic final, you have been world record holder and world champion. You know you are in the record books. Now you should be doing it for the same reasons David Hemery once gave me. He walked into my room for a chat at the Commonwealth Games in 1970 where I was running in my first ever international for England and he was already an Olympic champion. Eventually I asked him why he was still competing. He said, "Because it makes your life more exciting; it's better than sitting and watching." I would say to Jonathan: go to

Sydney, prepare as well as you can, then enjoy it, because you don't owe anybody anything. If Jonathan can overcome gravity, he will be all right. I think – in his words – if God's willing, he'll win.'

Edwards will undoubtedly seek inspiration from his faith, but he was also pledging to spend the winter and spring refining his technique, honing his body to try to crown his career with an Olympic gold medal. 'That is my hope,' he says. While his ambition has not been diminished, however, in the last rites of the summer of 1999 he sounded like a man who had brought home from Spain a legacy more valuable than a gold medal. 'The strength of my marriage and my family life with my boys has to be more important than my sport.'

Chapter 2

In the Beginning

You don't raise heroes, you raise your sons. And if you treat them like sons they'll turn out to be heroes, even if it is just in your own eyes.

WALTER SCIRRA SR

From the school reception, a yellow line has been painted diagonally across the quad. At intervals there are other lines with words inscribed next to them. 'HOP' is written first, then comes 'STEP', and finally you see 'JUMP'. The trail ends just in front of the tuck shop at West Buckland School, the furthest point from the reception and where the quad ends. The line measures precisely 18.29 metres.

This is the distance which Jonathan Edwards travelled before landing in a sandpit in Gothenburg on 7 August 1995 to establish a new world record for the triple jump.

Andy Edwards was a clerk with the Phoenix Insurance Company in the City of London when his first son was born. His wife Jill was a nurse who had trained at the Westminster Hospital, which is where she gave birth to Jonathan David Edwards on 10 May 1966. Their home was a top-floor flat in Herne Hill, a congested suburb in southeast London, coincidentally not that far from the athletics track at Crystal Palace.

Neither Andy nor Jill had been brought up in families with strong religious convictions. As a boy, Andy estimates he went to church three times a year; Jill suspects she went even less, but her mother, bringing her up alone, instilled in her a belief in God and she attended a convent school in Swanage, Dorset. By the time their son was born, Andy and Jill Edwards had become regular worshippers in the congregation of St Stephen's, South Lambeth, making the 10-minute journey from Herne Hill on the No 2 bus each Sunday morning. Their address was to prove of great fortune when Andy decided to apply, for a second time, to enter the ministry.

Although his family were not churchgoers, Andy belonged to a Bible class during his schooldays in Exeter. Their sense of fellowship was heightened by camps, house parties and an annual trip to Bembridge School on the Isle of Wight. 'Each time you went, you were asked what it meant to be a Christian and quizzed as to what Christ had done for you,' says Andy. When he was just 15, the question took on a tragic, new pertinence for him, for his mother died from a brain haemorrhage. 'I thought round that time about going into the ministry, but it had much to do with the trauma and the pain of losing my mother.'

His belief in God was challenged and, in his words, he floundered around for the next five years. 'It was only after I went to London in 1960 that I came back to the Lord. I made a fresh commitment to him, the call of the ministry started to come and I met the young lady who was to become my wife. Certain events occurred and you could say they weren't coincidences, and you start to think, "God

is trying to say something to me here." You talk to someone a bit further down the road and get told, "You need to
pursue this, push the doors further ajar." I did and it
seemed to be right; I felt I was being called. I went before
the selection conference and, aged 21, I thought I was
God's gift to the Church of England.'

It was not a view shared by those who mattered,
however. Andy was advised by those on his selection conference to broaden his experience. He was recommended
to work within the Family Centre in Canning Town, in the
East End of London. Andy went there, and his year in
Canning Town coincided with the time David Sheppard
was there. Like Sheppard, Andy Edwards had a love for
cricket, if not quite the same talent as a man who played
for England. Sheppard was to become the Bishop of
Liverpool, but in those days he worked closely with Andy
in what was, traditionally, a tough neighbourhood, where
the law of the streets tended to cut more ice than the
Metropolitan Police Force. 'I got to know David and I
really enjoyed the year, but it was hard, very hard.'

Soon after the birth of his son Jonathan in 1966, Andy
felt it appropriate to apply again to enter the ministry. He
was told by his local vicar of an obscure charity that
existed to fund young men during their studies. 'To qualify
you had to have lived in the Borough of Lambeth for three
years and be under the age of 25. When I first went to
London I had lived at the YMCA in Stockwell for 2½ years,
and when we got married we had planned to live just
round the corner from St Stephen's Church. A couple of
days before we were married, everything fell through and
we had nowhere to live. Then we found the flat in Herne
Hill, a 10-minute bus ride away from our church. When
I applied to the charity for a grant to enter the ministry

I qualified on age, and we discovered the flat was 50 yards inside the Borough of Lambeth. I was given a college grant of £250 a year; it was the first time it had ever been given to an ordinand. It was just a marvellous provision.'

His father had not been worried about Andy entering the ministry, but he was anxious about his son's financial vulnerability now that he had a family of his own. 'When I got the letter saying that we had this grant I showed it to my Dad and from that day to the day he died, he never questioned or concerned himself about how we would cope as a family. He saw that it was provided for – God provided in that way. This was thrilling to me, confirmation of going forward into the ministry.' By now, Jill Edwards had already spent a year in Bible College on a local authority grant and, with Andy going into college in Bristol, the foundation for Jonathan's devout faith, to be so vividly expressed through his prowess as a world-class athlete, had been laid.

The path ahead in those early summers of family life was to be far from smooth, especially for Jill. Their new home at Clifton, close to where her husband was at college, was a top-floor flat reached by climbing 58 stairs. In the second year of Andy's course, Jill gave birth to a second son, Tim. He cried constantly for the first six months of his life, and with two young children and all the paraphernalia that accompanies infants, climbing those 58 steps felt for Jill like encountering the North Face of the Eiger. 'I kept going to the doctor, but all they would say was, "Babies cry,"' recalls Jill. 'I knew he was unwell. Eventually, they took a blood test and found out that Tim was anaemic. Once he was on a course of iron and vitamins, he was a happy baby, full of smiles. But this was all hard on Jonathan; it's a big thing for a first child when a second comes along, let alone one that cries all the time. It was a difficult time for me, too. I had two babies to look after and Andy was never there, not for meal times or bath times.' Andy concedes, 'College life was geared for single men, not married men with babies.'

Jill remembers Andy being warned against getting married at all. 'When we got engaged the vicar of the church that we went to told Andy that this was an earthly entanglement and he shouldn't possibly consider it when he was called to the ministry. But it's interesting that God bringing us together coincided with Andy's calling and we have done it together.'

Yet Jill is convinced that those years when her husband was studying in Bristol impacted on Jonathan's personality. Certainly, he describes himself as a shy boy. 'I wouldn't even read a lesson in church,' he comments, by way of endorsement. Jill says, 'It was an unsettling time for Jonathan; he became quite clingy. He didn't like me going anywhere. We had moved home three times, then Daddy was away most of the time in college. Timothy came on the scene and just cried. You get harassed, don't you? From 6 o'clock in the morning until late at night, you know, you were just doing the essential things.'

She is not a woman given to self-pity, yet there is an unmistakable poignancy in her voice on this spring afternoon. She is seated in the lounge of their Cumbrian vicarage, with rich, panoramic views across the Irish Sea from their parish on the northern fringes of Whitehaven. She talks of tearfully revisiting Bristol with her daughter Rachel, who was born eight years after Jonathan. 'On two or three occasions I returned to Bristol and just wandered across the Downs. I just sat down and cried, thinking back to those days when Andy was in college, and remembered my feelings. I am sure this was what made Jonathan have this sense of insecurity as a boy, this lack of self-confidence. I can't think of any other reason, because he was always very clever.'

Andy Edwards' first living was to be in Blackpool, and the family moved north to a small house in Talbot Road. His ordination was conducted at All Saints, Preston amid the traditional pomp and ceremony and Jill remembers the effect it had on her young son. 'He asked me in total innocence, "Is Daddy still my Daddy?" An interesting concept for a little mind.' And now Jonathan's mind was about to be broadened by the beginning of his formal education.

She can still picture with disapproval the Devonshire Road Infants' School where Jonathan began his education. 'I hated the look of the school. It was a big, old-fashioned Victorian building with railings all the way round. I thought, "Dear God, have I got to send my dear little boy there?"' Her voice is self-mocking, however, and she still recalls with fondness the head teacher, Miss Ford. Three years later, the family had to move again, transferring almost the entire length of the country as Andy accepted a position as a curate in Teignmouth, South Devon.

According to Andy, Jonathan's switch to Inverteign Junior School was less than successful. 'In Blackpool, there was one teacher to one classroom,' he says. 'Inverteign was open plan. Jonathan is quite an orderly person in terms of his thinking, so he was safe and secure in one classroom. In an open plan, there was a lot of movement.' Jill concurs. 'The children could choose what to do when they first arrived in school. They could go to the maths place and do what was on offer there, or they could go somewhere else. Jonathan hated it; absolutely. He would get quite upset.' Eventually, one of the staff structured his school day. 'Then Jonathan found football and was selected for the team ... that made such a difference!' laughs Jill.

Andy Edwards had played ball games in the garden with his sons from the day they could walk. 'Every house we lived in had a window broken,' says Jill. Andy had been a more than competent batsman at Exeter School, worthy of a name check in *Wisden*, the world-renowned cricketing almanack, and he was selected for Devon Colts in 1959. One member of that team, Roy Kerslake, graduated to professional cricket with Somerset. Andy also won the long jump in the intermediate age group at Exeter. The genetic line had been established. But if Andy – an avuncular man these days possessing the comfortable girth of a tenor – introduced his sons to sport, as well as to Christianity, it was his wife who provided the bedrock of family and spiritual life for Jonathan, Tim and Rachel. Reverend Edwards could have wished for no more devoted a partner, striking out as he was on the demanding road of a clerk in holy orders.

Jill, though slight of stature, was a strong, resilient influence in the household. She ensured an atmosphere of calm and their home, like their lives, was without clutter or disturbance. The Edwardses' childhood revolved around family, the church and school and they were sheltered from all else, or that is how Jonathan tells it at least. 'I stayed within the confines of my own experience,' he explains. 'I was unworldly, isolated and sheltered in a backwater in Devon and that suited me. I was pretty one-dimensional in enjoying sport and not expanding my mind much beyond that.'

His mother remained a point of reference for Jonathan through adolescence and beyond. He looked no further than her for an anchor. At junior school in Teignmouth, he always came home for lunch. 'He didn't even want to stay when it was Christmas dinner and there was a party,' says Jill. 'We would never press Jonathan to do anything he didn't feel comfortable with. If it was necessary to be done, then you would explain that this was necessary and then, fine, he would do it.'

Jonathan was a child who liked routine and distrusted change. His mother tells an illustrative story. 'When we lived in Blackpool my mother was also living there, and having Gran on hand was lovely. One day I had to tell Jonathan we were moving to Teignmouth and he was distraught, absolutely distraught. He didn't want to move and cried and cried. I wondered what I was going to do, but there was nothing I could do other than pray. I think it was the next evening we were doing his Bible reading and it happened to be the story of Abraham being called to Canaan. He had to leave his home and God said, "I will be with you." Jonathan instantly remarked, "That's all right then, isn't it? God's going to be with us." There were no more tears, no more worries. He had accepted that God was going to go with us and he was happy.'

Jonathan had asked Jesus into his life when he was six years old, a fact Jill recollects very clearly. 'With all the children, we read the Bible to them at night and prayed until they were old enough to read it for themselves. One evening Jonathan asked a question and I said to him, "You need to have asked Jesus to come into your life for that to be true." Jonathan replied, "Oh, I've done that. I did that the other day." That was his answer. He had done it all by himself; he always was a thoughtful boy from the beginning. I have always prayed that the children would never

34

have a time when they didn't know that God loved them; and I feel God has answered that prayer.'

Rachel was born when the family were still at Teignmouth, but within a couple of years Reverend Edwards was appointed vicar of St Philip and St James's in Ilfracombe, on the North Devon coast. Andy and Jill felt that a major requirement on them as parents was to settle their sons into a stable school environment. Jill says, 'We weren't sure how long we would be in Ilfracombe, so we looked at West Buckland since there was the option of boarding. In that way, the boys would have the opportunity to stay at the same school for the rest of their education.'

Today the fees at the school for day pupils from Year 10 is £2,070 per term, excluding lunch. In 1976, the thought of finding the funds to send their two sons to an independent school 20 miles away on Reverend Edwards' £2,000-a-year salary would have sorely exercised their imagination. Jill was already keeping a tight rein on the monthly budget, and it was not uncommon for her to take a calculator with her when she shopped for groceries. 'It embarrasses me now, to hear Jonathan and Timothy reminisce about their packed lunches for school,' she admits. 'I used to buy a packet of chocolate digestive biscuits and give them a couple wrapped up, because that was cheaper than buying Trios or Penguins. They have also said they remember being allowed only one drink of squash a day, and that's right. Rachel says, "I used to think to myself, now when shall I have my drink of squash today?" and I think, "Oh, what an awful mother!" We laugh over these things, but we had to be careful what we spent.

'I see people loading their trolleys in the supermarkets today with massive packets of crisps and know it's the norm. When the children were growing up, the only time we ever had crisps was if we went for a picnic. That made it more special. The children obviously didn't have a lot of the things other children had. They say they didn't have much pocket money, but they never complained, not once. I didn't even hear them say, "So-and-so gets goodness knows how much," and if you go to an independent school there are obviously people there with money. An added expense was their sports gear and we could never pass on from Jonathan to Timothy, because Tim caught up in size. So it was always two pairs of football boots, two pairs of trainers.'

They were able to send their sons, and later Rachel, to West Buckland due to the fact that the school offered bursaries to children of clergymen. When Jonathan started there, the headmaster was the Reverend George Ridding and the school records show that, having attended the prep school without charge for a year, Jonathan received a £200-a-year bursary when he began in Form I in 1977. That was increased to a 75 per cent remission of fees from the following year, a grant that was to be extended for the duration of his education at West Buckland. A similar remission of fees was received for Tim. Without such assistance, Andy and Jill Edwards would never have been in a financial position to send the boys to the school.

West Buckland was a school rich in tradition from its foundation by Lord Fortescue, a local landowner of great importance, and Joseph Lloyd Brereton. In the front entrance the foundation stone, laid in 1860, bears the following inscription:

In humble hope that the Great Architect of the Universe and the Maker of Heaven and Earth the giver of all Good, will bless and proffer the work this day commenced, and that the School to be raised will prove, under the Divine blessing, an institution for the promotion of God's glory and the extension of sound and practical education, in the diffusion of useful knowledge, upon the imperishable foundation of Divine truth.

Jonathan proved to be the near-perfect pupil, adhering in fine detail to the aspirations written in stone more than a century earlier by Earl Fortescue, KG. He was accomplished in the classroom and on the sports field at the school, a grey stone building lost in 100 acres of North Devon countryside about 10 miles from the nearest sizeable population, Barnstaple. 'At different times I came top in most subjects,' says Edwards without a trace of boastfulness. 'I was the objectionable boy; good academically and good at sports. As a swot and a Christian, school could have been a less than happy experience! I think sport to a large degree was my saviour. I didn't have a particularly charismatic personality to make me popular, but sport gave me some street cred.'

Michael Downward, now retired as headmaster, became accustomed to greeting Edwards. 'I got to know Jonathan's right hand remarkably well, in the sense that I was so often congratulating him publicly on the stage,' he says. Downward, who took the headship in 1979 and retired in 1997, adds with clarity, 'I remember Andy Edwards bringing the boys to school for sports matches on Saturdays in a fairly battered old car. He had chosen to be vicar in a town which is pretty poor. Ilfracombe was a very popular holiday destination once and I remember when I was a boy in Surrey there was the Devon Belle, which was a Pullman train that went there. Well, Ilfracombe is now at the bottom end of the coach market, though there is determined effort to fund economic regeneration. Jonathan, though, grew up in a town with a lot of social problems and Andy was a dedicated churchman.'

Jonathan feels his childhood in Ilfracombe was idyllic: a classically English private school of unblemished reputation, an endless supply of sport and a strong sense of fellowship within the social group of his father's church. The vicarage was a large, rambling, Victorian house with two staircases that provided the boys with an uninterrupted racetrack round their home. Certainly, the school – whose motto was 'Read and Reap' – was to provide Andy and Jill Edwards with exactly the rounded education they had prayed that their children might receive. For Jonathan, small classes and a sense of tranquillity that has remained undisturbed to this day were to prove a blessing.

Lawrence Whittal-Williams is an archetypal sports master. His uniform on this brisk morning in late spring is shorts and a polo shirt. His arms and legs are muscular and tanned from years spent on the playing field. His manner is breezier than the wind rushing in from Exmoor, and his age is hard to define. He was already a member of staff at West Buckland when Edwards entered senior school as an 11-year-old in 1977 and now, 22 years later, Whittal-Williams is showing me the pit where the boy who would become world champion learned to jump into the sand.

The school sports fields are on a hill, like everything else in West Buckland, a tiny North Devon hamlet which lost its public house almost 70 years ago when it was demolished by Lord Fortescue, who did not believe in his farm workers getting drunk. According to local folklore, if you can see Dartmoor from these fields it is about to rain; if you cannot see the moor, it is raining already. To get to

the running track and the sandpits you walk past the first
XI cricket pitch and disappear through an avenue of
beech. 'You'll feel the climate change,' warns Whittal-
Williams, and this is not a lie. 'Character forming, we like
to say! Jon didn't much like training out here.'

Whittal-Williams offers an unsolicited angle as he goes
on to confide, 'To be honest, there has been a total role
reversal between Jonathan and Timothy. His younger
brother was by far the more obvious sportsman; hell, yes.
Really, Jonathan was more of the academic, early on
anyway. The one thing that Jonathan had was this fantastic
sense of timing and rhythm. Timothy was chunky – the
sprinter, the ball player, highly competitive. Jonathan was
much more laid back. It would be wrong to say he didn't
care, but he certainly didn't show it too much.'

I have a question for Whittal-Williams: 'If pressed,
which of the brothers in your estimation was destined to
be a sportsman of world-class calibre?'

'Timothy,' he replies without hesitation. 'He seemed
keener for it; and Jonathan was so small, you see. A will-
o'-the-wisp, minute.'

As well as brothers, Jonathan and Tim were best
friends. They would leave home together on the 7.45 a.m.
bus from Ilfracombe to West Buckland and return most
evenings together, having played one sport or another.
Unmistakably, they were boys cast from the same mould.
In manhood there remains a strong resemblance and they
sound uncannily alike.

Like Jonathan as a schoolboy, Tim's sporting credentials
were indeed impressive. Three times he went to the
English Schools Athletics Championships as a sprinter,
finishing fourth in the 100 metres in his senior year. Also
in his final year, Tim scored an avalanche of points for the

first XV rugby team as a winger capable of covering 100
metres in 11 seconds. He was timed once at 10.7 seconds
wind-assisted on a downhill grass track. During his college
days at Borough Road, Isleworth he would later attract an
invitation to train with Wasps, a prestigious rugby club in
North London. This was in 1991, when England had
reached the final of the Rugby World Cup and the game
was beginning to embrace professionalism. On a couple
of occasions in his student days, Tim had sprinting sessions under the tutored eye of Ron Roddan, who coached
Linford Christie to Olympic gold and a host of other
championship-winning performances. Yet Tim was not
motivated to treat sport as anything more than recreation
– and nor was Jonathan in the first instance, it must be
stressed – but one particular rugby training session in his
college days extinguished the flame for ever.

'I was known at school as Little Ted,' says Tim, now the
father of three young daughters, taking a summer vacation
at home in England while studying for a Masters in Jewish
Civilization at the Hebrew University in Jerusalem. 'I
never resented or felt overwhelmed by Jonathan's success
at school. In my own way, I was just as successful in sport.
In terms of academic work it never entered my mind that I
could be like him. Mum and Dad were always careful not
to compare us academically. I probably took a little pride
in *not* being as intelligent. I didn't put in the work I should
have done. I wasted that academic opportunity.

'At school, I played rugby for the county. At Borough
Road, Isleworth I played first-team rugby and had one
game for Middlesex; and in the final year I played rugby
league and we won the British Students' Championship –
hugely enjoyable. At the end of that season, the rugby
union team asked me to come back and play sevens and I

40

played in the Middlesex Sevens at Twickenham. Our last match in the first round was against Harlequins in front of some 40,000 people. After those sevens, I accepted an invitation to train again with the rugby union squad. Unfortunately, the coach proceeded to shout at me for an hour and a half. I came off and said to the team captain, "Sorry, I'm not doing this any more." I haven't played a game of rugby since. Wasps had been on the phone, saying I should come down – informally, you understand. But in that one training session, something died inside me.'

Tim does not regret his decision for a second. He is not in the least envious of his brother either. 'Being known as the brother of Jonathan Edwards doesn't bother me,' he says. 'Perhaps because I succeeded in sport and we're very close. He *is* my brother. I never look at him competing and wish that were me; not at all. Once that competitive instinct died in that training session, it was a very defining moment in my life. You know, when I was teaching later I saw that coach when I took my school team to the Rosslyn Park Sevens. He asked me if I was still playing and I told him I had stopped, but not the reason why. "What a waste of gas," he said. I had been his speed man, you see. The funniest thing of all was that I knew him shouting at me had not been personal, as he liked me, but as I say, something inside of me died.'

He admits that he never supposed for a second that his brother would actually make his career in athletics, let alone conquer the world. 'I don't imagine Jonathan would have predicted that either,' he says, smiling. At West Buckland Jonathan was a fresh-scrubbed, cherubic-looking boy who answered to the nickname Titch. He was coltish, all legs and little else. On the rugby field he was a composed, agile and intelligent fly half who could kick with either foot; yet in the depths of winter he risked ridicule by playing in gloves.

For a long time, Whittal-Williams refused to select him for the school senior XV, not for a lack of ability but on the grounds of safety. 'Jonathan was a lovely little fly half,' he says, 'but I was unable – frightened is the word – to play him in the first XV as I seriously thought he would get hurt. We didn't have that good a pack of forwards and to put him at No 10 would have been foolhardy to say the least. It wasn't until his final year that he made the team. He has a good brain and he understood the game, and that generally kept him out of trouble; but you can never tell in a game like rugby, can you?'

Throughout history, the good fly halves like Welsh icons Barry John and Phil Bennett have managed to protect themselves with their speed and wits. At schoolboy level, Edwards had the same inbuilt mechanism. 'I was a bit soft and didn't like to tackle, but I was fast and I could kick,' he says. 'You wouldn't call me brave, but I never worried about getting hurt.'

In Jonathan's final year, Tim, two years below him in school, made the first XV on the wing. 'The stopwatch would tell you Tim was faster than Jonathan,' says Andy Edwards, who was to be found consistently on the touchline or behind the boundary ropes encouraging his sons. 'Sometimes I didn't have much of a voice left!'

What Jonathan was lacking in physical presence was more than compensated for by his natural – many would suggest God-given – gift for sport. Throughout his schooldays he played in the cricket team, a bowler who could bat, or a batsman who could bowl; he was the best tennis player at West Buckland, even though he rarely picked up a racket; he played basketball, never mind his height; and he excelled, of course, at athletics. In the lower sixth Jonathan won the 200 metres in 24.3 seconds, took the long jump with a leap of 6.31 metres and travelled 13.05 metres to win the triple jump. He came second in the 100 metres in 11.89 seconds – behind Victor Ubogu, later capped as a very mobile prop for the England rugby team.

Steve Ojomoh, like Ubogu from Nigeria, was another contemporary of Edwards who would play international rugby for England. Edwards briefly played in the same school rugby team as Ubogu. 'He played on the wing then, when he returned to West Buckland to do his Oxbridge entrance exam,' says Edwards. 'Steve Ojomoh was four years younger than I was, but in the same house. He was a big, able sportsman; skinny, more of an athlete in those days than a rugby player. He did the triple jump too.' Amusingly, Ojomoh, not Edwards, holds the senior boys' home triple jump record at West Buckland.

Like Edwards before him, Ojomoh was a talented all-round young sportsman, who created a successful career for himself in rugby after the MP Chris Patten intervened in the late eighties to get him a British passport when he was threatened with repatriation after his schooldays. Ojomoh, whose father is a chief in the Nigerian city of Benin, won his England caps playing for Bath, the club he served for years before transferring to Gloucester in January 1998.

After all the bruises he has collected on the rugby field, Ojomoh explains how his triple jumping days at West Buckland have left their own, painful legacy. 'The event is very hard on the knees and even now, from those years of triple jumping, I still get back trouble,' he says. 'It's very, very hard on the joints. Somehow, though, Jonathan seemed to glide over the ground.' It is a description of

Edwards' style that will be echoed by those he has encountered in the world arena. 'It came easily to him. He was a role model at school. He set the standards we aspired to match. Jonathan was a natural. No disrespect to Lawrence Whittal-Williams or anything, but other boys in city schools would have had access to more qualified coaching every day. With us, we had our schoolmaster and that was it.'

Whittal-Williams would take no offence. He is a conscientious master, who for almost a quarter of a century has taught rugby, cricket, basketball and the various disciplines of athletics. He remains constantly available and a tireless enthusiast. He understands the different facets of his profession, takes seriously his responsibilities and treats his pupils – girls as well as boys these days – with a kindly but authoritative manner. Those who want to improve their level of performance at sport prosper in his lessons and benefit from his willingness to coach and cajole after the final school bell has sounded for the day. Whittal-Williams effectively demonstrates all this, walking around the athletics field with the wind stiffening.

He halts by the sandpit. The runway is marginally uphill and is wearing thin in places, having been trampled underfoot seemingly for an eternity. He points to the hedgerow beyond. 'I used to tie a piece of cloth there to make Jonathan look ahead on the runway, not down at the take-off board,' he explains. 'Even then, he had natural rhythm; a blind man could have coached him. He was a competitor. You have to be, don't you?'

Yet Edwards was definitely not devoted to training or practice, as Whittal-Williams testifies. 'It's the old British thing, isn't it? It's okay to be good at something as long as you haven't really practised. It's the barbarian factor ... yet Jonathan didn't avoid training simply because it was uncool to train. He didn't train because he didn't like it. Perhaps you can understand why, when on a typical summer's day the rain is lashing down and the wind is Force 9 from Exmoor or off the Atlantic. It frustrated me, because at 4 o'clock anyone could come up to this field and find me. I mean, my javelin throwers were all hitting their lines, and there was this flaming jumper who, if he got one run-up out of three right, you were lucky, all because he had no consistency in his approach to the take-off board. He wouldn't practise enough. When he did practise, Jon was a joy because you'd tell him something and he would do it.'

That complaint would shadow Edwards through university, through his days cutting a mark with Gateshead Harriers, through to the World Championships and the Olympics. It would be voiced by a whole collection of coaches. Fifteen years after he had left West Buckland, Edwards was still experiencing problems with his run-up in the countdown to the 1999 World Championships in Seville; and still, resolutely, he refused to work on corrections in training. His reasoning? 'Whereas I plead guilty to the charge of being a lazy schoolboy on the training field, that's not a factor now. I completely recognize the need for technical training, yet the reality of the past few seasons is that I've had to nurse a succession of injuries. Perhaps more significantly, the elements that I worked on in training didn't transfer into the competitive arena and that became very demotivating.'

When Edwards was running on this windswept playing field at West Buckland, with its grass track and a sandpit unsheltered from the elements, he could never have envisaged that he was running towards his place in athletics history. There were no clues, certainly not when Edwards, in common with all first-year pupils, was taught to triple jump from a standing start. In the second year, the children are allowed to take two steps before jumping, and it is only in the third year that they are permitted a run-up. Nonetheless, Whittal-Williams says, 'It just looked so easy for Jonathan from the start.' He had to organize for a new take-off board to be installed two metres further back, specifically for Edwards in the sixth form, because he was stepping into the sandpit. Edwards' world record jump of 18.29 metres is marked out here as well as in the school quad. To indicate where he landed that night in Gothenburg it has been necessary to draw a line across the paving stones on the far side of the pit.

As you would suppose, Whittal-Williams and Edwards shared as healthy a friendship as any teacher can have with a pupil. Yet the master had occasion to administer summary justice with a slipper on the one day Edwards is known to have stepped out of line. Whittal-Williams had tired of a group of boys fooling around with a rugby ball as he tried to prepare for a match. He warned that the next offender would be punished. 'Imagine my disappointment when I looked round to find the ball at Jonathan's feet,' he says. 'Him of all people; he was never one to cause trouble or be disobedient. Yet I had to be as good as my word and I did give him a slap with the slipper. Honestly, it hurt me more than him!'

Whittal-Williams appreciated the support Andy Edwards provided for his sons throughout their schooldays and was glad to have the company of an adult on away trips to Plymouth or Exeter, Taunton or Brixham. Reverend Edwards' great enthusiasm, coupled with his belief that Jonathan could only improve if he took his jumping more seriously, would later provide the impetus for his son to seek coaching at university. 'There is no hope in hell of his parents telling you anything adverse about him!' smiles Whittal-Williams. It is a truism, of course. Andy and Jill tell stories of a boy diligent about his school work, devout in his faith. 'Jonathan was unable to go to bed until he had completed his homework,' says Jill. 'He did French, Latin and German and on the nights when he was revising his languages I had to test him on every single word. He never got one wrong.' However, his equilibrium was unsettled during the first couple of weeks of each new academic year. 'He was tetchy and it was a bit like walking on egg shells with him until he knew what was expected of him,' she explains. It was Edwards' insecurity from his early childhood raising its head in another guise.

'I didn't like not being able to do things,' he says. 'I think it had more to do with wanting approval, rather than competitiveness. I really put a great deal of effort into my academic work, yet I remember that before my mock O levels I was a complete nervous wreck. I suppose it was a fear of external exams; a fear I couldn't do it.'

Those fears were misplaced. 'Virtually anything Jonathan turned his hand to in school he could do,' reports Michael Downward, headmaster for most of Edwards' schooldays. 'But he was also very modest and he had a lovely sense of fun and cheerfulness. He did, though, need a degree of reassurance. He needed to hear that you thought he was going to get high grades.'

There are staff members still at West Buckland who taught Edwards, like deputy headmaster David Clark, Mike Tucker and Chris Ponder, who continues to teach religious education after 26 years at the school. There is not a harsh word to be heard of him. 'At Christian Union Jonathan was

full of life, yet deeply committed,' says Ponder over coffee
in the staff common room, buzzing with gentle gossip and
school politics. 'Jon's always been so open, so transparently
open. He disliked any form of bullying, or when the
humour threatened to go over the top. He liked to see
people treated fairly. He felt injustice passionately. I wouldn't
presume to say this school is responsible for either
his faith or his athletics. I hope we encouraged him in
both. Obviously, he worked immensely hard on his own.
He is self-driven, but at the heart of it all is this wish – he is
an athlete and he wants to use that ability to the full in
God's service.'

Yet Edwards' insecurity would arise again, when he
rejected the opportunity to be house captain in the sixth
form. 'That would have involved boarding and I knew I
would not have enjoyed that. I spent much of my time at
school with my brother; we would even play snooker at
lunchtimes. As we lived so far from school, our social scene
revolved around our group at church. I was neither prepared nor confident enough to give that up.' Tim, in
contrast, accepted the role of house captain when the invitation was extended to him two years later. 'I look back and
wish I had taken the opportunity when it was offered,'
admits Jonathan now.

Despite his anxieties, Edwards' exam results produced
predictably high grades. He received A grades at O level in
Maths, Physics, Chemistry, Latin, French and German, a B
grade in English Literature and a C grade for English
Language. He applied to Oxford University, with this confi-
dential written reference from Michael Downward preceding him to Lincoln College:

Jonathan is a very pleasant, polite young man of diverse

interest and abilities possessing a well-justified self-confidence without a hint of arrogance. He combines an inquisitive mind in his academic pursuits with a dislike of being beaten by a problem. This latter characteristic is also evident in his athletic endeavours, where he is undoubtedly the best sportsman the school has had for several years.

Downward predicted A grades at A level for Edwards in Physics and Maths and a B grade in French, before concluding his assessment:

Jonathan has strong ideals based on a secure and happy background – his father is Vicar of Ilfracombe. He is a prominent member of the Christian Union, and has already shown qualities of leadership as captain of athletics, a House prefect and as a school prefect. Although uncertain yet about his future plans – his first idea of being an engineer has waned in favour of something more akin to a vocation, even perhaps as a missionary – he brings to all his activities a cheerful determination which is not given to many. I feel confident that he has the ability and attitude to benefit greatly from continuing his education to degree level, and would give much in return.

Edwards sat an entrance exam for Oxford, applying to read Physics but also writing a French paper. 'I was told I did quite well. My French master Richard Baker thought I might get offered a place to read French on the basis of my translation paper.' Indeed, he was invited for an interview – though all these years later Edwards is still suspicious that he may have been the beneficiary of an administrative mistake. 'The college was stunning,' he says. 'Manicured lawns, old quads; a sense of history and tradition ran through the place. I must admit I thought it was cool. But, though I have no reason to know if this is true or not, I think I might have been interviewed only because I had left home a day earlier than the college anticipated to accompany a friend, also going up to Oxford for interview. I discovered later that the college had mysteriously called my home after I had already left. I wonder to this day if someone had been trying to reach me to tell me not to come up.'

Not long after his interview, a letter arrived from Lincoln College and for the first time in his life Edwards was confronted with failure. He was not being offered a place. In typical Edwards fashion, he rationalized his rejection. 'If I'm honest, I don't think I'm especially intelligent,' he suggests. 'I just worked hard. I didn't have the capacity for independent thought. I would tread the steps of others. I guess a university like Oxford was looking for a little more.' He has never ceased applying frank analysis to his work, or to the application of his faith. Edwards duly made the A level A grade in Maths and gained B grades in Physics, French and General Studies. He applied with more success to Durham University, where he was awarded a place to read Physics.

If the Oxford experience briefly sucked the wind from his sails, however, Edwards' first flirtation with athletics glory was beckoning. In the lower sixth he qualified for the first time for the English Schools Athletics Championships. He came ninth in the triple jump, with a jump of 13.76 metres. A year later the National Schools Championships were held at Thurrock and Andy Edwards accompanied both his sons to the competition. Jonathan became national champion, jumping 15.01 metres. His triumph was witnessed by schoolmaster John Crotty, who was then national event coach for the triple jump. Without knowing it, Edwards had embarked on the odyssey that was to change his life. He had left his footprints in the sand.

Lawrence Whittal-Williams was also at Thurrock that summer's afternoon in 1984 and, naturally, he was a proud man. 'We just gave Jon an opportunity, that's all,' he says now, standing all these years later beside the sandpit on the sports field where the wind never takes a vacation. 'But after he broke the world record in Gothenburg, Jon did write to me. We have always kept in touch.'

Michael Downward has one final anecdote to share from Edwards' schooldays. During his day, the headmaster's house was in the midst of the school, overlooking the quad at the back, and he used to invite the school prefects to dinner with him and his wife Patricia. 'It was always difficult to find a date,' he recalls. 'In Jonathan's time, we chose a Sunday evening. Very, very politely, Jonathan said he would rather not come.'

In the Edwards household Sundays were different. Jonathan was not to appreciate then that his 'Never on a Sunday' stance would create headlines across the nation, nor that ultimately his reassessment of that stance would lead to the collapse of one of the values he once held closest to his heart – the values that had been established by Andy and Jill Edwards.

Chapter 3

Never on a Sunday?

Most people are bothered by those passages in Scripture which they cannot understand; but as for me, I have noticed that the passages that trouble me most are the ones I do understand.

MARK TWAIN

The fresh-faced, skinny student looked incongruous standing by the sandpit wearing a long raincoat over his street clothes. As other young athletes drawn from all over the country careered into the pit, the kid in the coat assisted coach John Crotty in measuring their jumps.

At lunchtime the teenager wrapped up against the chill wind that whips through the Crystal Palace Stadium in winter, picked up his bag and went to King's Cross Station. Ahead of him was a long journey back to Durham University. Those taking part in the training weekends at Crystal Palace in the mid-eighties could never have supposed that one day the kid in the coat would be the best triple jumper the world had ever seen.

Jonathan Edwards volunteered to help with the measuring on Sunday mornings when he was called to London for weekend training with the elite squad that used to assemble under the watchful eye of Crotty. The reason for this was simple: Edwards resolutely refused to train, or for that matter study, on Sundays. He was being consistent with his schooldays, with his upbringing in a household where his father and mother instructed their three children to observe Sunday as a day reserved for worship and time together as a family. No organized ball games, no television, no academic work.

Crotty had watched Edwards win the triple jump in the National Schools Championship in 1984 and invited him to attend national squad training at Crystal Palace the following year. 'The difficulty with Jon was that he didn't always do a lot!' says Crotty dryly. Edwards still calls him on the telephone to this day, specifically if he wants a trained eye to analyse his technique. Crotty possesses a large video library, often shot with his own camera, and he has much footage of Edwards dating back to his earliest competitions.

'Let me give you an example of Jonathan's programme when he came down to Crystal Palace in those days when he was a student at Durham,' Crotty continues. 'He would arrive on Friday night, more often than not going to bed early at the hostel. The next morning he would stretch a bit, jog a bit, but he was very fragile and we had to be careful with him. He was very quick and he had lots of potential, you could see that. He was springy and fast, but at that time he didn't have the endurance strength to train for the triple jump, let alone compete. On the Saturday morning we would do technical work because you need to be at your freshest to do that kind of work. Usually, after about three jumps Jonathan had had enough; he was aching somewhere. So, in the afternoon he would do very little. We would do a number of tests as a group, like a sprint test. Jonathan was always polite, always nice, and he would come and say, "Can't quite make this today, not quite up to it."

'We'd play some volleyball later. In the evening we used to play a lot of cards – I'm quite a gambler. Of course, Jonathan was polite, but he never played. He read his Bible and looked after himself. Don't get me wrong, he mixed with everybody, he got on well with everybody, but he had time for himself and we respected that. But the next day was the best day from my point of view ... and looking back you still have to giggle. Of course, Jonathan didn't do anything on a Sunday!' Except pace the sandpit in his raincoat.

Edwards' position was clearly entrenched, at least then. Still, he had no idea of the commotion ahead.

Edwards recalls that he first rebuffed the international selectors by rejecting an invitation to compete for an England A team because the match was being staged on a Sunday. He would not attract nationwide attention, however, until the day he declared that he would miss the trials to determine the team the British selectors would send to the Olympic Games in Seoul in the autumn of 1988. Olympic Games or no Olympic Games, Edwards would not compete in trials that were to be held on a Sunday. His faith, his dedication to be a servant of God, was more important than any athletic ambition.

Edwards recollects that one Sunday afternoon, as a sports-mad schoolboy, he was at a friend's house watching televised football highlights on a programme called *The Big Match* when his father came to fetch him home. Reverend Edwards denies this, chuckling. Yet he explains the sanctity in which Sunday was held within his house. 'I don't remember ever having to go and get Jonathan, but it would be fair to say that we thought Sunday was a day of rest, a day that was unlike any other day of the week,' he says. 'Sunday was to be kept as a holy day to be used for family time, to be given for worship. From that point of view we wouldn't do anything which we could normally do in the rest of the week.' One of Jonathan's vivid memories is of watching his mother peel and prepare the vegetables for Sunday lunchtime on Saturday evening.

Tim Edwards confirms that with his brother he would 'try to get a sneak look at television if Mum and Dad were in the kitchen'. He explains a typical Sunday in the Edwards household: 'Church, big dinner, Dad would have a rest and perhaps we would take a family walk. Sometimes it was boring!'

Jonathan would later appreciate the value of his parents' position. 'As I got older, it became a very positive thing; I believed this was right,' he argues. 'If I had an exam on a Monday, I wouldn't revise on a Sunday. That was it. Jesus, when he healed on the Sabbath, said to the Pharisees, "Sabbath is made for man, not man for the Sabbath." It's a day given to man as a gift, a rest.'

Jill Edwards, rightly so, is unapologetic about how her children were taught to observe Sunday, but she says now, 'With hindsight, I look back and think we were probably more rigid than we needed to have been. But you also have to see where we were coming from – that was our background from the time that we were converted. That was very much the era when people didn't do anything on a Sunday. I mean, Sunday sport...' Basically, sports fixtures were not held on a Sunday back then.

At the time when the British trials for the 1988 Olympic Games were scheduled for a Sunday, Edwards was completely certain of the course of action he had to adopt. He would not jump. He was 22 years old and working by day as a scientific officer in the cytogenetics laboratory of the Royal Victoria Infirmary in Newcastle, where he analysed chromosomes for diagnostic purposes. By night he was training at the Gateshead Stadium. He had already jumped the Olympic qualifying standard (16.65 metres) that summer and had jumped the furthest of any British athlete prior to the trials, but apart from catching the eye of those who read the small print of the athletics press Edwards had competed almost anonymously. Until now.

Suddenly, he was being portrayed in nationwide stories as a modern-day Eric Liddell, the man whose fabled stance of placing his religion before his sport had been the inspiration for the Oscar-winning film *Chariots of Fire*. Somewhat predictably, Edwards had not seen the film as his life in North Devon had revolved almost exclusively around school, church and sport when the film was released in 1980. However, millions had seen the movie and had been entranced, and for journalists there was too much of a parallel to ignore between Liddell's principled boycott of the 100 metres race at the 1924 Olympic Games in Paris and Edwards' decision to imperil his hopes of going to the Seoul Olympics in 1988.

One writer called Jean Rafferty graphically encapsulated the spirit Edwards had engendered as she suggested,

A religious athlete is a contradiction in terms in our psyched up, hyped up, drugged up days of sport. Eric Liddell, of *Chariots of Fire* fame, was already an anachronism when he refused to compete on a Sunday in the Paris Olympic Games. But that was 1924 when there were still a few Christians left in Britain. They have become an endangered species who surprise the rest of us with their eccentric belief in God and the soul and other such things you can't buy with a credit card. Jonathan Edwards might as well be a time traveller, hundreds of years old, who's come along in his personal Tardis to shake things up a bit.[1]

Edwards was overwhelmed by the fuss. If the trials had been on any other day, he would have jumped. As they were on a Sunday, he would not – as his coach Carl Johnson informed the selectors on his behalf. There was nothing sinister in his decision, nothing preplanned, no attempt to hijack publicity. He knew that the rules of selection guaranteed places on the Olympic team to the athletes who finished first and second at the trials. He would take his chances of being offered the third, discretionary place. This was a matter of principle, no more, no less.

Besides, he was not alone. Barrington Williams declined to compete in the long jump because that event at the Olympics was scheduled to be staged on a Sunday. Instead Williams, a lay preacher for the Elim Pentecostal Free Church in Chesterfield, Derbyshire, made himself available for the 100 metres. Williams made the Olympics in his alternative event. 'In athletic terms Barrington was a total enigma,' says Edwards. 'His story was amazing, it was the stuff of schoolboy comics.'

Williams was a wonderful, colourful character, but Edwards as the younger man was the athlete who caught the imagination of the country. In explanation of his unwillingness to compete in the trials, Edwards said at the time, 'I see my Christian life as the most important thing and I realize I have to make certain sacrifices. I was

1 *Plus* magazine, 31 January 1990.

brought up in a Christian family and happen to believe the Sabbath is holy. I will watch the trials on television and think, "I could have been there," but it's just one of those things. It wasn't a difficult decision not to compete. My Christian beliefs are much more important to me than athletics. Some of my friends think I'm foolish. They say I'm throwing away my chances of getting to the Olympics. But I feel this has given me a chance to demonstrate the sincerity of my Christian beliefs and to show to other people just how important Christianity is. I will get another chance. Athletics is not everything to me, but my faith is. I hope that God will repay me in the same way that I have repaid him and I stick to my decision even if it means missing out on the Olympics.'

It was little wonder that the media should want to present Edwards as a throwback to Liddell. Of course, the Scotsman was among the favourites to win gold at the Paris Games, while Edwards would have been the first to confirm that any expectations he might take on the plane to Seoul would not extend much beyond walking out in the opening ceremony. Edwards was in the rookie phase; Liddell, who won seven caps on the wing for the Scotland rugby team, was already an outstanding athlete.

Liddell, like Edwards the son of a clergyman, would have been selected for the 100 metres and 200 metres at those Olympic Games in Paris, as well as the two relay teams. But once he discovered that the heats for the 100 metres were to be held on a Sunday (contrary to the screenwriters' licence in the Hollywood version, he knew that before he caught the boat for France) Liddell withdrew from that event. His religious convictions would not allow him to compete on the Sabbath, and through the scheduling of the Games this meant that he also had to excuse himself from the relay squads. Instead, he entered the 400 metres, an event at which he was a relative novice.

The 100 metres was won at the Stade de Colombes on 7 July 1924 by the Englishman Harold Abrahams who, controversially for the times, employed a professional coach, Sam Mussabini. Twenty-four years later Abrahams, who had been to Repton and Cambridge, wrote poignantly, 'I have often wondered whether I owe my Olympic success, at any rate in part, to Eric's religious beliefs. Had he run in that event, would he have defeated me and won the Olympic title?' In the event, Liddell did defeat Abrahams in the Olympic 200 metres final, the Scotsman winning the bronze medal as the Englishman laboured home sixth.

Abrahams' success in the 100 metres was a prominent part of the plot of *Chariots of Fire*, but the central, heart-wrenching theme was Liddell's eventual triumph. Abrahams' account of the Olympic 400 metres final race – and his eulogy – is worth recounting:

I remember that as the seats allotted to Olympic competitors were in a very unfavourable position – at the start of the 100m – I paid my ten shillings (50p) to have a seat near the finish. Liddell was drawn in the outside lane, which meant that he had to make all his own running. The 400m in Paris was run round two bends only, that is to say there was a starting straight of, I should think, very nearly 200 yards. From the crack of the pistol Liddell ran like a man inspired. Indeed, the thought in my mind as he started off as if he was running 100 metres instead of 400, was 'He can't possibly keep this up'. But Eric never seemed to slacken in his pace, though of course he must have slowed appreciably, and he won that glorious Olympic final by a good six yards in the new Olympic and world record time of 47.6 seconds.

His name will for ever remain as perhaps the most famous and most respected and loved athlete Scotland has ever produced. His style was about as unorthodox as it could be, but the main thing is that he always displayed the greatest courage, and he will be remembered as one of the finest sportsmen who ever donned a running shoe.[2]

According to folklore, Liddell ran that 400 metres Olympic final clutching a piece of paper that was pressed into his hand on the start-line. On it was written, 'Them that honour me I will honour – 1 Samuel 2:30.' Whether this is an apocryphal story or not, Liddell's devotion to his faith superseded all else. He left Scotland, where he had grown up as the son of a Church of Scotland minister, to become a missionary in China. He died of a brain tumour in a Japanese internment camp in February 1945. He was 43 years old.

To mark the seventy-fifth anniversary of Liddell's gold medal in Paris, Donald Walker wrote in *The Scotsman* in the summer of 1999,

The 100 metres title did go to a Scotsman eventually. Allan Wells was asked after winning the blue riband of the 1980 Games if he would dedicate his 100 metres gold medal to Harold Abrahams. 'No,' replied Wells, 'this one was for Eric Liddell.'

The grave where Liddell rests in China was unmarked until 1991, when it was located by ex-pat Charles Walker, and a slab of Mull granite was shipped out as a memorial

2 *World Sports*, June 1948.

befitting a national hero. 'Everyone has a different view of Liddell,' said Walker. 'Some see him as an athlete, some as a Christian, some as simply a fine human being.' This weekend, we should see him as all those things, and as a true sporting hero.[3]

Edwards admits that at the time of his refusal to participate in the Olympic trials he was not consciously following the example of Liddell. 'I was vaguely familiar with his name, but I didn't draw any parallels. When others chose to write about me in company with Liddell it was obviously flattering, an honour to be thought of alongside him. But I think the biggest challenge to being likened to Eric Liddell is having to live up to what he achieved beyond the athletics arena. He committed himself to serve God and, though he could have used success by staying in Scotland and sharing the gospel, he bravely went as a missionary to China. He was an exceptional man. He won Olympic gold, but we remember him as a man of faith. It would be something if the same could happen to me.'

Unlike Liddell, Edwards was naturally targeted by the media. There was a rush to interview him from the moment his objection to competing on a Sunday became known. 'I was really a nobody, yet there was this incredible media attention. I wasn't prepared for that.' Nor was Val Davison, at the time head of department in the cytogenetics laboratory where Edwards was working. Her department came under siege.

Television crews and a posse of reporters and photographers were dispatched to the Royal Victoria Infirmary to try to get Edwards' story. There were more newsmen

3 *The Scotsman*, 10 July 1999.

attempting to dial into the hospital. Davison recalls, 'We ended up blocking the telephone calls. It's a very sensitive type of work that we do and I was unimpressed to have all the lines tied up. Frankly, the last thing you want in a genetics department is a lot of media attention for whatever reason.'

Edwards could not grasp the scale of the interest. 'It was unbelievable! I had piles of messages saying phone, phone, phone, phone, phone.' On the day of the trials, television crews turned up outside his church, the Heaton Baptist Church, with the ambition of filming him going in to worship. Unfortunately for them, Edwards had kept a prearranged appointment and gone away for the weekend.

The next day the media was still on his trail. Would the selectors award the third, discretionary place on the team to Edwards? Eventually, he took a call at the laboratory from a member of the British team management, telling him he had been selected for Seoul. 'I can remember being ecstatic and jumping up and down. I was going to the Olympics...'

Davison, now the director of the regional genetics laboratory at Birmingham Women's Hospital, shared his joy that afternoon in Newcastle. She had been a loyal supporter of Edwards from the day when, against all odds, she had appointed the youthful-looking Physics graduate to her department on an initial six-month contract. 'We were delighted; everyone in the lab wanted to help Jonathan because he's so genuine, such a lovely person,' remembers Davison, who in the early summer of 1999 had just returned from trekking in the Himalayas. 'We were quite a small group and all of us were athletic, in our own pathetic little way. We all did things like the Great North Run, gentle sort of running, and we all went to the gym at lunchtime. We were a fairly fit group, so I think to have somebody there who had the potential to be a real athlete was quite exciting for us. I remember at the time having an argument that went on and on with our personnel department over trying to get Jonathan leave on full pay for the Olympics. I think he had to have a period of about six weeks off. Personnel said fine, he can have the time, but we're not going to pay him. It was an ongoing argument. I think we won, if not totally, then almost, and that was an achievement.'

Those Olympics were never destined to offer Edwards anything other than experience, but the concept of competing on a Sunday was to remain anathema for him for another four years. He missed the Europa Cup when it was held at Gateshead on a Sunday in 1989, and he declined to jump at the World Championships in Tokyo in 1991.

He was now ranked No 1 in Britain. 'I've had lot of encouragement from the public,' Edwards said at the time. 'The decision not to compete was very much between my conscience and God. What I do in sport comes out of my dedication to God. The coverage I've had through not competing on a Sunday has been immense. That's given me a chance to share with people how important my faith is. God has used it, I'm sure, to give me a chance to tell people what a difference being a Christian has meant to me. Even though it upsets me to miss out on competition I'm being true to the thing that's the most important part of my life. It will get harder as it goes on. If I come to 1992 and the Olympics beckon and the event's on a Sunday, that will be hard. But I would accept it because that's what has been decreed.'

In their parish of Bearwood in Bournemouth (they had moved from Ilfracombe in 1989), Reverend Andy Edwards and his wife Jill were quietly proud of their son. 'One of the tragedies of our environment today is that a principled stance has become rare,' said Reverend Edwards. 'Unless you go with what everyone else does, you're a stick-in-the-mud; funny. Obviously, from a practical view there was some disappointment because there was an increasing number of competitions on a Sunday. Here's a person who has ability, a gift God has given him and he is unable to use it and that seems a frustration. But there is a principle and Jonathan felt if he honoured God, then God would honour him.'

Imagine, then, Edwards' relief and gratitude when the schedule for the Barcelona Olympics was published. The qualifying rounds for the triple jump were to be held on Saturday 1 August 1992, the final on Monday 3 August. 'A miracle, divine intervention,' he smiled. As it transpired, Edwards had a wretched Games in Barcelona, failing to make the final, and it caused him to reassess his relationship with God. Seven weeks later, however, he finished the year with a courageous victory in the World Cup in Havana, Cuba, despite being ill.

It was through the ensuing winter months that Edwards was to arrive at a momentous crossroads. Every major triple jump competition in 1993 was to be staged on a Sunday. Edwards was stunned. He still looked as if he could have been a fresher at Durham University, but he was 26 years old and in control of his own destiny. He took a far-reaching decision. At the beginning of 1993, he told the world that from now on he would compete on a Sunday.

In the summer of 1999, Reverend Edwards sits in the lounge of his vicarage in Cumbria and admits, 'At times, if

I'm really pushed, I wonder how completely right it is what Jonathan has done.' For Jill Edwards, her son's decision was a huge surprise too. 'Initially, I was disappointed, but it did make me go back to the drawing board,' says Jill. She read the Bible with new purpose, seeking explanations.

There was also genuine anxiety on their part that their son might have erased all the good work he had done. They feared that he might now be held in scornful contempt, dismissed as just another guy on the make. 'I think we were worried that Jonathan would completely spoil the good witness that he has of being a truthful man,' adds his mother. 'We never stopped respecting or loving him in any way, though, and we knew that he wouldn't have made any decisions lightly.'

Edwards knew that his change of heart would distress his parents, but he could not allow this to influence him. He was now intending to be accountable for his own actions. His own wife, Alison, had counselled him hard before he opted to go public with his radical U-turn. 'I was terrified mainly because of what other people would think and the effect it would have on his Christian witness,' she says. 'But this was Jonathan's stand; he was the one who didn't jump on a Sunday. I remember saying to him he had to be sure what he was doing.'

Alison confirms that her husband's parents found the decision difficult to accept. For Edwards this would have been especially hard, given how exceptionally close he has been to his mother throughout his life. He would have hated to cause her any pain. 'It was something Jonathan prayed through and it was very difficult for his Mum and Dad, probably the one real major difference they have had. They didn't agree he was doing the right thing, but this was Jonathan making his own stand. This was him saying, "This is what's right for us." We made the decision, gently told people and battened down the hatches waiting for this barrage of criticism – "How could you?" or "You hypocrite!" – but, by and large, nothing came and we were grateful for that.'

During the time that Edwards was changing his mind, dismantling a once strongly held principle, his brother Tim was on a six-month devotional stay at a Bible School near Lancaster in the company of his wife Anna. Tim wrote to his brother, posing a set of penetrative questions. 'Although there was no way that he could be a fully professional athlete and not jump on a Sunday, I wanted to know: Does that make it right? Could he still be a Christian athlete and make that stand? Was what he was doing wise? I thought I'd ask the questions that perhaps hadn't been asked. That was my thinking when I wrote, not that I didn't agree with him.' Jonathan would admit years later, 'When I got a letter from Tim, I realized this had to be a really serious issue because we're both notoriously bad at corresponding.'

Like Jonathan, Tim had been brought up by his parents to acknowledge that Sunday was to be preserved for worship and the family. Tim, however, has since taken his wife and three young daughters with him to Israel, where he will complete his Masters in Jewish Civilization at the Hebrew University in the year 2000. 'I work on Sundays now,' he explains. 'The church I attend meets on a Sunday because that's when the English-speaking services are held and Anna doesn't speak Hebrew. After church, I'm straight to the university. I don't work on Friday evening to Saturday evening as no one else does. It's the Sabbath and the libraries are closed.' So for Tim

Edwards and his family the board has moved, just as it has for his brother and his family.

In the summer of 1999, shortly after hearing the lingering worries of his parents, Edwards ventures, 'At some point towards the end of 1992, I came to the realization that it was not wrong to jump on a Sunday. Then the issue of course became: Was it wrong for me? Having made such a public stand, people would accuse me of convenient compromise. A bit of success, and I could hear people thinking, "Okay, here we go, another guy chasing the dollar." People could suppose it was easy for me to turn my back on jumping when I wasn't anybody, but now I'd started to jump reasonably well, my athletics was going to take over.

'I was very, very worried because that was not the case. But there's a verse in Proverbs 29 which spoke very directly to me about my circumstance. It states, "Fear of man will prove to be a snare" (v. 25). I think what that means is simply that being worried about what other people think of you can compromise your commitment to God. I'd gone into athletics to serve God. That had been very recently challenged with the whole Barcelona experience and I felt I'd come through to a closer walk with God and a stronger, more deep-rooted desire to serve him. I felt I could make the decision with integrity within the context of my Christian faith and the fact that I'm doing athletics to serve God.'

Also at around this time, Edwards received a visit from a friend who felt compelled to tell him of a dream in which he had featured. Extraordinarily, Richard Taylor's dream seemed to confirm Edwards' interpretation of the quotation from Proverbs 29. Taylor, a fellow member of the congregation at Heaton Baptist Church, had seen his friend standing on the edge of a runway on an athletics track. Edwards was waiting to jump, but could not because the runway was blocked by a host of people. Taylor came and cleared the crowd. Edwards says, 'After the people had gone, I was able to run and jump … and I jumped miles. That was Richard's dream, so vivid that he felt he had a responsibility to tell me.'

The two men had not discussed Edwards' reconsidered feelings to competing on a Sunday, but the athlete made a near-instant connection. 'I think this was the fear of man as a snare, the fear of other people's reactions that was stopping me from doing what I believed was the right thing to do. You read often in the Bible about God speaking directly; I do believe that God spoke directly to me there. I think this was because it was such a big decision, potentially the worst decision I could ever have to make. The press could have been forever cynical about Jonathan Edwards, which rightly or wrongly would have coloured the whole of the nation's impression of me.'

Edwards chose the quarterly *Christians in Sport* magazine in which to publish his decision. Unbeknown to Edwards, the director of coaching for British athletics at the time, Frank Dick, also sent a letter to be published in the same issue of *Christians in Sport*. Dick wrote,

I'm writing comment because, without knowing what he will write, I do know that he will be unwilling to state just how hard it was for him to balance all the factors involved and make the decision he did. You will, I hope, have gathered that I am talking about Jonathan Edwards, the young man who overcame food poisoning to win the triple jump in this year's Athletics World Cup in Cuba. He's a very special person. He'd fight to the death for his team-mates, the flag he proudly wears on his vest, and for his deeply held beliefs. He fought even harder in reaching this decision. I'm very proud to know him. He is a most outstanding ambassador for his sport, for his country – and most important of all – for his beliefs and the values he holds highest.[4]

Alison Edwards' assertion that her husband escaped all criticism is not quite true. Colin Hart from the *Sun* newspaper recalls, 'We were at the World Indoors Athletics Championships in Toronto and I remember Jonathan sitting down with a group of writers and he came out with a story that God had spoken to him in a dream and told him that now it was quite all right for him to jump on a Sunday. And, of course, being the old cynic that I am, I thought, "Oh yeah, it's suddenly dawned on this young man that most of the major events are going to be on Sundays. And if he doesn't jump on a Sunday he's never going to make it as an international athlete, nor is he going to make any money at his business. When he first made his decision not to jump on a Sunday the sport was not as professional, there wasn't the money to be won. What a wonderful way to get round the problem, through a dream someone else had." Whether we were cynical or not, however, he was obviously a nice young man and you couldn't get away from that fact. He was so genuine, he believed it, so because of who he was there wasn't a great song and dance made of it.'

Surprisingly, the most barbed attack on Edwards' re-evaluation is delivered by Norman Anderson, a close friend of the family as well as his weightlifting coach. In

---

4 *Christians in Sport* magazine, March 1993.

advance of my meeting with him, Anderson told Edwards
that if he spoke, he would want to speak from the heart.
To his credit, Edwards told him he would want him to do
just that, and so we hear Anderson, unabridged and raw.
'It's a complete myth to compare Jonathan with Eric
Liddell,' he says. 'There is no comparison. He wouldn't
compete on a Sunday, Liddell, and he stuck to it. Jonathan
decided that perhaps he could.'

Anderson is registered blind and over 60 years old, but
he is regularly lifting weights in the gym at Gateshead
Stadium as he still competes in power-lifting in his age
group. Before he began working seriously with Edwards in
1995, Anderson was part of a group who lifted in the gym
at times when the athlete was present – men
like Peter Gordon and Arthur McKenzie, both international discus throwers in their prime, and Bob Morton,
who owns a gym they sometimes used. There was a lot of
good-natured humour, as they tried to persuade Edwards
to jump on a Sunday.

Ironically, once he had established in his own mind
that he would be no less a Christian for jumping on a
Sunday, Edwards' decison was met with a wave of cynicism within that same band of men, according to
Anderson. 'The cynical view was, "Hallelujah, one of
Jonathan's friends has had a dream, so now it's all right to
jump on a Sunday,"' says Anderson. 'How convenient,
when you knew you had to jump on a Sunday if you were
going to make any money.'

Yet perversely, Anderson insists he does not wish to
sound critical. 'I think Jonathan has made the right decision,' he says. 'I think he's absolutely right. He's a talented
man and he has made a good living. If he had been my
son, I would have told him to get out there, for goodness'

sake. So I'm not criticizing; I'm just saying how his decision is seen by some of those around here.'

Edwards' decision was bound to stir emotions in those
closest to him. His coach at that time was Carl Johnson,
who had been with him since he arrived in the Northeast
to attend Durham University. Now Johnson says solemnly,
'His decision to compete on a Sunday perturbed me
greatly; it perturbed me greatly because I felt it was wrong
for him to make what was a decision that altered the principle of his life. I didn't want him to regret it 10 years
down the line, and I'm still not sure about it.

'It was necessary from the point of view of his athletic
development because he was being denied opportunities
in major competitions. His development was being
slowed down. Now once he opened that up, he was able
to develop as an athlete, but that's not the be-all and end-
all, you see. It's to become a right and comfortable person,
to be eventually comfortable with yourself. What worried
me at that time was, all right, he was comfortable, he
could rationalize, explain it, but what happens in 10
years? What's he going to think at the moment he comes
to die? None of us know this, do we? But is that not where
your actions in this life are really quite important?'

Edwards has continued through the years to receive letters
from Christians expressing both disappointment and
encouragement over his change of heart. With the passing
of those years, he has also come to articulate better how
he arrived at the point where he felt able to compete on a
Sunday. On 30 October 1999, he offered the following
thoughts for publication in this book.

*　　*　　*

The editing of this chapter, reliving some of the events surrounding 'Sunday' and my athletic career, has been a sobering experience. I have had to smile as well as wince at some of my comments and, indeed, those of my biographer: 'He was 26 years old and in control of his own destiny...' At 33, I probably feel less in control of my destiny than I ever did.

What still amazes me is that not-jumping-on-a-Sunday is an image that endures seven years on. 'You're that athlete who doesn't jump on a Sunday,' said the man who came to fix our oven recently. 'A real Christian, you are; not like the rest of them who are only in it for the money.' He spoke in a manner that did not invite response, so I smiled and mumbled a 'thank you' and let the conversation pass to another subject.

Unknowingly, that gentleman had hit on the heart of the issue; an issue that this book has brought to my attention again. Because I do now jump on a Sunday. Because I am still a 'real Christian' ... or am I?

The one major fault I now see in the manner in which I handled the announcement of my 'Sunday' decision was that I never gave a clear biblical basis for it. If this foundation does not exist, then I am very much open to the criticism of not being the genuine article.

I initially wrote a much longer, more detailed article that outlined what I see as the biblical justification for my change of heart, and this now appears in an appendix at the end of the book. I hope that this briefer, less technical piece will serve as a more accessible insight into my thought processes, as well as providing a reassurance of my continued commitment to serve God with my whole heart.

The crux of the matter, I believe, hinges around the application of the Old Testament Law to New Testament believers.

The Law that God gave to Israel after her deliverance from Egypt, the Law that contains the Sabbath commandment, delineated the way he wanted the Hebrew nation to live their lives. The question is this: Does God call those who follow him today to live by the same set of commands?

The Bible is not a theology textbook; it is not a book we can just casually pick from the shelf, choose a random passage and apply it directly to our lives. Some thought is needed. To whom was the passage originally addressed? What were the unique historical circumstances? How does this relate to other portions of the Bible? This is not to assert that God can only speak to us through certain parts of Scripture, but only to say that care is needed when we try to understand and apply God's written Word.

These considerations come to bear directly on the Sunday debate. The Old Testament is clear: 'Remember the Sabbath day by keeping it holy' (Exodus 20:8). The New Testament seems ambivalent: 'One man considers one day more sacred than another; another man considers every day alike. Each one should be fully convinced in his own mind' (Romans 14:5). Which one is right?

Well, both are; they just apply to different groups of people living at different points in history. The first command, from the Old Testament, is part of the Law given to Israel and the second, from the writings of the Apostle Paul, is directed to the church in Rome. But what about us, believers living in the third millennium?

As Christians today, we are part of the Church, the worldwide group of followers of Jesus Christ, and we share a direct and vital continuity with those believers whom Paul was addressing. Therefore, it would be my belief that it is the latter command, the New Testament imperative, that is applicable.

It was this conclusion that I reached at the end of 1992: as a present-day believer, it was not wrong for me to jump on a Sunday. I cannot emphasize strongly enough that I would never have made the decision if I did not have this belief. The verse from Proverbs and the dream played their part in helping me overcome the fear of making a U-turn, but its foundation rested firmly on God's Word.

So when the man who repaired the oven noted that I was a real Christian, one who would not compromise his beliefs for personal gain, I hope he was mistakenly right!

Reverend Andy Edwards and his wife Jill had not read this piece prior to their own review of their son's decision. 'Jonathan will always give an honest answer about his trust in God,' says his mother. 'Quite clearly, people who write about him and interview him realize that. His integrity has never been questioned.' Reverend Edwards admits, 'We had to look at ourselves and discover why we felt like we did, think about what we believed. There was also a duty to see it from Jonathan's perspective. I understand what he does and I value what he does. If he's going to be the witness that he wants to be as a Christian in the athletic world, he's got to be where they are. I totally understand that and fully endorse that.'

His parents, of course, were both in Seville in August 1999 to support Edwards' fruitless attempt to regain the World Championship title. The depth of their commitment to their son cannot be overestimated.

Edwards himself places great importance on the fellowship he now receives from the friends he has made at Holy Trinity Church, close to his home in the Newcastle suburb of Gosforth. He still attends church on most Sundays and when he is at home he is a devotee of the midweek fellowship meetings that are held on Wednesdays. Spiritually, he was feeling strong in the autumn of 1999.

He smiles, too, at the recollection of the first competition he entered on a Sunday. 'It was the European Cup in Rome and on my first jump I was given a white flag. But the television replay showed that it was a clear foul – you could even see the mark in the plasticine. If I had been struck by a bolt of lightning, one might perhaps have drawn the conclusion that God wasn't too happy with me! Instead, I got a gift.'

Edwards is drawing a humorous line in the sand, of course, but the reality is this: the issue is closed. He can stand on the track on any day of the week with a clear conscience.

Chapter 4

Howay the Lad

You begin well in nothing except you end well.

THOMAS FULLER

Jonathan Edwards has always suspected that he read Physics at Durham University by default. He disliked the thought of studying Maths – too abstract. He might have read French but for one distinct problem – he had an allergy to French literature. He had never really taken much interest in Physics until the time of his O levels. 'I did a degree because that's what you did on the academic conveyor belt. I was on a conveyor belt, all right. I did what was expected of me, and shuffled along. I had a very secure home, strong set of beliefs, close relationship with my brother Tim.' Having been interviewed but not accepted for Oxford, Durham was his next choice, and Physics it was.

The routine at Durham suited him: three meals a day at Van Mildert College, someone to clean his room once a week. For Edwards, sport was still a recreation in 1984. He trained a little more coherently, but there was still no sustained attempt on his part to take athletics more seriously than he had done before.

His father, however, was more curious. He sensed that his son might possess rare ability and he wanted Jonathan to explore his potential at least. Reverend Edwards wrote to a man called Malcolm Arnold, who was national coach in Wales. Arnold would one day coach Colin Jackson to the 110-metre hurdles World Championship and become director of coaching for the British Olympic team in Atlanta, but Reverend Edwards chose to write to him because he had coached a young triple jumper in Ilfracombe. Scott Balment was two years younger than Edwards, but they had developed a friendship through competing on the same Devon team.

On receipt of Reverend Edwards' letter, Arnold recommended that they contact Carl Johnson, national coach in the Northeast. Andy Edwards still has a copy of the letter he wrote to Johnson on file in his vicarage. The letter, which effectively pushed Jonathan Edwards to contemplate giving more priority to athletics, reads:

Dear Mr Johnson,

I am writing to you at the suggestion of Malcolm Arnold over the matter of encouragement and coaching for my eldest son Jonathan Edwards.

To fill you in with the details to give you some understanding of the situation: Jonathan is at present at Durham University (Van Mildert College) reading Physics, he started last October. He came first last year in the ESAA Senior Boys triple jump with a distance of 15.01m. He went to the UAU Championships last week at Crystal Palace and came second at 14.99m. As you are no doubt aware members of the university come to Gateshead for training on a fairly regular basis which Jonathan has done but he has not been able to benefit from any encouragement or coaching there. He did attend the Great Britain Junior Commission in January, which he greatly appreciated.

The change from school to university is quite traumatic and results in a loss of continual encouragement and coaching and personal supervision and I feel that if he had some sort of help from a possible coach at Gateshead it would be a greater incentive for Jonathan. The particular area where he needs some expert help is in sorting out his run-up – he has always had difficulties. He has achieved a lot despite this handicap.

I trust you will not have minded me writing to you in this way. I feel that after the promises made last year following his success at Thurrock in the ESAA he has almost wasted a season – my desire is not to see talent wasted.

Carl Johnson arranged for Edwards to meet him. Johnson is a methodical man. To him coaching is a science, to be continually researched. His records are charted, no detail too small. When we met – and he has never spoken about Edwards at length before – he produced carefully printed and chronicled notes which made it possible to understand the scale of his working margins.

The first pages are entitled 'Nurturing the Gifted Performer. A Case Study. Athlete "A" – Triple Jumper'. In bold type, Johnson has written, '**Autumn 1986 he came under my influence and responsibility.**' Edwards is not named once, but the notes unmistakably apply to him. They offer an insight into Johnson's earliest contact with Edwards, still an undergraduate at Durham. The notes make fascinating, compelling reading and disclose how one medical expert even advised him to quit triple jumping.

Initial evaluation
Slight, naturally quick, reasonably springy, but not greatly so in my estimation – no real experience of athletic training (had so far succeeded on natural talent) thus athletically rather naive – moreover (and more importantly) did not give the impression of being prepared to accept hard training (he found reasons, usually slight injury, for stopping work, or not doing it).

Action
Check out real propensity towards injury by referring to local sports injury specialist orthopaedic surgeon.

Specialist advice – 'Stay away from the triple jump, the configuration of the bones of the foot suggests that the event will prove a recurring source of injury.'

Coach's advice to athlete – 'Which other event can we find for you to do which doesn't have these indicators?'

Athlete's response – 'But it's triple jump that I'm good at, and that is what I wish to do, despite the prognosis.'

Coach's resolution – train quietly to each point of stress, then back off. The athlete, despite previous indications and reservations, must be allowed to determine the rate of progress in this respect.

* * *

Actualization

Initially the rate of progress was slow. The pace was dictated by reluctance to 'pitch-in' to hard work, and adverse reactions to aches and pains, and genuine minor stresses of feet and ankles.

At each stage we advanced at a pace that he was prepared to accept, rather than that which my training and experience felt was necessary. My rationale was that it was better to keep such talent 'on-board' than to chase it and lose it. I was very conscious that I was handling quite a unique product, i.e. a 20-year-old triple jumper of talent, who was clear of chronic injury and was anxious to keep it that way for as long as possible. I was quite prepared to delay his optimum development by a year or two in order to meet that goal.

One early, and necessary management decision, was to facilitate instant physiotherapy treatment when minor ailments arose. Fortunately, I had maintained contact with an athletics injury insurance scheme and this he benefited from until he left college and became a worker.

Training frequency at this stage of his career was relatively intermittent; much was done on his own at college, and part of the weekend was denied us because of his religious convictions. He remained 'a novice' for quite a long time.

On that work he improved to 16.05m in 1986.

Edwards trained periodically with Johnson at the beginning, at most once a week during his nine-week-long terms. He certainly gave more prominence to his Bible study group at university. 'Around the college, he was known as *That's Jonathan Edwards*,' says Graham Rainey, a Law student at Durham in the same period. 'He represented the college at things he had never played before. He would try them and win. He was very visible around college, yet he was as he is now, bright and smiley and generally very pleasant. I suppose Jonathan is – and I mean this as a compliment – a very uncomplicated person. What you see is what you get.'

Rainey, now chaplain at Reading University, arrived at Durham from Northern Ireland a year after Edwards. Their friendship was forged at that Bible study group at Van Mildert, which involved between six and eight undergraduates. After growing up in the troubled Province, Rainey brought with him a perspective on religion and its impact that was beyond Edwards' experience. 'We had family friends who were killed,' he says. 'Yet as a child you tend to assume whatever is happening is just normal. It wasn't that you went into town and you'd dive for cover from flying bullets.' By contrast, Edwards' own childhood and adolescence had been sheltered and to a large extent privileged.

The diversity of background within the group led to an interesting forum, recalls Rainey. 'Jonathan would say what he thought, but I think as a group we gelled. No one voice was louder than the next. The concern for each other as human beings was underlying all that we did. We disagreed – and I had a few run-ins with Jonathan over politics because I was at the other end of the spectrum, or at least further to the left – but I don't remember any major arguments. Jonathan is a child of Thatcherism, whether he identifies himself as that or not! That's just my opinion. We used to have a good bit of banter about that, with me telling him he came from a privileged background and him telling me that was rubbish. But he was an easy person to befriend, a warm and attractive person. He was also self-sufficient.

'To say he kept his cards close to his chest is making too much of it, but he wasn't the type of person who would readily sit down and talk about his whole life experience. Sometimes, we imagine people must be more complex and there must be something lurking under the surface, and I think with some people there just isn't. I suspect Jonathan was one of them. I think his life was fairly simple and I don't mean that in a pejorative way. He came across as someone who'd had a relatively easy life.'

Another undergraduate in that Bible study group was Tony Davis, who was attracted to becoming a Christian by Edwards' strength of character. Unlike Rainey, Davis was a sportsman like Edwards, a footballer and a team-mate in the college cricket XI. In the cricket team Edwards fulfilled the role of all-rounder, remembers Davis. 'He was one of these guys that some people find annoying because whatever he tried he was good at. As a batsman he was more David Gower than Ian Botham.'

Looking back on that time, Davis says, 'Jonathan didn't stand on any type of soapbox. He just had this peace around him and he was very much respected. He didn't have to go into a bar and have six pints to be one of the gang. I think that was one of the reasons why he was respected. He held his views very highly and stuck by them. I used to go to church before I went to university, but Jonathan took me to one or two Christian events and that was how I became a Christian.' He later asked Edwards to be his best man.

Davis, now a Midlands-based chief accountant and company secretary for a couple of subsidiary companies of ICI, saw Edwards angry just once at Durham. That was the morning after someone had spiked his drinks at his twentieth birthday party. 'The only time I ever saw Jonathan drink alcohol, the poor man didn't know about it until afterwards! As I say, he had a lot of friends and he was respected, if you like, by the sports guys who frequented the bar on an average evening. A group of us took him down into Durham for his birthday – and some despicable characters spiked his soft drinks. It was sufficient to give him a bad head the next day. When he came into the breakfast hall, he was genuinely upset. It was a none too harmful university prank, but it wasn't part of Jonathan's make-up to do such a thing. I can't remember if I was involved – and I put my hand on my heart when I say that.'

Davis observed a subtle but meaningful change of emphasis in Edwards' approach to athletics during their university days. 'I think he went from being lethargic to being more dedicated. His training stepped up a gear and became much more part of his routine. I guess that mirrored the fact that he had moved up through the rankings by the time we left university.' Edwards, in fact, came an unimpressive ninth at the University Games in 1987, with a distance of 16.30 metres. 'No great shakes really,' Edwards says. He remembers the distances of his jumps like other people remember family birthdays and anniversaries – something he is not too hot on.

When Edwards was nearing the end of his degree – he gained a 2:1 in Physics – he realized that for the first time he had a responsibility to make a decision that would shape the course of his life. He started to fill out application forms to try to forge a career in banking, but he did this without any sense of fulfilling his destiny. 'I was on the point of being unceremoniously dumped off the conveyor belt at the top – or bottom,' he says. 'What was I going to do? I felt very strongly that the right thing to do as a Christian, what God wanted me to do, was to be an athlete. He had given me a gift and I should use it. How was I going to do that? I spoke to Carl Johnson and asked him if he thought I had the talent to consider giving this a go. He said, "Yes."'

That response created a sense of direction that would indeed shape Edwards' life, although the early signs were not encouraging. His confidence underpinned, Edwards decided to make the Northeast his adopted home. He would train with Johnson and search for a job. Paul Jones, the team manager for Gateshead Harriers, was a bachelor and offered him a room in his house for the short term while he got himself established. It all seemed to make sense, and Edwards headed for the West Country to tell his parents of his plans.

For Jill Edwards at home in the vicarage at Ilfracombe, the news came as a bombshell. 'Jonathan had spent a little while at home, then just announced he was going up to the Northeast to live. There was not much discussion and I was stunned. I found it very hard to accept and I was very upset; yes, very upset. It just came out of the blue. It seemed to happen without rhyme or reason. He didn't seem to have a career plan and I couldn't understand why he had to go so soon. He could have thought about working for the summer at home. I was devastated.'

Edwards certainly did not have a career plan as he stood on the railway platform in Devon with a one-way ticket to Newcastle. His mother hugged him tearfully as the train drew into the station. 'We didn't expect him to stay in North Devon because there would not have been anything for him. It was just that it all happened so quickly. It was a *fait accompli*. It would have been different if he had come home and said that he'd got a job. But he had nothing in place. He was just going.'

Those were the worries rushing through Jill's mind as she waited to see him onto his train. Her son was now a man of the world, but what world was he entering? He was leaving for the opposite corner of the country without a job or permanent accommodation. 'I won't ever forget Mum's face as we said goodbye,' says Edwards. He shed a tear or two of his own, but he felt an overwhelming wave of independence and anticipation. He would make it on his own or fail in the attempt – and Jonathan Edwards was not a young man conversant with failure.

His search for a place to live did not prove too difficult. At the rear of the parish church where he worshipped there was a book listing houseowners with accommodation to rent. Edwards selected a flat, placed a call and the owner obligingly offered to collect him for a viewing. Edwards confesses that as the car drove into Heaton his heart missed a beat. As rain drilled against the windows, all he could see was street after street of dreary-looking terraced houses. For a young man spoiled by the wild, rural beauty of the North Devon coast and then the quaintness of Durham, this urban landscape was a culture shock. Still, Edwards needed a roof over his head and the accommodation was clean and affordable. He was to discover that his first impressions did not necessarily provide a fair reflection of the area. He found a friendliness and warmth in Heaton and, with his wife Alison, later established their first marital home in the street that had provided him with such an unflattering view of the suburb on the day he came flat-hunting.

Edwards may have found himself a room, but as a just-graduated student, finding work was to prove more arduous and depressing; a scenario that thousands of other young men on Tyneside would doubtlessly recognize. He took the sensible course of action and went to sign on the dole. When he arrived at his nearest DHSS office, he was told he was in the wrong place and redirected to the other side of the city. One image persists: 'I was always speaking to someone through a glass panel,' he says. The harsh reality of unemployment was a fleeting experience for Edwards, but the exposure showed him how the system can so easily dehumanize those on either side of the reinforced glass panel. The unsentimental tone of the questioning from the stressed-out DHSS staff also opened his eyes to a hard, unforgiving environment which was alien to him. 'It was horrible, desperate.'

Edwards returned to his rented room deflated and dispirited. 'I cried my eyes out. I felt alone. I probably also thought at some point, "God, what am I doing up here? And what are you doing bringing me up here?" Quite what I expected God to do in 24 hours, I'm not sure.' He was 21 years old, looked younger and wore round-framed glasses like the late John Lennon. He was adrift in the ocean of a big city hundreds of miles from the safe harbour of the family home.

'I'd never experienced life, real life, like this. After I'd moved into the flat in Heaton, my first attempt at cooking involved making an omelette and putting it on a lettuce leaf. Grotesque. The first time I cooked spaghetti I must have done enough to feed an army. I look back and think, "How did I survive?" In fact, I can still hardly believe that I ever had the courage to move up to the Northeast at all. Consider the facts: I wasn't confident, I wasn't someone who liked the unknown, and yet I got on that train and set off for Newcastle with no more than the bags I had in my hand. If you ever wanted proof that the age of miracles wasn't dead, this was it! I believed that this was what God wanted me to do and trusted that he would look after me; I would never have done it without that belief.'

In those first, lonely weeks his search for a job proved to be as successful as his culinary efforts. Each Thursday, Edwards would rush to get an early copy of the *Newcastle Chronicle* as soon as it hit the streets. He would scan the employment section and, after circling appropriate-sounding jobs, he would write out his applications. 'I applied for any kind of clerical job.' As well as filling out an application form, Edwards inserted a covering letter. He wanted prospective employers to know that he understood that he was vastly overqualified for the position being advertised, but that as an aspiring athlete he had no ambition to climb the corporate ladder.

Edwards never got so much as a reply – until he wrote to the Royal Victoria Infirmary for a job that he knew nothing about. 'I read the advert and I didn't know what it meant, but it said they wanted a science graduate, so I fitted the bill.' He was invited for an interview and that was when panic materialized. The job on offer was for a scientific officer in the cytogenetics laboratory and Edwards had not an iota of knowledge about genetics. Two days beforehand, he called for help from an old university friend, Zoe York (now Hyles). Zoe had read Zoology at Durham and in Edwards' book that made her a genetics professor. Even though the post was advertised as a six-month contract, Edwards discovered that he had five rivals at the interview, all of them with genetics-related degrees.

To his great surprise – and relief – head of the laboratory Val Davison offered Edwards the position on a salary of £13,000 a year. In the space of an afternoon, he had become a scientific officer who would be charged with performing diagnostic analysis on chromosomes. As they walked down the hospital corridor after he had been appointed, Edwards had just one pertinent question for Davison: 'Why did you appoint me?'

Davison says now, 'I'll always remember Jonathan asking me that question. Well, the truth is, we were advertising just a locum post, to cover maternity leave, and I have to say the applications for those are usually fairly poor. Obviously, Jonathan wasn't searching for a career in genetics, or in anything other than triple jumping, and we appointed him because he seemed as though he actually had a brain. I thought that as he was bright we could get something out of him.' Her hunch was to prove correct.

A large aspect of the work in the laboratory involved prenatal detection of genetic handicap. If a woman is carrying a baby who is genetically handicapped, she may decide to abort the pregnancy. Due to his religious convictions, Edwards found that part of the job morally unacceptable. His feet are strongly in the pro-life camp. Davison, however, ensured that he was never asked to perform diagnosis on a foetus. 'We always discuss this at interview,' she says. 'He didn't come on very strongly, but we knew that he would not want to do this section of the work. In general terms, Jonathan was one of the brightest youngsters that you would come across. He was very assured about where he was going and what he was doing. I think a lot of that strength he got from his religion.'

Edwards now had a structured and ordered existence. He would work, then he would be given a lift to Gateshead Stadium by a newly made friend in the laboratory. After training he would make his own way back to Heaton, riding the Metro to Newcastle town centre and, on occasions, walking several miles if a bus did not come along. 'It could take over an hour, then I'd cook an evening meal. I look at myself now and think, "Did I do that?"'

He still went home to Ilfracombe when he could, as did his brother Tim, who was now studying at Borough Road, Isleworth. 'We were playing table tennis one day when I asked Jonathan what his chances were of getting to the Seoul Olympics,' says Tim. He had worked with an organization called Youth With A Mission during a gap year and knew that there were opportunities to return to YWAM at the Olympics in South Korea. He duly applied and was accepted.

For his brother, the selection process to get himself on the plane to Seoul was marginally more complicated, of course. Having refused to enter the Olympic trials because the competition was being staged on a Sunday, he had to wait to be called up. When the selectors eventually nominated him, Edwards appreciated that his career was moving in the right direction. The brothers arranged to meet in Seoul.

Those Olympics are to be forever remembered as the Games that died of shame. Canadian Ben Johnson, the winner of the 100 metres in a new world record, was unmasked as a drugs cheat. Johnson went from hero to zero in 9.79 seconds and the reverberations were felt around the globe. Athletics was front-page news from Argentina to Australia and all places in between, for all the wrong, contemptible reasons.

Edwards can still vividly recollect the race, billed beforehand as a duel between Johnson and his American rival Carl Lewis, with Britain's Linford Christie competing for the minor medal. Edwards had seen nothing to compare with it at an athletics stadium before – how could he have done as an international tenderfoot? 'Everything was quiet before the race ... then, bang! and suddenly there was this huge eruption of noise. Johnson was amazing. He just flew. His pick-up from the blocks was amazing. There were two races – Johnson in one, the rest in another.' Johnson took the gold medal place, with Lewis second and Christie third. In Canada, the population was ecstatic, with the *Toronto Star* hollering the message, 'BEN JOHNSON – A NATIONAL TREASURE'.

Lewis had shaken Johnson's hand as protocol – and his own integrity – demanded, but he was raging inside. He would later reveal that as they crossed the line, his initial thought was, 'Damn. Ben did it again. He got away with it again.' Only he had not.

Three days after the epic 100 metres final, Edwards was waking up to the buzz going round the athletes' village: Johnson had tested positive for an anabolic steroid called stanozolol. 'Everyone was talking about it.' Little wonder. The fastest man in the world was a chemically enhanced fraud. We had watched him travel like no man before, we had celebrated the beauty of the moment and now we were told it was a falsehood. 'Yet I'll never forget the memory of him running,' says Edwards. 'The emotion I felt, the image of him powering down the track, is not changed by what subsequently happened. It's overshadowed, of course; but he still ran an amazing race.'

Edwards was never going to be in contention for a medal at these Games. He was 22 years old, the new kid on the team, watching, learning, finding his feet. If the truth be known, he was a little overawed, a fact endorsed by one recollection he offers from the Seoul Olympics. At the British holding camp in Japan, the athletes were rooming in a village of log cabins and Edwards, who liked to sing Christian choruses, discovered that the team manager had brought a guitar with him. He asked to borrow it. He was told which cabin to visit to get the guitar and when he knocked on the door it was answered by Daley Thompson.

Edwards' legs turned to jelly and his tongue refused to function. Thompson was the reigning Olympic decathlon champion and a larger-than-life character. Eventually, Edwards managed to splutter the reason for his visit. He disappeared into another room in the cabin, played and sang for about 30 minutes and then went to leave. Nervously, he thanked Thompson and apologized for any disturbance he might have caused. 'Bye, Jon, see you later,' said Thompson. Edwards was amazed. 'I walked away incredulous that Daley Thompson, *the* Daley Thompson, knew my name. I was just overwhelmed.'

Another veteran campaigner on that British team was Kriss Akabusi, who had become a Christian just two years earlier. Initially, Akabusi was on a crusade to convert everyone. 'I wanted to share this good news with everybody,' he says. 'I was what the Americans call a fundamentalist; the Bible was very important to me. Hell and brimstone ... got to do the right thing ... I was very evangelical.' He collared anyone within his orbit. '"Please, listen, you're a friend..." I wanted to see all my friends become Christians.' Akabusi laughs uproariously as only he can. He had gone from one extreme to another; from being one of the lads to being a Bible-punching Christian zealot on a mission to save mankind.

Inevitably, Akabusi and Edwards were drawn into the same Christian circle in Seoul. 'Jonathan looked very angelic and bookish. Out of all us Christians, he looked like a Christian! Line us up against the wall and demand that someone name the Christian: he was the Christian. He was the antithesis of the person I was, except for the Christianity part. He was middle class, well educated, obviously white. I was a black boy who had grown up in a children's home.'

Akabusi knew Edwards' type, he says. One of his closest friends is Roger Black, public school educated, son of a doctor who also ran 400 metres rather successfully in a British vest. 'So that was my immediate rapport with Jonathan. Though we were different, I could relate to him because he was a Christian and because I thought I understood his cultural background.' Had Edwards not been a Christian, the truth is that Akabusi feels they would never have fallen into the same social group. 'One thing that athletics and Christianity have in common is that they bring people together from different backgrounds. If I hadn't been an athlete, I wouldn't have met a Roger Black sort of person; if I hadn't been a Christian, I would never have met a Jonathan Edwards type of person.'

In Seoul, Akabusi, Edwards, Barrington Williams, Vernon Samuels and Judy Simpson often met to worship in Akabusi's room. 'We were quite open; we wanted everyone to become Christians,' says Akabusi. 'We were worshipping God unabated. There is a story in the Bible of David when he danced in front of the whole crowd before God. I was thinking it was very much a similar situation. Jonathan played guitar and Vernon played the portable keyboard and we were praising God, dancing and singing. When I say this was a holy moment, it's not the same as when God said to Moses, "Take off your shoes, you are standing on holy ground." We would keep our door open and we would let this celebration of God flow into the corridor and just hope people's hearts would be touched a little bit.'

Edwards, who shared a room with Barrington Williams – as well as 'never on a Sunday' convictions – certainly found spiritual inspiration within this self-contained Christian group. 'Good times, and from then on a kind of Christian presence in athletics was established,' he says. 'Kriss is a great guy and an extrovert. What really impressed me was that he never had a victim mentality, never felt sorry for himself despite the severity of his upbringing. He used to just explain that he had made the best of what had been available to him. There was no resentment, no attitude problem. I drew a lot of strength from Kriss.'

His abiding memories of Seoul and the Christian worship group were further heightened by the presence of his brother. Tim had asked one of the Koreans on his Youth With A Mission team to buy his ticket for him so that he could attend the Games on the day his brother was competing. 'The ticketing was very complicated and you couldn't choose where in the stadium you sat,' he explains. 'I know it was selfish – but I prayed I got a good view of the triple jump.' His prayers were answered. His ticket was for a seat towards the sandpit end of the runway. 'Jonathan saw me and we chatted before he competed. Surreal. Later we were able to spend a couple of days together in the city.'

Seoul was to be a seminal moment in Edwards' development as an athlete. He did not qualify for the final, but he left those Games appreciating that this was the level of stage on which he wanted to perform. 'I thought, next time I come to an Olympics I want to have a chance of competing for a medal, and not be an also-ran.'

Back in England, Edwards continued to train with Johnson and the next year was to be critical. 'The summer of 1989 was a watershed,' says Johnson. 'The conservative approach to training had paid off. He rapidly established

British ascendancy that summer.' Edwards won the UK Championships, but would not represent Britain in the Europa Cup, which was being staged on his doorstep at Gateshead, as his event was programmed for a Sunday. He did not even attend as a spectator. The British team triumphed nonetheless, and that enabled Edwards to pitch up in September that year in the World Cup, where he would announce himself as an athlete of international calibre.

The World Cup was held in the Montjuic Stadium in Barcelona, later the venue for the 1992 Olympic Games. Johnson admits that he advised Edwards to miss the competition, as he did not believe there would be sufficient time to prepare for the Commonwealth Games, which were scheduled for Auckland in January 1990. Johnson thought he should end his summer season early and commence winter work by mid-August, creating time to recuperate from a long season. This would also provide an ample time frame to travel to and acclimatize in New Zealand.

Unsurprisingly, however, Edwards could not resist the attraction of the World Cup. His reward was his first-ever legal jump in excess of 17 metres. He came third with a leap of 17.28 metres, leaving Johnson to confess, 'This was his breakthrough into world class.' Yet Edwards could not repeat that performance in Auckland, although he finished with a silver medal for a jump of 16.93 metres – an experience that was to repeat itself down the years on more demanding days in Atlanta and Athens. He was deprived of a Commonwealth Games gold by two centimetres.

The medal he carried on board his flight home from New Zealand may not have been the colour he had hoped for, but his disappointment in Auckland registered a low

mark on the Richter scale compared to the distressing
news awaiting him when he landed in London.

Edwards cleared customs and looked forward to being
reunited with his parents and brother. He was bursting to
tell them stories of his time in Australia and New Zealand.
On reflection, the mood in the car seemed a little more
sombre than it should have been as they drove away from
the airport, but he hardly noticed then. He was still
buzzing.

Edwards did not have to wait long to hear what the
family had to tell him. In his absence, his 15-year-old
sister Rachel had been rushed to hospital. She had been
found collapsed at home, and was undergoing therapeutic
counselling. There was a fault line in the family's solid,
Christian foundations that he had not envisaged. 'It was
pretty shocking news,' says Edwards. 'I think I had this
assumption that we were a perfect family. Everything in
the garden seemed so rosy.'

Not in Rachel Edwards' garden. A childhood spent
following in the footsteps of her brothers' success at West
Buckland School and listening to her father's acclaim for
the boys had proved to be a daunting journey and a
haunting melody. She demanded to be recognized in her
own right. 'It wasn't just Jonathan, it wasn't just Timothy –
it was my father, it was my mother, it was my entire family
unit,' she says. 'Particularly the male figures in it. I think a
lot of it stemmed from a real lack of belief in my own self-
worth. West Buckland was great for Jonathan and Tim, but
it didn't work for me. I never felt I was affirmed for who I
was. I was an Edwards rather than Rachel Edwards. That's
why I rebelled. That's what led to my breakdown. At that
time, it was incredibly traumatic. I went through a time of

incredible self-reflection, counselling, therapy, whatever you want to call it. But I reflect on it now more positively; 1990 was a pivotal year in my life.'

Now Rachel Edwards-Grundy, she spoke to me at her home in Oxford just before her twenty-fifth birthday in the autumn of 1999. She is a self-assured graduate in Fine Arts from York, exceedingly comfortable with her own identity, happily married for one year and leading a hectic and rewarding lifestyle. She is a printmaker, a creator of handmade greetings cards, and also a part-time support worker in a residential unit for psychiatrically disturbed adolescents. 'I think I'm heading for a lifelong commitment to the mental health service,' she says. She fervently believes that art can become an excellent line of therapy for psychiatric patients. Retrospectively, from her closeness to disturbed young people, she has a greater understanding of her own illness, diagnosed as a 'juvenile breakdown'. 'When I look back at my difficult time, I didn't have a psychiatric illness. I was just soul-searching.'

Eight years younger than Jonathan, six years younger than Tim, she grew up in the same household but inevitably had limited interaction with her brothers. The boys played with a ball in every available hour of daylight, then moved the game to the basement when darkness fell. 'We loved her, of course,' says Jonathan. 'But the age gap was a big factor and Tim and I had already forged a strong relationship before Rachel was born. Before she was three years old, we had already begun schoool at West Buckland and this meant we left home at 7.45 a.m. and often didn't return before 6.00 p.m. Of course, on Saturdays we invariably had school matches. So little sister just wasn't part of everyday life; after all, she was too small to go in goal!'

Rachel's own enrolment at West Buckland School, where her brothers had carved enormous reputations in sport, was calamitous for her self-esteem. 'I was never called by my first name. I was an Edwards and apparently that was good enough. I don't think I thrived on that. I don't think anyone does, really. I don't think Tim thrived on it, but he had more obvious channels to deal with it because he was a bloke. I think there was very high expectation and I reacted to that.'

She tells one story to illustrate her case. There were to be trials for the hockey team, but she was not required to take part. 'You don't need to go and trial, do you – you're an Edwards,' she was told by one master. Rachel was indignant. 'Pardon? I don't know if my brothers played hockey, but I think probably not and, besides, that's hardly the point.' The master insisted she did not have to attend the trials. For Rachel that was breaking point. 'From that moment, I thought: "You've got to be joking."' At around this time she developed a knee injury and completely abandoned sport. She immersed herself in art and drama instead.

Rachel found it especially difficult to be around her father when Jonathan was competing, and she suspects she probably still would. 'I don't remember what it was, but I didn't enjoy watching athletics with my father. Don't get me wrong – I'm very proud of what Jonathan has achieved, but I also think it's important to keep it in perspective. I think Jonathan himself has the same kind of attitude. He's thankful to God for the success he's had, but also recognizes triple jumping for what it is. Hence, he deals with it more modestly, perhaps, than people around him do.' Diplomatically, she does not elaborate.

Jill Edwards admits quietly, 'I guess it's our fault as much as anybody's because she was that much younger, and there was always something sporting going on. People would come in and say, "What was the score at the rugby?" or, "What did you jump?" So the conversation was always about sport and Rachel was growing up with it all the time. With hindsight you can see that, but it was just part of family life. Andy's always been keen on sport.'

Contrarily, Reverend Edwards comments, 'I look back and I didn't help Rachel, but I wasn't conscious that I wasn't helping her. I realize now that she has other gifts, other abilities which I admire. She's made her mark.' When she was a youth worker at Lee Abbey, he says proudly, children with special needs always gravitated towards his daughter for comfort and care. His wife adds, 'Yes, she's got a wonderful gift. She's artistic and the boys found that was something they didn't particularly relate to. She likes to write poetry and they didn't relate to that either! I think there is a little lack of understanding of Jonathan for Rachel, and vice versa.'

Perhaps that sentiment should now be expressed in the past tense. 'Jonathan and I had quite an interesting relationship; at times we were quite ambivalent towards one another,' says Rachel. 'I don't think we had any real insight into how each other worked. We had never been able to meet on a level, mainly because he was the older one and I was the younger sister. There were times when I thought he was quite annoying. Once I wrote to him to say sorry for aggravating him. He replied saying it didn't matter. I think he was aware I probably had comparative comments when I was still at school and it's hard to know how to respond to that, how to put that, without sounding egotistical. I'm much older now in the way I view these things. I would have to say that Jonathan's impact on my life was much more profound at school than the impact on my life of what he achieved in 1995.

'I'm closer to Timothy. I think, with him being that little bit younger, my relationship developed with him in a slightly different way. I think that's typical of family dynamics, that younger–older syndrome. Either they're inseparable or there's this mysterious wonder and ambivalence. We're very similar, Jonathan and I, both quick thinking. We both love word games.' There is a strong physical resemblance, too, and both have dark, piercing eyes.

She has grown accustomed to being introduced in company as 'the sister of...'. 'Yes, it happens. There was a time when I used to find that quite difficult. I wanted to tell them I was a person in my own right – it was irrelevant who my brother was. Now, I don't mind at all and sometimes have a bit of fun with it. People will often say what a lovely bloke Jonathan is, and I reply, "Oh really, is he?" It's weird, though, hearing strangers express opinions about my brother when they have no idea what he's really like. Of course, he *is* lovely!'

Edwards smiles at a private image of his sister. 'Tim and I were so strait-laced; Rachel definitely provided the alternate side to the Edwards family. When she was away at camp, she would always befriend the Gothic with a ring through his nose...' Rachel admits that a rebellious streak resides in her nature. She is not a slave to convention, refusing to accept at face value any kind of doctrine, theological or political. She poses questions, demands answers. It is why, in adolescence, her faith came under serious threat. She took unkindly to the move from the family home in Ilfracombe to begin afresh in her father's new parish of Bearwood, near Bournemouth, and failed to settle in a large, robust senior school.

Her unrest culminated in her 'breakdown', as Rachel explains. 'I wasn't in hospital very long, but I spent most of 1990 getting back on track and getting back into school. I'm thankful to God that I went through that because I had to face questions that I had ignored, as predominantly people do. I didn't want to take my faith from the family, accepting that was your DNA, as it were. I'm the sort of person who questions everything. As a result, my faith became something that was a living reality.'

A move to an independent school provided Rachel with a fresh beginning, and that was integral to the discovery of her own self-worth. 'Once I changed school and went to Clayesmore, I found my niche. I was my own person – and I absolutely flourished. All three of us had tremendous opportunity in the education we had and the people we met; and each of us has expressed that opportunity in different ways. I believe succcess, in whatever terms you like to measure it, is within the grasp of anybody. I would say that a lot of what Jonathan has done has enabled me to step out with confidence in my ability. By that, I mean he has shown that you don't know what you can do until you have pushed the doors and tried to open them. I think he would be surprised at that, that he's affected me, but he has.'

She staged her first art exhibition in the summer of 1999, a triumph in her terms. She is effervescent, full of life and quite obviously caring. Her brother's big date at the World Championships in Seville prompted her to telephone him on his mobile phone after he had arrived in Spain. 'He was very much on my mind. I had a very bad dream that things were going to go disastrously wrong, which I didn't tell him. I wanted to have a positive conversation and we did. I just felt so sick for him when he didn't win – I know that it affects him profoundly when he doesn't perform how he should. Jonathan and I are quite similar; there's no in-between, it either goes well or it doesn't. I was so pleased when he got it into perspective so soon after he came home. Jonathan and I do get on very well. As I was becoming an adult, I was no longer fazed by the things that he was doing, but more interested in who he was. I wanted to be close, but there's always the little sister syndrome, isn't there?'

Rachel, whose husband Tim is a primary school teacher, has a finely identified sense of her self-worth. She is proud of the fact that she was the first in the Edwards family to visit Israel. 'My family has always been interested in the Jewish roots of the Christian faith,' she says. She grew bored of hearing about it and took off for Israel in 1994 to see the country for herself. She survived for one year on a total budget of £600 and worked with various Christian organizations. 'I lived in about 17 different places, and made it to North Africa as well. I lived on a shoestring, but I thoroughly enjoyed it. The Middle Eastern culture is absolutely lovely; I'd happily live there. When I went out there I had no intention of coming back.' When her father later visited Jerusalem on a sabbatical, he found himself being introduced as 'the father of Rachel Edwards'. It was a novel twist; one he tells with pride and one that definitely amuses his daughter.

She feels an empathy with her brother's loss of privacy. 'Being a family in a vicarage, you're in a goldfish bowl all your life!' she says knowingly. 'That's how I described it from being very little. From that, Jonathan's position is worsened because as a Christian he seeks to be more accountable and more self-critical. Jonathan sees athletics as a gift and his responsibility in this life is to steward what he has been given.'

Challenge her as to whether her elder brother has changed, and she poses her own question in return. 'Since when? Since he was an obnoxious 16-year-old?' Rachel laughs, because the indifference that they experienced in childhood has given way to a love that she thinks will only get stronger and stronger. 'I think the success of 1995 has sobered him. He has become more modest in the way he has responded to things. I'm very proud of the way he has dealt with fame. Jonathan has always placed family first, and his beliefs, and he has held on to that. You wrestle like Job wrestled with things; everyone knows conflict, it's just relative, that's all. Jonathan's conflict is heightened by the nature of it being public.'

Rachel Edwards' 'breakdown' unquestionably shook the family in the early months of 1990 as her brother came home from the Commonwealth Games with a silver medal. Reverend Edwards had counselled other families when they experienced such trauma, but he had never for a second supposed that he would have to deal with it within the confines of his own home. They were desperately unhappy times, you sense; but Jonathan would have been spared most of their anxiety as he was living away from home.

'I was always aware that Rachel wasn't completely happy, but never realized how profound it was,' he says. 'I'm not sure any of us did until it was too late. I think we all failed her without meaning to, without even knowing. I think Rachel's insecurities were stirred when she followed Tim and me to West Buckland; and were brought more sharply into focus by my success and Dad's reaction to it. By the time she reached crisis point, I was living 400 miles away and preparing to get married. Even if I'd been closer, I don't think I could have been of much help. In Rachel's eyes, I think I was part of the problem rather than the solution. Tim certainly had a better relationship with Rachel; he spent a good block of time with her at home after I had left. Tim was also challenged during his time with YWAM and made a big effort to forge a relationship with Rachel.'

For Rachel, the road to recovery was lined with those wishing to assist and love her – counsellors, staff at Clayesmore School and her family, especially her mother, who was no less than a guardian angel in the really rough times. Jonathan adds, poignantly, 'We were all desperately concerned for Rachel; Mum and Dad in particular went through agonies. Now we're all incredibly grateful and relieved that she has successfully established herself. Without the commitment of Mum and Dad, who knows what might have happened.' Rachel has made her parents as proud of her as they are of their sons.

She has also found room in her life for sport. She plays badminton and cycles. 'I'm running at the moment … Jonathan would laugh if he knew that.'

He did. 'She's an Edwards, after all!'

Chapter 5

The Worst and Best of Times

Calamity is a man's true touchstone.

BEAUMONT AND FLETCHER

A year that had begun under a dark cloud for the Edwards family ended joyously as Jonathan married Alison Briggs at Heaton Baptist Church on 10 November 1990. Reverend Andy Edwards conducted the wedding ceremony, while his daughter Rachel acted as bridesmaid along with Alison's sisters, Margo and Lynsey.

Edwards suspects that his season on the track may have been overshadowed by the preparations for making such a fundamental change in his life, leaving his bachelor days behind him. 'Perhaps the fact that I was getting married meant my mind was not quite focused,' he admits. 'Anyway, I had a real dip in form. I was flat the whole season.' Unusually, Edwards cannot specifically detail his best distance for that year – '16.50 something,' he says. From a man who recollects his jumps more easily than he can recite family birthdays, perhaps we can put this particular lapse down to a case of selective amnesia. As an athlete who had cleared 17.28 metres in 1989, perhaps subconsciously he had decided that any jump not registering above 17 metres was to be locked in the vaults of his memory and left to gather cobwebs.

For further evidence, ask Edwards how his season began in 1991 and this is the response: '17.21, 17.36, 17.43...' and the numbers come tumbling out faster than Guinevere can deliver the balls in the draw for the National Lottery. He could even give you the wind readings. Yet, in reality, this was to be another year tinged with disappointment for Edwards. Still unwilling to compete on a Sunday, the 1991 World Championships in Tokyo were disappointingly off limits to him, as the qualifying rounds were to be held on that day. Edwards watched those Championships on television and saw the triple jump title being annexed by an American called Kenny Harrison. 'He was red hot,' says the Englishman. Harrison had dominated the world stage for the previous two years, and Edwards knew he was a genuinely talented athlete and he would not forget the name. The rest of us, if we had not already done so, would have occasion to learn it soon enough.

Edwards, in truth, may not have been much of a match for Harrison in Tokyo. He did not sustain his early form through the season. His coach Carl Johnson says, 'General management problems arose in 1991. The World Championships were denied him and he also needed a summer invitation meet programme for financial reasons. This imposed a change in training routine involving a reduction in strength work and resulting in a rapid loss of strength and decline in performance, which had related side effects which he or we had not envisaged. Promoters were not really interested in using poor performers and promotions officers are not keen to fight the case of below-form athletes. It provided a salutary lesson for both of us.'

These were hard times for Edwards. He was dedicated to making his young marriage prosper, but his training was disadvantaged by the hours he spent in the laboratory. He understood this even more clearly after attending a men's retreat organized by his church. 'The speaker challenged me very directly,' says Edwards.

The speaker asked him, 'What do you feel God wants you to do?'

'Be an athlete,' Edwards told him.

'What do you spend most of your time doing?'

'Working in a laboratory.'

The starkness of that conversation brought the reality of Edwards' ambition into focus. He had to make a fundamental change, or else ignore every instinct that had been drawing him to the track. With Alison's blessing, he went part-time at the laboratory. 'At first it felt really odd; I thought I was skiving,' he smiles. 'I worked from 8.30 a.m. until 11.30 a.m. four days a week, then one day a week I worked from 10.30 a.m. until 4.30 p.m.' His name was not yet on the lips of promoters looking to attract a hot ticket. Edwards was in no-man's-land, a part-time athlete, a part-time employee. Where would he find that critical breakthrough?

To Edwards, the Olympic Games in Barcelona the following summer were now at the forefront of his planning. 'Please, please,' he pleaded, 'please, please,' he prayed: *Do not let the triple jump be on a Sunday.'* When the schedule landed on his doormat, he tore it open with the urgency of a child unwrapping a gift at Christmas. 'Qualifying was on a Saturday. My heart dropped.

I thought the final had to be the next day, but as I scanned the programme there was no mention of the triple jump on the Sunday. I looked at the Monday programme – and there it was, "Triple Jump Final". This was a miracle as far as I was concerned. I thanked God. The day I rest was the day that the Olympics rested the triple jump. I was quite overcome.'

As spring passed into summer, as those Games came into focus on the horizon, Edwards figured out a game plan. He had to join the elite athletes who were going to finalize their training in Monaco, where the climate and facilities were of the highest calibre. Linford Christie and Colin Jackson would be in the Principality, high rollers of the track with no aspirations to break the bank in Monte Carlo, but with ambitions to strike gold in Barcelona. In particular Kriss Akabusi, along with Roger Black and John Regis, would also be in Monaco. Edwards knew he had to get there – but how? Who would pay the bill?

He called Andy Norman, promotions officer (and de facto top dog) of British athletics, to plead his case. 'I pestered Andy to take me,' says Edwards. His argument was that Norman should speculate to accumulate. With typical bluntness, Norman used to tell Edwards in the early days that he was as marketable as a car with a set of flat tyres. Nevertheless, he always had a belief and a suspicion that Edwards was an athlete who would one day succeed in the grand arenas of the world. He agreed to make the investment. Edwards would be included in the camp in Monte Carlo, and he knew he could ask for no better preparation for the second Olympic Games of his career.

His appetite for this level of training had been whetted on a trip to California earlier in 1992, made possible by a

£5,000 grant from Northern Electric. Instead of being left to his own lonely devices in Gateshead, he had been in the company of Black and Akabusi on a university campus near Los Angeles. He was in the company of men of a like mind and ambition, ensuring that the quality of his work was intense and competitive. Alison took unpaid leave from the physiotherapy department of the Royal Victoria Infirmary in Newcastle to travel with her husband to California. She looked around a few hospitals, did some research, soaked up some sun and provided support for Edwards in an alien environment. 'It was a really difficult time for Jonathan to break in at this level – at least I felt that,' she says. 'Everyone else there seemed to have achieved so much. People were nice enough, but I felt we were regarded a little as outsiders. Jonathan showed them that he was fast and that he was impressive in the weight room, but there was just this sense that he was being treated as a new boy; and nobody really took the triple jump seriously.'

Yet Akabusi and his wife Monika left an impression on her. 'Kriss took Jonathan under his wing and Monika, in particular, was so good to me. They were lovely and we will never forget that.' Akabusi was on the countdown to his last Olympics. He was the most well-known Christian in athletics and, with his full-throated laugh, certainly the most audible. He was looking to pass the baton to another Christian and the likeliest candidate was Edwards. Akabusi had befriended Edwards at the Seoul Olympics and they had developed a strong bond. There was an obvious intimacy between these two men, brought together by their faith.

Akabusi's own conversion to Christianity had occurred just six years earlier, and not long after the death of newborn twins. 'We lost the babies on 5 November 1985, a date I'll never forget,' he says, his voice uncommonly solemn. The couple already had a baby daughter, Ashanti (and would later have another child, Shakira), yet the deaths of his infant children caused Akabusi more than grief. They made a spiritually profound impact on him. 'It was a catalyst to get me thinking about the great things in life,' he explains. 'Prior to having the twins, I was happy-go-lucky, nothing fazed me. Life was all, "Go on, enjoy yourself!" I'm still happy-go-lucky, but with a little more purpose, a little more *raison d'être*. Jonathan was good to be around; in those days he knew so much more about the Bible than me.

'When he came to California, to see what the big boys did, it was evident that he had lived quite a sheltered athletics existence. He was still looking to make his mark. He was blisteringly quick – a surprise for us, as he looked so weedy. He was challenging Roger and the boys in a sprint, so he knew he had a lot of potential there.'

Edwards benefited hugely from the exposure to full-on training, living, breathing and thinking his sport. As the Olympics approached, his confidence was on the rise. To go to Monte Carlo with Akabusi, Black and the others was just putting the final piece of the jigsaw in place, or so he thought. Once in Monaco, he met daily to study the Bible with Akabusi. 'One of the topics of conversation was Kriss's retirement. He was the most recognizable Christian in athletics and it had given him a great platform to share the Christian faith. We discussed how this responsibility would likely pass to me. We also assumed that my success in Barcelona would be an important part of this puzzle, spiritually speaking. Remember, I was in good shape, so we had physical as well as spiritual hope that it was going to be my year. I was going to Barcelona with great hopes.'

After nine days in Monte Carlo, Edwards arrived in Spain two days before the triple jump qualifying round on Saturday 1 August. While Edwards had been in Monte Carlo, his parents, accompanied by their youngest son Tim and his wife Anna, had begun the journey to Spain by road from the South of England. They had scheduled a leisurely drive through France in Andy Edwards' Peugeot 405 estate to reach their base for the Olympics at a house in the Pyrenees owned by a friend of Anna. The location was around 140 miles from Barcelona, but that was deemed an acceptable commute to have the opportunity to see Edwards participate in the Olympics. They were working with the constraints of a tight budget, but their journey through France was immensely pleasurable. In the suffocating heat, they occasionally wished the car had air conditioning, but otherwise they were uncomplaining.

Alison Edwards had made separate arrangements. She had a ticket to fly from England to Spain, to arrive on the evening of 1 August. She would meet the others in Barcelona and then return with them to their retreat in the Pyrenees. The entire Edwards family had tickets for the triple jump final in the Montjuic Stadium on the Monday evening, but they felt they could only buy one ticket for the day of the qualifying round. With Alison not expected in the Olympic city until the qualifying had ended, Reverend Edwards was deputed to be their representative in the stadium.

The temperature in Barcelona was excruciatingly hot, so much so that most journalists found on arrival that an essential early assignment was to purchase an electric fan to provide a modicum of relief. The terraced houses in the media village had been constructed without air conditioning, but the organizers had sought to compensate for that oversight by providing us with a 24-hour bar.

From the athletes' perspective, you could only imagine how brutal the heat was. The qualifying competition for the triple jump began at 6.00 p.m., a time when the sun could still scald unprotected skin like a branding iron. On that Saturday evening, Reverend Edwards took his place inside, believing the qualifying to be a formality. 'Everyone expected Jonathan to be a finalist at the very least. Certainly, we did.'

The Olympic Games in Barcelona will be remembered by most of us who were present as a feast of sporting excellence and a celebration of the human spirit. The Games were a beautiful carnival, running from dusk till dawn, when the entertainment switched seamlessly from the stadium, the pool or the basketball arena to the bars and restaurants that apparently never closed on the avenue called La Rambla. For the Edwards family, however, the Olympic Games in Barcelona were to be nothing less than depressing.

On that August evening, Andy Edwards had no reason to know that as he took his seat in the stadium. His wife, son and daughter-in-law had gone to explore the sights and sounds of the city and he would meet them again soon enough to bear witness to his son's progress into the final. Andy's seat was behind the spot where they would start the 100 metres final, but a long way from the sandpit. His son had no clue where to look for him, as they had not spoken since the family had left England. Still, he was in the stadium, and after all those years of driving around the West Country to support his son playing rugby, cricket or competing at athletics, he was now going to see him jump in the Olympic Games. He was a proud father, no doubt about it.

Jonathan Edwards entered the stadium in good heart. His preparation had been close to perfect. Unlike in Seoul four years earlier, he was now an experienced international athlete. He could cope with the enormity of the occasion, or so he believed.

What actually happened was that Edwards never, ever got into the competition. He ran through his first-round jump. This description for fouling a jump has a repetitive ring to it, but there are no better words to illustrate the way in which a triple jumper responds to an aborted take-off. Edwards never left the ground for more than a split second and was putting on the brakes as he ran into the sand. His second jump was reduced to a shambles when he 'collapsed' on landing the second phase and leapt a distance that was unmemorable. Edwards was stunned. He was in the invidious position of having just one jump left to gain a place in the Olympic final. He had produced a big jump on demand before; could he do so again now? He had no option.

Edwards' plight was barely registering with the British fans in the stadium. This was the night Linford Christie was to prove himself the fastest man on earth and, with a wicked sense of irony, the climax to the 100 metres was being staged just as Edwards was failing. 'The atmosphere was tremendous in the sense that Linford was doing well,' says Andy. 'All the Brits were going mad and there was my son competing and not competing, just not achieving.'

It was to grow worse. Edwards' final jump was abysmal. His Games were over. He was distraught and the tears ran down his cheeks like summer rain. 'I was devastated from moment one. I didn't even have the energy to make an effort to somehow hide that fact.'

Across the track, Christie's celebrations were underway. The old man of the track had won the gold medal in the blue-riband event. This was an awesome moment for Christie. His Games had begun horrendously. As captain of the British team, he had been faced with the unenviable task of trying to console young sprinter Jason Livingstone, who was sent home before the track programme even began after it was announced that he had tested positive for anabolic steroids. Christie had to lighten the dark mood within the British team's quarters. A positive test has a debilitating effect on everyone within the camp and, from the moment Livingstone was banished, there was a palpable uneasiness and an increase in tension. Christie had pledged to lead by example, and now there he was in the stadium, draped in a Union flag, smiling and letting the applause wash over him like a tidal wave. You savour moments like that, or go to your grave regretting it.

Andy Edwards was not feeling like celebrating with the other Britons who had made the journey to Spain. 'I just wanted to give Jonathan a hug,' he says. 'My son was going through agony and pain and I couldn't get to him; that's what really upset me.' He left the stadium to search for his wife and Tim and Anna. On the track, Jonathan was trying to come to terms with his failure. 'I'd no idea where my Dad was sitting – only that it would be agony for him as well.'

As Edwards was being ushered from the stadium with his fellow competitors at the end of qualifying, one of them came to introduce himself. His name was Rogel Nahum from Israel and he would become a tried and trusted friend, but at this moment Edwards was fighting to keep control of his fragile emotions and was not of a mind to make small talk. 'I'd noticed Rogel's results and I wanted to meet him because I had a strong interest in

Jewish people, from biblical history. I was genuinely pleased to meet him, but it wasn't the moment I would have chosen. I think I managed to retain a semblance of politeness!' Edwards then made his way through to the mixed zone, where journalists from the Northeast of England were waiting to quiz him. He was wearing dark glasses to hide his tear-stained eyes.

His coach Carl Johnson was swiftly in attendance. He wanted to comfort Edwards. He also had cause to shield him from Frank Dick, in those days the redoubtable British team boss. 'I knew Jon would be feeling quite emotional, filled with terrible disappointment,' says Johnson. 'I had great respect for Frank and I don't think British athletics has been the same since they lost him. He was ahead of his time and always pushing people. He was like the hare that's always running ahead of the hounds, always running as if he's afraid for people to catch him. Frank used to give motivational talks, making reference to the mountain people and the valley people. Valley people never get anywhere, never aspire to anything, whereas the mountain people are always on top. We all had to be mountain people. Frank wanted to see the British athletes as they came out of the stadium, but I didn't think Jon needed to see him in the condition he was in. With Linford winning gold, I managed to get to Jon before Frank did. I grabbed Jon and said, "Come on, come with me." I wasn't aware of it at the time, but Frank got quite annoyed with me afterwards. I shouldn't have done it, but I wanted to protect Jon.'

Edwards was eternally grateful. 'Carl probably thinks he didn't help that much, because he didn't have the answers. There weren't any at that stage. But he was great, he was there when I needed him.' Once outside, they just walked round the stadium, passing unnoticed in the crowds. Edwards was a broken young man and Johnson sensed he needed to be with him. 'In those circumstances I think I'm the world's worst because I never know what to say when people fail like that,' explains Johnson. 'But over the years I've come to feel that just being there to support, to share, to empathize with them is enough. You don't have to say a lot; being there is all that's important.' He had read the signs correctly on that evening.

Round and round Edwards and Johnson walked, for an hour, Edwards desperately hoping that he might find his family in the crowd. It was a forlorn hope – the perimeter of the stadium was a sea of humanity, as it was throughout the Games. Andy Edwards, however, had no difficulty locating Jill, Tim and Anna, as they had a prearranged rendezvous point. Jill did not need her husband to tell her that her son had failed to make it into the final. 'I could see by his face,' she says. 'We just couldn't take it in.' She would have met a ransom demand to have been with her son in those moments. 'I understood how he would be feeling and that was what was worrying. He would have been devastated and we had no way of getting in touch with him.'

As his parents fretted outside the stadium, Edwards' wife Alison arrived to meet them as planned. She had flown into the city and met Mark McAllister, a long-time friend from the Christians in Sport organization. Alison hugged everyone, presuming that her husband had successfully made it into the final. Eventually, Tim Edwards broke the disappointing news. 'I thought he was kidding,' admits Alison.

'I can still see the look on Alison's face,' says Andy. 'She looked at me as if to say, "What have we been doing these past four years?"' Alison's emotions were fried. Mostly she felt helpless, as she did not know how to find her husband.

The Edwards family had no option but to depart without seeing Jonathan. They had to take a coach from the stadium to the station, in order to catch a train to where they had deposited the Peugeot 405 in the park-and-ride system. 'It was awful because we were just being swept up with the crowd, being taken away when we didn't really want to go,' explains Jill. 'When we got to the station, Alison and I tried to contact Jonathan. We rang through to the Olympic village and when we reached the British team's headquarters all they could talk about was how wonderful it was for Linford Christie. Yes, it was wonderful, but frankly, we didn't care. All that concerned us was finding Jonathan. No one could.'

Andy, Jill, Tim, Anna and Alison were confronted with a three-hour drive back to the mountains. The journey was made in almost total silence. 'It was an awful drive, just dreadful,' says Jill. When they reached their accommodation it was almost 2 a.m. Alison went to her room to discover that it was rotten with damp. She did not even unpack. 'That night was just a disaster. My room was sticky and humid, the bottom parts of the bed were damp and I didn't sleep a wink. I was consumed by a real sense of disappointment. You have to work so hard, you're dedicated and committed and you have this sense of hope, and the hope comes to nothing. It knocks you flat. There's an emptiness inside and you try to think, "Why? Why didn't he at least qualify for the final?" Everyone has waved you off from work and now there's the humiliation of having to go back and explain what happened.' Her stark recollection is not a cry of self-pity. She is simply expressing a lack of understanding of what had gone wrong.

Edwards was equally disturbed, back in his room in the Olympic village. Unsurprisingly, he too was unable to sleep. 'I honestly thought it must be a bad dream. It was a profound experience. You can be upset and disappointed, but think that there is always another day. But this went to the core of me. It got to me in a way I probably didn't anticipate much could.'

In the morning, still feeling wretched, still feeling like an emotional time bomb, Edwards went to find Kriss Akabusi. He needed solace and he needed the wise reflection of a man who had been through the fire and emerged unscathed. Akabusi – competing in his last major event, remember – recalls how he interpreted Edwards' failure. 'I said to him, "Jonathan, I don't know if it's God speaking to me, or if it's just me, but I feel that you have gone through a heartrending moment and we're handing over a baton here. You have got something to learn. Be still before God and just listen."

'I likened it to what happened to Elijah and Elisha. Elisha didn't want to leave until he saw God take away his master, Elijah. I wasn't comparing Jonathan to Elisha, but what I wanted to say was that I felt like Elijah – I would pass the baton to Elisha. I had had my moment in the spotlight and the focus would pass to Jonathan, like the sun coming after the moon. I just advised him to hang in. He was in a bad period, but you can't know the picture unless you get outside the frame. He was passing through a dark shadow, but there would be a day when he would come out of that shadow and become an achiever. In time, he would be able to communicate, to empathize with other athletes – some Christians, some not – because he'd been there, seen the darkness.'

Then, on that August morning when Edwards shamelessly cried in front of him, Akabusi added with prescience, 'You will see other people's tragedies from both sides. You will be at the centre of things as a great athlete...'

Akabusi, who was to leave Barcelona with two Olympic bronze medals to carry into retirement, also felt that Edwards' career might have undergone a shift of emphasis in the hours after his bitter disappointment. 'The funny thing was, all of us as Christians were saying the results don't mean much, we're here to glorify God. Jonathan had always had his faith which told him that he was there serving God and athletics was the vehicle. The end result didn't really matter; what really mattered was Jonathan being a Christian in his environment. But I think at that moment Jonathan realized that the result *is* important. Okay, I'm here to glorify God – but I don't want to be a loser. I want to go on that rostrum. I want to show my gifts to the fullest. I think that really hit him then.'

Ironically, Edwards would later reach a conclusion in direct conflict with Akabusi's theory, but that was not something he could manage to get his head around just yet. He was in the same kind of emotional distress as his family, in their accommodation three hours away in the Pyrenees. 'We spent Sunday mournfully,' says Jill. Jonathan recalls eventually reaching them on a telephone in a communal hall within the athletes' village. Naturally, the area was a hive of activity. He was strong and resilient in conversation with his father and tearful wife, assuring them that he was fine and that he would meet them the next day to share some time together in the city. But his brave facade was shattered when his mother came on the line. Neither Jill nor her son could speak for crying.

When the family drove back into Barcelona to meet Edwards the next day, however, they found a young man in complete control. 'I'd come through it to a degree,' he explains. 'I'd quantified what had happened and I thought I'd seen the way forward. Fine, I'd jumped badly, but a large proportion of the season still remained. I felt I could show everyone what I was really capable of. Alison wasn't ready to move forward quite as fast. She was upset because I'd had this huge disappointment and, suddenly, here I was, fine and in control. She had experienced the pain with me but hadn't been there when I was putting it all back together, establishing some kind of perspective. She takes my failures very hard. She feels it's unfair. She feels I deserve more – more for my commitment and dedication, more even for my commitment to God.'

Of course, Alison does not hold such a simplistic view and nor does Jonathan truthfully believe that to be the case. Her problem is like that of anyone who is related by blood or marriage to a sportsman or woman. She knows how hard her husband has worked, she knows the sacrifices that have been made. She comprehends that sport is not a science and cannot be interpreted as such, yet she cannot suppress that sense of injustice she feels when events do not go as anticipated. 'We had been to America to enable Jonathan to train for Barcelona, and this was his big chance to prove that he could be good at what he did.'

With her husband out of the Olympics, she had no stomach to remain. All she wanted was to go home to Newcastle, but she was forced to leave alone. 'I was desperate for Jonathan to come back, but he thought it important to stay and face people. He didn't want to run away from his failure,' she says. 'It was a horrible journey home, but I wasn't cross with him. I just wanted to be with him, to come home together and put the disappointment behind us.' It was late at night when she finally walked into their first-floor flat in Heaton. She closed the door behind her and collapsed in a heap.

Edwards' own show of strength was built on a bed of straw, it transpired. He presented himself around Barcelona, smiled and accepted all the good wishes that were offered. He is not the type of man to run for the hills when he has taken a flesh wound, yet he is introspective, and there were few waking hours when he was not dissecting his performance, not analysing the ramifications. Once he did return home, he discussed his thoughts with Alison as he always did. She is his partner, his friend and his sounding board.

He had been mortified by his failure in Barcelona, but he felt that he could consign the Games to history. It is how sportspeople have to behave. When you reach this altitude there is a necessary harshness of self-judgement. They work to a balance sheet with a bottom line that is defined as sharply as in any financial institution in the City. There is one column marked 'Win'; there is another column marked 'Loss'. The figures cannot be laundered.

For Edwards there was more to evaluate than just victory or failure. Where did this performance, this result, fit in conjunction with his faith? Had he been an unworthy servant of God – or had God betrayed him? These are not subject headings that you can write on a scrap of paper and have a dialogue about with your coach. These questions go deep within the man; they challenge the essence of what Edwards feels is his calling. This is what troubled him weeks after he had left Spain. He had the questions, but no answers. 'I think this was a process of maturing for Jonathan,' says Alison. 'He was trying to come to terms with a lot of issues. It wasn't easy for him. As I look back, it was one of those defining times in our lives.'

Edwards says, retrospectively, 'I'd got through the Barcelona experience – and it had been desperate – and I felt that it had been a real test of faith. At first, I thought that I had come out the other side and was ready to move on.' He was dreadfully mistaken. When he continued to jump poorly, the desolation of Barcelona returned to haunt him. Athletically, he was in a mess. Spiritually, he was confused.

He began to keep a note of his innermost feelings, what he felt God was saying to him. One particular comment from his notes is worth repeating here: 'Despite what I was feeling, something inside me told me it would not always be like this.' Later, there was a resounding clarity in something he read. 'I found a passage that said just when you think the test of faith should be finishing, that's just where it begins.'

For Edwards, those words had a ring of truth. The lingering fallout from his unsuccessful bid to win a medal at the Olympic Games was striking at the heart of his Christian faith. 'It was terribly hard for me to admit to myself, but I began to realize that a huge part of me was only in it for me, for selfish reasons.' In other words, he was afraid he was jumping for gold not for God. Sometime, somewhere, something had to give. It turned out to be in Turin, in early September 1992.

His jumping was still in this slough of despond when he reached the Grand Prix final in the Italian city, famously home to Fiat motor cars and the Juventus football club. Edwards was horrified when the triple jump overran and the last round began when all other events were completed. 'Everybody was looking at the triple jump – there was nothing else going on – and I just did not want to be on the runway. I felt humiliated; all my confidence in my ability had been drained by jumping badly.' His self-worth had evaporated. 'I felt like a nobody.'

In that instant Edwards suddenly worked things through in his mind. He knew the root of his dilemma. His perspective had become twisted and distorted, as though it had been rearranged with a crowbar. 'On that runway I realized how important success was to me and the recognition that it brings, and how painful failure was. I began my jumping career by saying that I competed to serve God, come what may. And on that runway in Turin I rediscovered my focus and told myself, "I'm doing this for God. I could be the worst triple jumper the world has ever seen, but this is what I'm going to do. This isn't about me."' Edwards ran down the runway, Edwards jumped and Edwards came last.

To study the result, to analyse his technique, was to miss the point. Edwards would later identify that night when he stood on the runway petrified, like a rabbit trapped in the headlights of a car, as a profound moment in his Christian life. 'I felt I'd come through something very significant. I'd made the jump, when it would have been so much easier to have walked away from it. The Apostle Paul talks about Christians presenting their lives to God as living sacrifices; you die to yourself and you live your life to serve God. I think there was a process, a very profound process, of dying to myself, making my own desires, wants and wishes in athletics die, at least in part, through that humiliation I experienced standing on the runway.'

Edwards would no longer mistakenly jump in pursuit of his own success. That was the vow he took away from

Turin. Looking back now, so long after what was unquestionably a bitter disappointment in Barcelona, Edwards,
now a father of two sons, concludes, 'It was a fundamental
moment for me as a Christian, in terms of having something very strong inside me broken. Whatever desire for
success, recognition, that I had, and all stated as a desire to
serve God, had been challenged in a very painful and traumatic way. I think God was disciplining me at those
Olympics, not to punish me but to bring me closer to
him. The same as I would do to my children, if I felt they
needed to be put right. As a father, I'd say, "I'm doing this,
Sam, Nathan, because I love you and I want what's best
for you." I look upon what happened to me in Barcelona
in the same way.' Edwards' belief was stirred, but never
shaken. He was made to think, but never encouraged to
wander from the path he had plotted for himself as a child
growing up in a vicarage.

There followed a wonderful, spiritually uplifting postscript to what had been mostly a summer of desperation.
He was selected in the British team to go to the World Cup
in Havana, the dilapidating monument to Fidel Castro's
vision of Communism. 'I didn't really want him to go
because he was jumping so badly,' says Alison, who was
seeking to protect her husband from any further indignity.
'But, rightly, he felt an obligation and responsibility as
part of a team.'

Edwards willingly boarded the flight to Cuba, but on
the morning of his competition he was violently ill and
running a high temperature. British long jumper Mark
Forsythe, who was also reserve for the triple jump, woke
up to hear Edwards vomiting in the bathroom. 'He
shouted, "Jonathan, are you all right?" Obviously, he was
beginning to think he may have to jump!' Edwards saw

the team doctor, Malcolm Brown, who examined him and then said he would take a final check closer to the competition. Edwards smiles when he says he never saw Doctor Brown again that day; and not for a moment does he suspect him of anything other than being conveniently busy elsewhere!

Edwards kept his warm-up to a minimum. He jogged a lap of the track and stretched out by simply touching his toes once or twice. He was afraid to exert himself further. His conservatism did him no harm. 'In the first round of the competition I jumped 16.89 metres, as good as anything I had jumped since before the Olympics. I felt weak, but quite good, if that makes any sense.' Edwards was fourth going into the final round and Olympic bronze medallist Frank Rutherford thought he held an unassailable lead. With only Edwards to jump, Rutherford was waving to the crowd, beaming, behaving like a man who felt he was already on the top step of the podium. His optimism proved to be foolishly misplaced. With a light breeze helpfully behind him, Edwards jumped 17.34 metres to win with something to spare.

Rutherford was crestfallen, Edwards elated. That jump would have been good enough for fourth place in the Barcelona Olympics. Andy Edwards can recall British team chief Frank Dick being complimentary of his son's performance in Havana. 'From a team point of view Frank was impressed that Jonathan came up trumps when it mattered,' says Andy. 'He knew that Jonathan wasn't feeling well – and he knew full well that he hadn't had a good season.'

Edwards felt he had garnered some reward, some consolation for the disappointments he had endured through the season. 'I was physically, emotionally, spiritually right at the top of my game in Barcelona and I was at the opposite end of the spectrum in Havana,' he says. 'I don't believe God gave me supernatural power to jump – I was easily capable of jumping 17.34 metres – but in God's plans and purposes, and this is only my interpretation, I think this was just a lovely encouragement. It was also an important lesson on what the focus was for me as an athlete. This wasn't about me, about me being successful. It was about me serving God, first and foremost.'

As ever, Edwards also found a source of encouragement from the Bible, in a passage from Isaiah which has served Christians through the ages:

> *Do you not know?*
>   *Have you not heard?*
> *The LORD is the everlasting God,*
>   *the Creator of the ends of the earth.*
> *He will not grow tired or weary,*
>   *and his understanding no-one can fathom.*
> *He gives strength to the weary*
>   *and increases the power of the weak.*
> *Even youths grow tired and weary,*
>   *and young men stumble and fall;*
> *but those who hope in the LORD*
>   *will renew their strength.*
> *They will soar on wings like eagles;*
>   *they will run and not grow weary;*
>   *they will walk and not be faint.*
>
>   (ISAIAH 40:28–31)

With that still as his First Commandment of Athletics, Edwards was to move into 1993 as an athlete now prepared to compete on Sundays.

* * *

Edwards' income from jumping into a sandpit was less than £5,000 a year at this time, while he earned around £8,000 annually from his part-time job in the laboratory. Alison's salary as a physiotherapist meant that their financial position was healthy for two young people with a modest mortgage, simple lifestyle and no family. By the dawn of 1993, however, Alison knew she was pregnant.

This wonderful news meant that Edwards would soon become the sole breadwinner. Happily for them, he began to make an impact on the athletics circuit. His earnings from his prowess as a triple jumper began to escalate way beyond anything he had imagined. He would soon be generating a salary comparable to, say, a Second Division footballer playing for a successful team.

That was the level of the couple's financial expectations when their first child, Samuel James Edwards, was born on 10 August that summer. As it so happened, that was not an exceedingly convenient date for his father, as he was due to compete at the World Championships in Stuttgart. 'Alison's due date was the end of July, so we didn't anticipate any problems for the World Championships,' he explains. 'In the end, Alison was induced and Sam's birth was rather too close to the Championships for comfort.' He was with Alison when she gave birth and, naturally, he was thrilled to become a father. But he had work to do, a living to earn. He had to be in Stuttgart.

He left mother and newborn child in Princess Mary's Maternity Hospital in Newcastle. Alison tells it like this: 'I gave birth on a Friday and Jonathan left on Monday. My Mum had come from Scotland to be with me, but she had to go home immediately as her mother suffered a stroke. I was on my own.'

Edwards jubilantly won a bronze medal at the Championships, a breakthrough into the big time, but nothing would run entirely smooth for him. Dave Martin, a Northeast-based journalist and a long-time acquaintance of Edwards, offered him his mobile phone at the stadium to call his wife in hospital. He broke the good news that he was a medallist, but there was some bad news for Alison too. The medal ceremony was not until the next day, he told her. 'She burst out crying and told me to come straight home,' he remembers. 'I seem to recall her mentioning something about the relative importance of wives and medals!'

As Edwards briefly wrestled with the dilemma, head coach Frank Dick offered his worldly experience. 'Frank emphasized the significance of the medal ceremony itself. In reality, Alison and I both knew I had to stay.'

His wife did understand, but this did not ease the anguish she felt at the time. 'I knew it was important for Jonathan to get his first major medal, but I just wanted him to come home. I had a temperature. I'd been ill that night. I just wanted my husband to be with me.' Of course, when Edwards did return as a conquering hero of a sort, he was anxious to hold his new son. 'I'd just got Sam to sleep and he wanted to cuddle him. I do remember pleading with him, "Leave him alone!"' Alison suspects that she suffered from postnatal depression, and Edwards had to learn to be a father in double-quick time. 'I was a complete wreck for those first few weeks. Jonathan had to take more responsibility than he might otherwise have done. His Mum came up to stay, which was a huge help.'

Meanwhile, Edwards' performance in the World Championships had not gone unnoticed. Brendan Foster, an Olympic medallist and now a promoter and broadcaster, as well as president of Gateshead Harriers, had his curiosity aroused. Foster spoke with a close personal friend called Ross Taylor, who was a kidney transplant surgeon at the time and chairman of the British Transplant Association. Foster's baby, the Great North Run, a half-marathon staged on the streets of Tyneside, raised money for Kidney Research. Taylor was a trustee of a foundation set up by Foster, to provide financial assistance for promising local sportsmen. Edwards was an obvious candidate.

'Ross knew of Edwards from the hospital and he used to tell me how busy Jonathan was,' says Foster. 'When you're doing medical tests you have to be on hand. I definitely got the impression that his medical job interfered with his training.' Unbeknown to Foster, Edwards' job was drawing to a natural conclusion in any case. Since going part-time, he had been paid from a research grant and this money was coming to an end.

Foster asked Edwards to meet him at his office. 'What do you need to help you get better?' asked Foster. 'What's going to make you jump 18 metres and win the Olympics?' Edwards was uncertain how to respond. Inwardly, he was still insecure about his ability to provide for his family as an athlete. Foster offered Edwards a grant from the Great North Run Trust, but this was not instantly accepted. 'Jonathan asked for time to think,' says Foster.

Edwards was uncomfortable about being the recipient of money that could be better used elsewhere. Foster remembers his reticence. He had to explain to him that the fund had been instigated to assist worthy, underfunded athletes. 'Jonathan asked what was expected in return,' says Foster. 'Nothing,' he told him: he had to do absolutely zilch. A day later, Edwards called Foster to accept his generous proposition. Effectively, he was being granted £30,000 for three years. 'When he wrote to thank us, Jonathan said he hoped he would one day justify our faith in him,' says Foster. Edwards would do that, and then some.

The signs at the beginning of 1994 were most encouraging. Johnson's coaching log, in which he measured speed/strength parameters under controlled tests, informed him that Edwards was moving impressively forwards. By late January, he was in the training form of his life. 'Then it all went sour,' says Johnson.

Edwards had been excelling in the gym and on the track when he went down with flu. For a man renowned for listening to his body, it was perhaps strange that he ignored the warning bells this time. He continued to train hard, nourished by his encouraging test results so early in the year. He was to pay a cruel price.

He performed without distinction during the 1994 indoor season, which was never truly representative of his form. Yet his sprinting also indicated that something was not right. At indoor meetings he would occasionally compete over 60 metres and his times were poorer than he would have expected.

When Edwards' season swung outdoors, he actually managed to jump 17.39 metres at the National Championships in Sheffield. It was a false dawn. He felt lethargic for no apparent reason. His jumping remained at a low ebb, and he finished a dispirited sixth in the European Championships. He came home from the Commonwealth Games with a silver medal after leaping 17 metres, a high point in his calendar that year. 'I was quite pleased with that, considering I wasn't feeling at all good.' Johnson calculated that Edwards' season average over 16 outdoor competitions had fallen noticeably.

Edwards was perplexed. 'Why had I suddenly become this very poor athlete, essentially without reason?' He made an appointment to visit a specialist in London to have some blood tests. When the results were returned, Edwards was told that he had been suffering from Epstein Barr Virus. 'They could tell from the antibodies in my blood.' He was prescribed rest.

He was not the first and would not be the last athlete to be struck with a virus when supposedly in the full bloom of health. 'There used to be a joke that viruses leapt out of the water jump and straight into Seb Coe as he ran past,' says Edwards. 'People do say that when you're ultra-fit you're vulnerable to a virus.' In retrospect, Edwards now knows he trained when he should have been resting. That set him back months. His 1994 season had been a virtual washout, so who could possibly know what sort of year 1995 was going to be?

Chapter 6

18.29 and All That

I think of it as a kind of time that cannot pass,
that I never used, so still possess.

TED HUGHES

Edwards entered 1995 grateful that he had been diagnosed as having had Epstein Barr Virus, but fearful of
Post-Viral Syndrome. Not for a moment did he fantasize
that he was ready to conquer the world.

In the dying embers of the previous year, he had been
on a Christians in Sport weekend near Northampton and
had shared a room with a javelin thrower who, as a junior,
had been competitive with Olympic medallist Steve
Backley. 'I remember very vividly him explaining to me
how he had got a virus and he was still struggling with
PVS 10 years later. He had been round the houses trying to
get to the bottom of the problem and even tried anti-
depressants. The point is, PVS is a very grey area medically
– some doctors don't think it even exists. I just didn't
know what to expect. I didn't know if I was going to be
okay ever again. I know that sounds a bit dramatic, but
that was my mental state. Will I be okay? Will this PVS dog

131

me for the rest of my life? Not that I'd notice living normally, but as an athlete I'd never be able to get back that
last 2–3 per cent.'

Edwards, training lightly at the beginning of 1995, felt
he needed a change of environment. In February, he left
Newcastle for Florida with his pregnant wife Alison and
son Sam. Unlike other British holidaymakers, their destination was not Disneyland. They were bound for the state
capital Tallahassee, so that Edwards could take advantage
of the camp that the British Olympic Association had
already opened to enable their athletes to train and acclimatize for the Atlanta Games, scheduled for the following
summer.

On an introductory tour of the facilities at Florida State
University, Edwards met jumps coach Dennis Nobles and
politely asked if he would mind watching him jump.
Nothing much else was said. Later that day Edwards found
a copy of the local Yellow Pages telephone directory, to
hunt for a church to attend. There were hundreds listed
and he selected one at random. 'Incredibly, at the first service we met Dennis and through him we made some great
friends during our stay.' Nobles became a point of reference for Edwards through to the Atlanta Olympic Games
and beyond.

After the warm-weather training in Florida, Edwards
came back to England determined to make some
fundamental changes. He had long felt a stagnation in his
relationship with Carl Johnson, the regional coach for the
Northeast who had provided the blueprint for his training
for the past eight years. Unquestionably, Johnson played a
significant role in the development of Edwards from
novice to world champion, and that is not a fact Edwards
would deny. On introduction, Johnson declares that he

was '95 per cent' responsible for the athlete Edwards became in 1995.

Yet by the spring of that year, before he jumped into history, Edwards was distancing himself from his coach's orbit, explaining, 'A relationship needs to develop and I don't think ours had. Carl's approach was scientific. He would have been happier in a laboratory. He was a man trying out experiments – would this work, would that work? It just wasn't dynamic, the chemistry wasn't working. Carl had been there, seen it, done it. He didn't seem to get excited about the performance end of the spectrum, or at least if he did, he didn't communicate it.' Johnson is renowned in the locality for being a man who marches to the sound of his own drum.

At no point did Edwards actually sever their partnership; he simply drifted into a different regime. In the gym at Gateshead Stadium where he trains, he came under the influence of Norman Anderson, the charismatic, blind power-lifter whom he would grow to treat like a 'second dad'. On the technical side, he began travelling to Jarrow to work with a man called Peter Stanley, whose daughter was a triple jumper. With Stanley, Edwards began to perfect a new technique. The seminal moment occurred one night as they watched video film together at Stanley's home in Lanchester, some 20 miles from Edwards' house. 'Mike Conley's action stood out so much, it was like a light bulb had been switched on,' says Edwards. 'For me Conley was always the man.' From then on, Edwards concentrated on whipping both arms skywards during his jump, rather than employing them singularly. On a day-to-day basis, Johnson could hardly have been surprised that his role was diminishing to vanishing point.

In the lounge of the Gosforth Park Hotel in 1999, Johnson broke his silence over Edwards to admit, 'I find young men quite difficult to work with because they're quite arrogant. They know best and they want to do it their way and most of them do it wrongly. Jonathan was always rather distant, aloof. I didn't make any contact when he came back from America and he was rather hurt. I said at the time, "Look, Jon, it wasn't my job. You're the athlete, you should make contact with me." He didn't like that. Now Norman [Anderson] is okay on his weightlifting, but at some stage he became more important on the scene than I was. As for Peter Stanley, I taught him most things he knows; he came on my courses.'

His memory is that Edwards became awkward about training times, especially after his first son Sam was born. He wanted specially organized sessions, according to Johnson. As director of coach education for British athletics at that time, second in command to director of national coaching Frank Dick, Johnson had set times to meet his athletes. These were not always convenient to Edwards, he says. There was clearly a fundamental breakdown in communication, too. 'I found it difficult to persuade him to take on new ideas and new forms of work,' insists Johnson. 'Maybe you have to understand him. He had a format, it was right, it was working and he was unprepared to change that format. Yet you have to move on, because if your training becomes monotonous, it deadens. There were still some ideas I wanted to try. I would talk quietly to him and he would say nothing back. He would just take no notice … I had no influence at all. In the end, I thought, well, if you want to work like that, let's just quietly walk away. Now it might have been that he was getting better advice elsewhere, but I don't think he was.'

Edwards' principal regret is that he did not address the deteriorating working relationship with Johnson much, much sooner. 'From my side, I hadn't been completely happy for over a year before I went to the United States. Emotionally, I had taken two or three steps backwards and Carl was unaware. The problem was my lack of backbone. I should have been strong and said I felt the time was right to move on.' His reticence was perhaps understandable, because down the years Johnson had become a friend of his family. Johnson has always held Alison Edwards in high esteem and she thought well of him. 'I suppose loyalty played a factor. Carl had done a lot for me and I will never deny that,' explains Edwards. 'It was a bit like trying to finish with a girlfriend when you stay for months longer than you should just so that you don't hurt her feelings.'

Johnson was made redundant with minimal compensation in 1997 in the meltdown of the British Athletics Federation (BAF), which went into administration. He now works in the Northeast region with elite swimmers including Sue Rolph, and admits to being far from blameless in the breakdown of his relationship with Edwards. 'If, as Jonathan says, we stagnated, there were faults on both sides. I'm prepared to accept I'm not an easy guy to get on with. I led a bachelor existence throughout my married life; I did what I wanted to do. I was always out, I was always coaching, I was always busy. I was always working. My wife had a teaching career and that preserved what little bits of home life that I had. So I didn't encourage my athletes to intrude and I felt, for the sake of my wife, I had to protect that. My wife's interests were in music and our girls were musicians. I kept my home life and sport and my work entirely separate. Because of that, I didn't develop very close relationships with my athletes except that the coaching contact, the interaction, was close.

'In certain circumstances I'm terribly impatient. I couldn't be bothered with colleagues, if you like, who didn't do a thorough job. I'm a slave of duty. I've always been that way. I tend to talk straight and, yes, I'm quite abrasive and no doubt there are many people in the sport glad to see the back of me. But it was a privilege to work with a world record holder, an even greater privilege to have worked with somebody who not only bust the record once, but bust it repeatedly through that 1995 season. Jonathan gave me a Parker pen with his world record inscribed on it and I still have it. Maybe to some extent I'm my own worst enemy because I tend to denigrate myself in public, yet inside I'm quite arrogant about my ability. That's maybe a strange mixture.'

Edwards, as became clear during subsequent years, is an athlete who requires a continual change of stimulus. His mind needs to be constantly challenged, but he likes to be master of his own destiny. If he was a public limited company, Edwards would be chairman and chief operating officer.

In that spring of 1995, Edwards' training diary told an illuminating tale. His notes show that he took a great number of days off: 'Very tired today, rest two days, very cautious … two days off, train, easy day the next day.' He admits, 'Looking back, I was amazed at how much rest I actually took.' Yet somehow he was contriving to arrive at peak fitness. He jumped 17.05 metres at a training session not long after his second son Nathan was born in May – and he had never exceeded 17 metres in training before. He also jumped more times in training for this season than ever before or since.

It was with a mixture of optimism and lingering uncertainty in his heart that Peter Stanley drove them both south to Loughborough for the first competition of the outdoor season. It was cold and drizzling when they reached the track. Edwards stayed in the warmth long enough to see Rob Andrew land the drop goal that brought England a stunning victory over Australia in the quarter finals of the Rugby World Cup, being broadcast from South Africa. In contrast to the raucous capacity crowd in South Africa, less than a couple of hundred die-hards braved the elements to watch events unfold at Loughborough. Those who were present can claim to have seen Edwards write the opening lines of a story that was to capture the imagination of the country before the summer was over. In his first round he produced a jump of 17.01 metres and, given that he had surpassed 17 metres just once through the misery of the preceding year, this gave him a fillip.

He aborted his second jump, but in the third round Edwards established a new British record, leaping 17.58 metres to erase Keith Connor from the records. This was 14 centimetres further than he had ever jumped before. After the jump had been measured, Edwards put on his tracksuit and, with no one noticing, he lay on the track, hidden for a moment or two under his waterproof top. He shed a private tear and offered a prayer of gratitude. 'It was a really huge breakthrough. First competition of the year, miserable weather, one man and a dog present, but I was like, "Wow! I'm back, and some."' Of course, with the Rugby World Cup stealing the ink in the newspapers, Edwards' effort went largely unnoticed. The headline writers would pay attention in due course.

The following week, Edwards crossed the Channel to compete at an invitation meeting in Lille. Again, it was raining. The competition, however, was red hot. His rivals included three men in form: Jamaican James Beckford, Brian Wellman from Bermuda and Cuba's Yoelbi Quesada. Beckford, who was later to concentrate on the long jump, had jumped 17.92 metres in Texas, although it was unclear from the detail emerging from the Lone Star State whether that was wind assisted. 'Everybody's a little sceptical about performances in Texas!' says Edwards. In the event, the Englishman mopped up the opposition, winning with 17.46 metres. Andy Norman told Edwards afterwards that on the right day the world record was a feasible ambition. Edwards was encouraged, notwithstanding Beckford's parting shot. 'I'll be ready for you next time,' said the Jamaican.

A few days later, Quesada and Wellman competed in Madrid and laid down some markers. Quesada equalled the world record with a wind-assisted 17.97 metres and Wellman leapt 17.72. It was extremely windy, +7.0 metres per second, but the numbers were impressive enough. At home in his three-bedroom flat in Newcastle, Edwards thought to himself, 'Goodness, and I really had them slaughtered at the weekend in the rain at Lille.' The next morning Edwards did a planned weights session in the gym at Gateshead Stadium. Over the years, he has grown accustomed to his performance with the weights providing him with a useful guide as to how he will compete. This session was woeful and he feared the virus might be stirring again. 'My state of mind was still very fragile. My weights had been going so well and they really are a fundamental indicator of where I'm at. I was under a cloud again. Was I going to be all right?'

He had to return to Lille at the weekend to compete for Britain in the European Cup and travelled independently

of the majority of the team, as they were leaving on
Eurostar 48 hours before he wanted to be in France. Once
in Lille, there was a good feeling of familiarity. Having
been there just seven days before, he had found a small,
deserted room near the warm-up track where he could
conclude his preparations. He did not know it at that precise moment, but he was warming up to dismantle his
event. For ever.

In his first jump, he sailed 17.90 metres. It was wind
assisted but, most remarkably of all, Edwards knew that
technically it had been a flawed jump. 'I knew there was a
lot more to come,' he says. How much more he could not
have predicted. In the next round, he timed his hop to step
to near perfection and, in his words, 'I flew.' The trackside
board flashed the distance round the stadium: 18.43
metres. French runner Elsa de Vassoigne, who married
Roger Black in 1999, rushed excitedly to convey the news to
her boyfriend and Steve Backley as they came into the stadium together. Black, now a broadcaster, then preparing to
win a treasured silver medal in the 400 metres at the Atlanta
Olympic Games, thought his girlfriend was confused. 'You
mean 17.43 metres, don't you?' he said. But she did not.

Black's enquiry was understandable. Edwards had just
gone from being Clark Kent to Superman without visibly
visiting a phone booth. Tim Layden, writing in *Sports
Illustrated*, the most prestigious sports publication in the
United States, described Edwards like this: 'He is a wisp of
a man, a shade over 5ft 11in, weighing less than 160lbs.
He has a miler's body. If you were to see him in a tweed
jacket and corduroys you might think him not an athlete
but a secondary school teacher.'[1] No one could possibly

---

1 *Sports Illustrated*, 13 May 1996.

argue with this, yet with that jump Edwards had grown in stature.

Even Edwards found the scale of his performance overwhelming. 'It was flabbergasting,' he says. 'When I came out of the pit I didn't know what to do with myself. The whole experience was almost surreal, dream-like.' Extraordinarily, the wind was only 0.4 metres per second stronger than the legal limit for record purposes of 2 metres per second. Amidst the furore of his wind-assisted jumps of 18.43 metres and 18.39 metres (in the fourth round), Edwards sandwiched a modest 17.72 metres to extend his own two-week-old British record by a further 14 centimetres.

A slave to the modern convention of his sport, he was required to take a drug test and he was accompanied by team doctor Malcolm Brown. He borrowed Dr Brown's mobile telephone – Edwards did not possess one then – to call his wife Alison. His next memory still causes him to shudder.

Back at the hotel, the post-meeting banquet was in full flow. Edwards did not get to savour it for too long. 'My whole body went into spasm. My hamstrings, calves, stomach, literally went pah, pah, pah. I had to stretch out my whole body or I felt I was going to roll into a ball and never be able to get out of it.' Two team physiotherapists had to carry Edwards from the banquet to the team treatment room and administer emergency massage. 'My legs had seized,' he says. 'One of the other physios brought my food to me and she was a bit drunk and she started nibbling my ear … I can't remember her name…' He smiles as he lies. His excuse sounds plausible and his reputation as a Christian and a gentleman guarantees that, even if he could remember, he would not choose to embarrass the lady here.

He had never experienced such violent cramping. 'I think my muscles had just been to a place they'd never been before. There was something about that day that was just incredible. I just ran down and jumped into the pit, and it was almost 18.50 metres.' Edwards had not simply moved the goalposts; he had uprooted the pitch.

What Edwards did not know was that at home in England his breathtaking performance in Lille had been witnessed in the most distressing of circumstances by his younger brother Tim. He sat in the lounge of his small house in Bath, cradling his five-week-old daughter Zoe. His wife Anna was catching up on lost sleep upstairs. 'Tim came to wake me and said, "You should come down, Jonathan's doing rather well,"' recalls Anna. 'So understated.'

If this was a big weekend in the life of Jonathan Edwards, in a sense it was of far more importance to his brother and his wife. The next day, Zoe was being admitted to Frenchay Hospital in Bristol for critical brain surgery. 'We had been allowed to bring Zoe home for the day on Sunday, and it just happened that we found ourselves watching Jonathan,' explains Tim. Zoe had been born on 22 May, three days after Alison Edwards had given birth to her second son, Nathan. Three and a half weeks later doctors diagnosed that she had hydrocephalus, exacerbated by a fluid-filled cyst. Her head had grown by five, even six, centimetres from the swelling caused by the fluid on her brain. Fortunately, those monitoring Anna and Zoe in postnatal checks identified the crisis. 'Babies don't usually have their head measured until they're six weeks old, but our health visitor and doctor were great and picked up on the problem,' says Tim.

On Monday morning, as Jonathan Edwards was being celebrated in newspapers across the country, 25-year-old Tim and Anna drove solemnly to Bristol. 'We left this precious, tiny baby surrounded by nurses and anaesthetists in this huge room,' explains Tim. 'Zoe was crying and you feel emotionally cut up, devastated. Just because you have Christian faith, because God gives you peace, it doesn't stop you from hurting for what your child is going through. You still suffer, still hurt, still struggle. But you pull yourself together to a certain extent. We bought a couple of papers and went and had breakfast and read about my brother. While our daughter was having brain surgery we were reading about my brother's success. You can't describe that.'

For an experienced neurosurgeon, the procedure to put a shunt into the cyst to drain it would be regarded as straightforward surgery, says Tim. 'But we were aware, as any parents would be, that when you operate on the brain there are risks involved. There were no choices. Had she not had the operation, she would have died.'

Reverend Andy Edwards and his wife Jill were in the unenviable position of watching one of their sons being heralded as a triumphant sportsman, while trying to ease the anxieties and fears of their other son. 'We cried with Tim and Anna and rejoiced with Jonathan,' says Jill. 'Never once did Tim and Anna ask, "Why us?"'

Andy Edwards takes immense pride from the manner in which his sons individually dealt with Kipling's twin impostors, Triumph and Disaster. 'It's all a facet of the joys and pain and suffering of living,' he suggests. 'But we were certainly proud of Tim and Anna and the way they coped. It was agony seeing them come back from the hospital when the diagnosis had been made. We would have just loved to have taken the pain away.' There was a determination by the family to keep the harrowing story of Zoe Edwards' plight out of the newspapers. 'Can you imagine what they would have made of it, had they discovered Jonathan's niece was having brain surgery?' asks Reverend Edwards.

Jonathan, exceedingly close to his brother, was concerned from afar. 'Alongside our joy and celebration was their heartbreak,' he says. Zoe required two more operations before Christmas 1995, when she was declared out of danger. In the summer of 1999, when she was at home in England with her parents, on holiday from Tim's postgraduate studies in Jerusalem, Zoe looked like any robust four-year-old, surrounded by her younger sisters Esther and Josie. 'Zoe has an annual check, but the doctors have been fantastic and as long as the shunts continue to work she has a normal life,' says Tim. 'But it's probably best she doesn't play rugby!'

From Lille, Jonathan Edwards returned to England to compete consecutively at home at Gateshead, in front of family and friends from Heaton Baptist Church, and at Crystal Palace. He won with 18.03 metres, wind assisted, at Gateshead; and with 17.69 metres at Crystal Palace, but needed physiotherapy on an ankle after three rounds of the competition in the tired old arena in South London. 'I was tense, trying too hard and my technique was not as solid as it had been.'

Edwards had sustained a niggling injury, but his reason for missing the AAA Championships at Birmingham, officially the British trials for the World Championships, was due more to a conspiracy hatched by Andy Norman. Unbeknown to the British team hierarchy, who demand that all athletes participate in the AAA Championships in midsummer, Edwards had been booked to jump elsewhere. Edwards entrusts Norman with the shaping of his competition diary. 'I pulled out of the trials with an ankle injury,' he recalls. Norman correctly surmised that his man would be selected – subject to fitness – for the World Championships in Gothenburg despite his absence from Birmingham.

Three days after missing the trials, Edwards arrived unannounced in Salamanca, an ancient, beautiful university city approximately two and a half hours' drive from Madrid. Remarkably, the extra treatment he had received meant he was already fit again. Edwards suggests, 'If I'm honest, I do resent the selection policy being made round one event. I think it's a policy which has evolved from the desire to ensure Britain's top athletes compete to satisfy the demands of television. It isn't a policy necessarily with the athletes' best interests at heart.'

Certainly, he has not committed himself through the mature years of his career to appearing at the AAA Championships as a priority. 'For me, it's an unnecessary hoop to have to jump through in a busy season. I do believe that those of us with a proven track record should be given the freedom to prepare for major championships in a way we think best. If I felt my selection was in any way under threat, I would be the first to want to compete in the AAA Championships. But since 1995, jumping in those championships has been an irrelevance for me. It's a little ironic that we have such a policy when 90 per cent of the team selects itself. An ideal selection policy seems to me to make sure your best athletes get to the championships in the best possible shape. Jumping in the AAAs doesn't prove that I should be selected, does it?'

Norman felt that Salamanca on a summer's evening could be conducive to Edwards breaking the world record. To call my presence top secret is pushing it a shade far, but Andy agreed with the promoter of the event that they would not announce in advance that I was competing,' recalls Edwards. 'Andy's reasoning for me going was that he thought if I could get the world record I might relax. He was absolutely right. I arrived and there was no pressure, no legion of British pressmen.' There was one man present to concern him, however: reigning Olympic champion Mike Conley. Edwards had last seen him compete the previous year in Paris, when Conley had looked a man apart, jumping prodigiously in an unfriendly drizzle. To Edwards, Conley was *the* man. 'I thought he had appeared untouchable that night in Paris; now here I was lining up against him having jumped 18.43 metres a month before.'

Conley was soon to understand the threat Edwards posed. In the first round, the Englishman hopelessly mistimed the final jump phase, yet his hop and step enabled him to leap 17.39 metres. Conley looked bewildered. Man, this is supposed to be the triple jump, not just two jumps!' Edwards smiled benignly, knowing that, had he mastered his jump, he would have been close to emulating his performance in Lille. The world record of 17.97 metres held by Willie Banks and set a decade before would not withstand the evening.

With his next attempt, Edwards emerged from the sandpit in Salamanca to be greeted as the new world record holder. He had jumped 17.98 metres. Norman was the first to hug him, and the newspapers back home in Britain carried stories about how Edwards had proved his fitness to be on the British team for the World Championships in Gothenburg by setting a world record

in Spain. Over dinner, Edwards was greeted by Mik
Powell, the American who in 1991 had broken Bol
Beamon's fabled long jump record, which had stood fo
23 years. 'Hey man, welcome to the club,' said Powell.

Edwards had seized the oldest field event record in th
book. He was also the first British male to break a jump
world record since C.B. Fry in 1893 (provided you accep
that Tim Ahearne was an Irishman competing under th
British flag when he set a triple jump world record at th
1908 Olympics). David Powell, athletics correspondent fo
The Times, suggested, 'Fry would have approved of Edward
as the man to follow him. An England cricket captain an
international footballer, Fry was a graduate in classics an
India's representative at the League of Nations.'[2]

Not a man to court controversy willingly, Edwards qui
etly relished the mischief he had perpetrated by missin
the AAA trials at Birmingham and appearing unan
nounced in Salamanca. He had executed a finely planne
coup. There was a news conference for him on his home
coming, of course, and it was staged at Newcastle airpor
His name was beginning to make an impact, with a
increasing number of messages being left on his answer
phone at home, still the small flat not far from Newcastl
city centre. 'I'd go out for an hour and come back and fin
10 messages.'

Edwards was moving into the Premiership Division c
athletes. 'I was waiting for Gothenburg,' he remembers. 'I'
got the world record, but what it boiled down to in m
own mind was that the season would have been for noth
ing if I didn't perform to my optimum at the Worl
Championships.'

2 *The Times*, 20 July 1995.

On arrival in Sweden with a brigade of British athletes, Edwards found himself being afforded special treatment. Along with Linford Christie, the reigning Olympic 100 metres champion, he was ushered to a waiting car while the other members of the team boarded a bus outside the airport. 'I know that Linford shared my discomfort at being treated as special. We were whisked through accreditation, a whole new world to me. I think the British team had made the arrangements and you know that they were trying to make things as easy as possible. They knew that we would have a lot of extra pressure on us, but it's a difficult one to call. I felt really awkward about receiving such treatment.'

The extra demands began when Edwards was drafted in as part of a Puma-organized press conference that included Christie and Colin Jackson in a city-centre hotel. The enormity of the occasion and the ensuing chaos is embedded in his memory. 'I think there were around 200 journalists and 50 photographers crammed into a room designed for half that number. I had to fight my way through and there was a constant flashing in my face. It was my first exposure to this high-profile hype.' Edwards answered some questions, then was directed to escape the madding crowd by going through the kitchens. 'It was awful, I hated it. It made me very, very nervous about the level of expectation.'

Edwards stayed in the athletes' village until he had qualified for the final, then accepted the offer of a room provided by Puma in a hotel. He had been unsure whether he could, in conscience, accept being singled out for further special treatment. 'I didn't want to come the superstar bit.' Roger Black told him he would be foolish not to take the offer. He was told he would find it more peaceful in the countdown to competing. 'I'd had a terrible night's sleep in the village before the qualifying rounds,' says Edwards.

As usual, there was a rest day between qualifying and the final on Monday 7 August – a day and a night to think; a day and a night when time never drags more slowly. Edwards played some chess with British middle distance runner Curtis Robb, knowing it was a trusted distraction for the mind. He had been attracted to the game largely by Gary Kasparov's charisma in his confrontation with Briton Nigel Short. 'There are so many options in chess and I just wanted to keep my mind off what was ahead.' Edwards also spent some time playing the guitar and singing Christian choruses.

He knew on the eve of the competition that he had been drawn to jump tenth out of the 12 finalists. Brian Wellman, who had been jumping most consistently throughout the season, would go immediately after him. He would also need to watch the others who trained at the University of Arkansas like Wellman – Conley and Jerome Romaine; and also the Cuban contingent led by Quesada. Edwards knew that he could count on one ally in the heat of the upcoming battle. His friend Rogel Nahum from Israel had made the last 12 after struggling for most of the year to recover from a knee operation, and they hunted each other's company in the countdown to the final.

'We did our warm-up together,' says Nahum. 'I like to have espresso coffee, but Jonathan just likes to go stretch straightaway. Everything he does is a little different. He eats less, rests more and his warm-up is more mental than physical. He is not like the other guys who have a very hyperactive warm-up – you know, running and jumping. Often Jonathan's warm-up takes an hour and a half, twic as long as mine. I join him when he gets to his middle phase. I do more drills, more run-ups, more jumps. Sometimes, Jonathan doesn't even jog. I remember in Gothenburg he only stretched, with one trial run-up. That was it. Jonathan saved everything for the big jump. Everything. Jonathan was hugely tense, but he was ready to jump far, everybody could see that. We were waiting for him to explode.'

The wait was not a long one. The Ullevi Stadium was full, bathed in midsummer sunlight, and there was a breath of a tailwind. Edwards was taut, never more confident. He came onto the runway and the crowd clapped rhythmically. Like a man fired from an invisible catapult, Edwards – wearing vest No 539 – was off down the runway. He devours the ground like no other triple jumper. There are two distinct species of triple jumpers: those who are muscular and rely heavily on their strength – men like Quesada, Wellman, Kenny Harrison and Denis Kapustin; and those who are dependent on their speed which allows them to skip over the ground – men like Conley and Edwards.

In Gothenburg, Edwards left the board and was airborne. He touched down momentarily and was airborne again before kissing the ground to jump into the pit. 'I knew it was a brilliant jump,' he says. 'I felt relief. Relief and exultation. There was always a chance I wasn't going to do it. And I had; it was a brilliant feeling. I was in a daze.'

Photographers flooded the runway. Edwards was looking at the board that would display the distance of his jump, but it remained blank. 'Suddenly, there was a roar from the crowd,' he says. 'I don't know what I've jumped but everybody else does. I don't know where they saw it. And then I see: 18.16 metres. And that's it, a world record and the world championship.' Ludicrously, Edwards wandered towards the end of the sandpit and started to mime questions to Andy Norman about his technique. 'Were my arms okay?' Swiftly, he appreciated that this was not the most relevant question he had ever asked. 'I think my over-riding emotion was relief as much as anything. Yes, relief ... and thankfulness.'

For Wellman, the man jumping next, this was a Doomsday scenario. 'The photographers were all over the place,' he recalls. 'They left their equipment in the middle of the runway. They were chasing Jonathan; and I'm supposed to jump and this guy's big old camera with the big old lenses and stuff is lying across the runway. What *is* this?' Unsurprisingly, when Wellman finally had an unhindered sight of the sandpit, he fouled his jump.

Edwards was what sportspeople like to call 'in the zone'. The competition was taking place, but he was oblivious to his rivals. He had entered a world of his own. His sprint down the runway was 18 strides, as always. His speed was estimated to be in excess of 25 miles an hour and he was covering 11 metres per second. Instinctively, when he took flight in the second round he knew he was travelling even further. 'I hadn't got a great step in my first jump, but this time my step was near perfect and I had a sensation of flying.' When he landed, sand exploded around his calves. He was beyond the number 18 on the board beside the pit and there were no more numbers after that.

He seemed to rise in slow motion. He walked out of the pit, looked in the sand in disbelief. He did not need confirmation from the judges. Edwards knew he had just taken the world record onto another planet. His smile could have replaced the electric grid and lit the city for the night. His friend Rogel Nahum knew instantly that he had

he best seat in the house for the greatest exhibition in
riple jumping the world had ever seen. 'Jonathan spends
ess time on the ground than anybody else,' he explains.
He is amazing. Jonathan is faster than the other guys and
ne retains that speed throughout the three phases of the
ump. Maybe this was the best triple jump event ever seen.'

Up went the distance on the board in the infield:
8.29 metres. Edwards had become the first man in his-
ory to jump over 60 feet – 60 feet and a quarter of an
nch, to be precise. Later, he received his gold medal from
he Queen of Sweden as the entire stadium rose to salute
him. The ovation lasted almost three minutes, until
Edwards motioned to them to resume their seats.
Afterwards he had a small, unseen presentation of his
own to make, as Rogel Nahum recalls. 'Jonathan gave me
nis watch as a souvenir and I still have it.' In truth, it was a
gift of gratitude.

In 1999, four summers later, Edwards' excitement at the
nemory of Gothenburg is still barely controllable. Catch
the breathlessness in his voice and dismiss the grammar as
ne relives his most-treasured moment: 'Yeah, really it was
a dreamlike feeling that I had broken the world record
again. I'd got all that pent-up emotion and nerves and will
t, won't it, go right out of my system – because I'd done it
– I'd broken the world record in the first round, and there
'd broken the world record again – and I *knew* I'd broken
he world record again. I'd just gone out there – I'd done
t. I shook my head and there was none of that, like, *Yes!*
ike last time. It was very calm, almost serene. Crazy. The
walk back again, surrounded by cameras. Brian [Wellman]
again standing on the end of the runway, waiting to jump.
Having to wait for an eternity – his concentration would
be totally ruined. Comes up 18.29 metres and I'm very

aware that it was 60 feet. It was just like a perfect day. It was just me ... just incredible.'

Pandemonium was not confined to the Ullevi Stadium in Gothenburg. Celebrations were taking place across England, memories being cast for life. In their first-floor flat in Heaton, Alison Edwards had been proving herself to be a notoriously bad spectator, as ever. Three friends, Linda Donaldson and John and Liz Hawksworth, were looking after her two young sons Sam and nine-week-old Nathan, while she pretended to garden. 'I was digging up the garden, just trying to keep my mind occupied, when Linda shouted down to me that Jonathan had broken the world record,' she says. 'I have no recollection of seeing any of it. I can never sit still when Jonathan's competing.'

She can, however, recall the bedlam that broke out as journalists began to knock on her front door, while other members of the media kept the telephone ringing as if the number had been misread for the emergency services. Alison was reluctant to comment until she knew that the competition was over. 'Some of the reporters turned up with champagne and they wanted pictures of me with the children. We were completely gullible then; I think I brought Sam down for them to get one picture. The BBC sent a news crew and one newspaper wanted to fly the children and me to Gothenburg for a reunion with Jonathan. We said, "Thanks, but no thanks."'

The telephone never stopped ringing until midnight, she says. Two hours later, she was up to feed Nathan. In the morning Linda arrived with all the newspapers and the gate at the top of the stairs was left open by mistake. Sam seized the opportunity to tumble down the stairs. 'I called my GP and he told me to keep an eye on him,' says Alison. 'Fortunately, he sustained no lasting damage!'

At the vicarage in Bearwood, near Bournemouth, Reverend Andy Edwards was at home with his wife Jill and her mother. They had hoped for a peaceful evening in front of the television, but Southern Television had other plans for them. Would they agree to be filmed watching their son compete? Reverend Edwards suggested that he would speak to them after his son had jumped. After Edwards' first giant leap in Gothenburg, there was a knock on the front door of the vicarage. It was the television crew. 'They had their van parked round the corner and were watching Jonathan on their monitor,' says Reverend Edwards. He invited the crew to interview his wife and himself in their garden. Later, a BBC film unit arrived. They filmed us watching the medal ceremony.' Reverend Edwards estimates that over the next 24 hours he was asked to give around 15 interviews, including a BBC radio three-way link with Jonathan in Gothenburg and Alison at home in Heaton.

In Leeds, Tim and Anna Edwards were visiting a friend called Steve, who at their request borrowed a television for the night as he did not own one. The owner of the black-and-white set, Billy, stayed with them to watch the athletics. Tim says, 'After Jonathan's first jump, we all let out a huge roar. As we went quiet, our baby daughter Zoe started to scream because she had been startled by the loud noise. Anna calmed her down and we looked back at the screen, and there was Jonathan on the runway again. Another huge roar. He'd done it again! It took a few moments for us to realize we were watching an action replay…'

At an airport hotel near Heathrow, Lawrence Whittal-Williams, Edwards' sports master from West Buckland

School, had just checked into a room with his wife Judith. 'We were going to Italy on holiday the next day and walked into the room just in time to see Jonathan take his first jump,' explains Whittal-Williams. 'That was fairly awesome to have managed to time it like that, and as we watched him it was still hard to believe.'

At Gateshead Stadium that night, they had rolled out the red carpet for a pre-season match involving Newcastle United. John Hedley, Edwards' regular training partner at the stadium, has black-and-white blood like most of the male population of Newcastle. 'They had turned the upstairs bar into an executive lounge – Sir John Hall [the Newcastle chairman] was coming and Kevin Keegan – you know, all the Newcastle hierarchy – the mayor and a lot of people,' remembers Hedley. 'They had a colour television in there, and so I'm sitting watching the athletics when all these people start to arrive. And I said to them, "No offence, but I'm not leaving." Jonathan did the first jump and – it was just like watching Newcastle – I couldn't control myself. I was up off my seat, punching the air. All these people were looking at me, asking, "Who's that?" And then Jonathan jumps 18.29 metres and does his lap of honour. I felt such pride for Jonathan. I'm happy for him and I'm happy for myself. Then I went out and watched Newcastle play an exhibition match in front of 12,500 people – a fantastic night, great!'

In Earlsfield, near Wimbledon, Jo Svarovsky, a student who had befriended Edwards at Durham University and who had accompanied him when he went shopping for his first-ever suit, had come home expecting her flatmate to have recorded the athletics. 'My friend had gone out, so I went to the kitchen where we left notes for one another. There was nothing there. I knew how well Jonathan had done – I had heard the news on the radio – but I desperately wanted to see it on television. As there was no note in the kitchen, I went into the lounge and sat and cried. When my flatmate came home she wondered what on earth was wrong. "I left you this message asking you to video Jonathan, that's what's wrong," I sobbed. To my embarrassment, she told me the tape was all set up in the machine. All I had to do was press "Play".

On the south coast, Kriss Akabusi was watching in the living room of his house in Southampton. 'I wasn't prepared for what Jonathan did,' he says. Akabusi is an ebullient man, with a contagious laugh that contributed to his popularity on the track and now does the same in his role as a one-man corporation and presenter of television shows like *Record Breakers*. He is also a profound, deep-thinking man, someone Edwards had leant on in the depressing hours after his failure at the Barcelona Olympics three years earlier. Now Akabusi was sitting at home with his family in Southampton and rejoicing at what he had witnessed.

'I remember watching him prepare, the little hops and things he does. He skips, skips, skips, hops, hops, hops, beside the track. He looks down. He puts his hands together over his head, watching, watching, watching, then *bam!* – off he goes. He has always been blisteringly quick, which is a surprise as he looks so weedy. He's certainly quicker than I was. You looked at how far he had jumped, then you looked again. Incredible. And then he does it again! It was one of the moments when the realization of what he has done comes very, very late, because there's this feeling of disbelief. You're scratching your head, thinking, "Did he jump that far, did he really?" I recognized at that moment what he had done – "Man, you've just jumped into the stratosphere!"'

In the meantime, a young woman in Jerusalem was excitedly scouring a Hebrew newspaper for details of Edwards' success. Rachel Edwards, aged 20, in the midst of a year-long stay in Israel working for a Christian mission and other voluntary organizations, was delighted for her brother. 'I saw the pictures on television a day late,' she says. 'But I read Hebrew and knew what he'd achieved. I was very pleased for Jonathan.'

Pity Brian Wellman waiting to jump for a second time, while the media fawned on and fêted Edwards. Wellman had arrived in Gothenburg convinced that he would make an impact at the World Championships. Now he was just in the chorus line. Somewhat predictably, Wellman ran through his next jump. For him, there was only one chance left to beat the halfway cut of the competition, and that was when Edwards made a gesture that Wellman will not forget. 'Jonathan realized what was going on, in terms of photographers everywhere, and he was nice enough to pass on his third jump,' explains Wellman, speaking in the summer of 1999 from his apartment in Arkansas, where he still trains. Even though Edwards had no need to make another jump, it would have been within his rights to have made his third-round attempt. It would have kept Wellman under intense competitive pressure, and he was probably the only man who believed he was capable of rivalling the Englishman. Had Edwards gone for his third jump, Wellman might never have gathered his concentration in the hullabaloo surrounding the runway of the triple jump. But such thoughts never entered Edwards' mind. 'Actually, Jonathan apologized for all the distractions,' adds Wellman. 'I mean, it was no fault of his, but still he said sorry. Big guy.' With the chaos receding as Edwards sat out the third round, Wellman posted a legal jump. He was still in the Championships.

'I think Jonathan may think the same as me,' insists Wellman, who believed until the end that he could steal the gold. 'When I win competitions I want to beat the other person fair and square on the day – give them that opportunity to perform; man to man, who's the better guy. I was still mentally in the game right through; I still thought I could maybe pull a big one off.'

There is a camaraderie amongst the triple jump fraternity, born from common knowledge of the hours, days, weeks, months, years spent trying to perfect an exceedingly complicated technique. Edwards' success did not evoke any jealousy, as Wellman confirms. 'In this day and age it's so hard to believe that people can be genuinely nice and honest and, you know, upstanding and live their lives in the way that it should be, and be nice to people. Yet I have no doubts that with Jonathan what you see is what you get. You spend two hours together as a group every time you compete against each other, so I think there is genuine respect.'

In the euphoria of the hour, Edwards jumped again by public demand that night in Gothenburg, but without any expectation. His champagne moment was behind him, the evidence for the world to comprehend was already on the leader board. *Position 1: J. Edwards (GBR) 18.29 metres*. The board might also have flashed the obvious message of the night: *The Rest, nowhere*. Mike Conley, the Olympic champion from the United States, said afterwards, 'I can't bring myself to get mad at Jonathan. I can only get mad at what he jumped.'

After his final jump, Edwards pretended to stagger as he left the pit, but, as a conservative man, he was still privately a little nervous of what Wellman might have left. 'I had to endure the last round – and Brian was unbelievably pumped up.' His fears were unfounded, of course; no one was going to get close to his excellence that night. Nevertheless, Wellman came out of the pit after his last jump with a great exhibition of what-might-have-been and he was graphically bemoaning his misfortune. 'Brian is a theatrical performer,' says Edwards. 'I think he got energy from his own belief, you know, very American. He had to convince himself in his own mind that he could jump that far.'

Once Wellman had made his departure, Edwards was soon in possession of a large Union flag, but not until he had first thanked all the officials who had controlled the event. 'Well, they work for free, you know.' Edwards had always wondered what it would be like to be in a full stadium doing a victory jig. Now he knew. 'It was fantastic,' he says. 'I received a lovely reception as I went round the track.' As he rounded the top bend, it was evident that the women's 100 metres final was about to start. An official intercepted Edwards and thousands in the grandstand on the straight started to jeer as they saw that his progress was being halted. 'I ducked the official and went on the inside of the grass and down the straight. I kept the women's final waiting!'

Naturally, the BBC was anxious to have an immediate interview with him. Des Lynam, the station's prime sports anchorman (later spirited to ITV in a huge transfer deal during the summer of 1999), was awaiting him. Edwards had begun to rehydrate, taking lots of water in readiness to provide a urine sample for the compulsory drug test he knew was on the agenda. Yet the BBC was persistent and managed to get Edwards to their studio before he went to doping control. By then, however, Edwards was desperate to go to the toilet. 'I don't think Des would have appreciated me taking a toilet break in mid-interview. It wouldn't have been a great end to the evening!' Before going into the studio, his 'minder' from the drug-testing personnel followed him into the toilet and watched him urinate, but this was still in contravention to protocol, not something that Edwards appreciated until afterwards. 'When I did get to drug-testing, we mentioned this and the guy in charge wasn't very happy. By this time I had taken so much fluid, the sample I gave was so diluted that the pH level was too low. I must have given 170 millilitres and you're supposed to give 70. My bladder was completely empty, but I was told I had to start again.'

Edwards spent the next one and a half hours sitting at doping control with world decathlon champion Dan O'Brien, and another American decathlete called Chris Huffins. They were hostages in the now-empty stadium until past midnight. 'Dan O'Brien is a superstar and suddenly, though you're no different a person, you're accepted in the club. That's what struck me as I sat there. You've gained entrance into sort of exclusive circles where you wouldn't have been noticed before.'

Doctor Malcolm Brown and press officer Tony Ward from the BAF had kept Edwards company. All three men were hungry, but an attempt to get a hamburger and fries at McDonald's proved fruitless as the staff cleaning up for the night would not allow them entry. Fortunately, the hotel where Puma had arranged for their athletes to stay was not far from the stadium and the kitchen was still open. Edwards did not wish to abuse this hospitality and, though his hosts would not have minded had he ordered a case of Dom Perignon, he ordered only light refreshment. 'I still chuckle at the bottle of good red wine and steak that Tony had no qualms about ordering!'

It was approaching 2.00 a.m. when Edwards at last retired to his room, where he found a note pinned to his door. 'Thanks, Jonathan, you have given me all the inspiration I need,' read the note and it was signed by Steve Smith, the young Liverpudlian who held the world junior high jump record. Edwards had one letter to write himself, tearing a page from the programme to send a message to Willie Banks, the effervescent American who had held the world record from June 1985 until the Englishman jumped past his mark in Salamanca. Edwards wrote, 'You are the man who made triple jump what it is today. It was very exciting to break your record and I look forward to meeting you in Atlanta.'

The next morning Edwards' story was circulating the world and the media assembled in Gothenburg wanted his whole life story, chapter and verse. Paul Hayward, the chief sports writer for the *Daily Telegraph*, gave an impression of Edwards' frenzied first hours as world champion when he reported,

At Edwards's umpteenth news conference of the day – and it was only 11 a.m. – [Tony] Ward read out a schedule of engagements that would have had a Bill Clinton or John Major blanching with guilt at his own laziness. 'At 8.05 a.m. we were at the New Opera House for Sky TV,' said Ward, taking a deep breath at the start of a long oration. 'Then we went up to the international broadcasting centre for BBC Radio, then we missed BBC Breakfast Time because of Swedish broadcasting problems. Then we went back to the Opera House for GMTV before going on to the Viking Ship to do BBC Everyman.' He was not nearly finished. 'Then we went back up to do BBC Breakfast Time, which we caught by a minute. Next was breakfast at The Sheraton and then on to this (for the press). From here we go to a news conference with Puma and then to ITN for the lunchtime news. I've told Jon to finish after that, because I think he's done everybody. Then we go to look at his new Mercedes.' The new Mercedes, in case anybody was on a day-trip to Pluto on Monday, was for breaking the world triple jump record, not once but twice.[3]

Through this whirlwind of engagements, Edwards was a model of politeness and modesty. It is his way. He was flustered just once, and that was when Anthea Turner, from her sofa on GMTV in London, told him she had a surprise for him. Ms Turner explained that his wife Alison was on the line from their home in Newcastle. 'It was a surprise, all right,' says Edwards. 'We had spoken the night before and I thought, mistakenly, that Alison wasn't going to give any interview until I'd got back. We didn't want the kids being exposed to the entire hassle and pressure. Our son Sam had been unsettled for about a week after I came home to a reception at Newcastle when I had first broken the world record in Salamanca a month before.'

Edwards' initial abruptness on that occasion passed unnoticed, however, and his meeting with the British media was an unreserved success. Stephen Bierley, writing in the *Guardian*, observed: 'Jonathan Edwards is about as far removed from a typical ego-driven superstar as it is possible to get.'[4] David Miller wrote in *The Times*, 'I suspect that his real secret, which neither he nor any coach or

---

3 *Daily Telegraph*, 9 August 1995.
4 *Guardian*, 9 August 1995.

sporting psychologist can define, lies in his head. His faith, he says, is the basis of his whole life.'[5] Neil Wilson, the vastly experienced athletics correspondent for the *Daily Mail*, posed a significant question: 'One wondered whether he has taken it [the triple jump] beyond the imagination of others, as Bob Beamon did the long jump with a single leap in 1968, a jump not to be matched for 23 years.'[6]

Mike Rowbottom from the *Independent* began his dispatch, 'Donovan Bailey, Canada's new 100 metres champion, wandered past the Hotel Opalen here yesterday morning and paused to shake the hand of an athlete surrounded by cameramen and autograph hunters. His arrival did absolutely nothing to alter the focus of attention. Jonathan Edwards, the world triple jump champion and world record holder, is now officially "A Star".'[7] Inimitably, the *Sun* concocted a variation on the regular column they provide when someone is breaking news. Instead of '20 things you don't know about…', they scaled down the column on Edwards to '18.29 record things on our triple jump champion Jonathan'.[8] The sports desks on what was once Fleet Street were finding Edwards a refreshing story line.

For Edwards, there was still a clarity – some might suggest a beautiful naivety – about what he had actually achieved. 'It's only jumping into a sandpit,' he said. There was also an acceptance, nonetheless, that his life was changing for ever. When he was questioned as to how he

5 *The Times*, 9 August 1995.
6 *Daily Mail*, 9 August 1995.
7 *Independent*, 9 August 1995.
8 *The Sun*, 9 August 1995.

would equate wealth with the fundamental principles of his Christian faith, Edwards replied, 'Paul was writing a letter to Timothy in the Bible and said, "Charge those that are rich not to become high-minded and trust in uncertain riches, but in the living God who gives all things to be enjoyed." I will enjoy this success and what it brings, but I won't trust in it. I'll aim to be a good steward of what I have been given.' He would discover in the coming years precisely how challenging that would prove.

In Gothenburg, however, Edwards was quite properly revelling in his triumph, comfortable and confident in fielding all enquiries from the British press contingent. There was a sense that everyone was sharing his celebration. Light questions filtered through the more serious enquiries. Edwards admitted, for instance, that he could see no harm in an occasional glass of wine. 'I'm not teetotal and I don't think there's anything wrong in that. It says in the Psalms that God gives wine, which makes glad the heart of man – Psalm 104, verse 15, I think.' In the *Telegraph* Paul Hayward wrote humorously, 'This met with much sage nodding.'[9]

In the midst of his chaotic schedule, Edwards had stopped for breakfast at The Sheraton with Andy Norman and Fatima Whitbread, who was to become Andy's wife. Also present in the breakfast room were Jeffrey Archer, later to become a Tory peer, and Sir Michael Belloff QC, Principal of Trinity College, Oxford. Both men were avid supporters of athletics. Edwards and his wife Alison would later join the guest list at the Archers' fabled champagne and shepherd's pie Christmas party at their Thames-side penthouse. 'Extraordinary man, Jeffrey,' smiles Edwards. 'He can relate to anyone, chat with anyone, but, to be

9 *Daily Telegraph*, 9 August 1995.

honest, we felt like fish out of water. The guests included Lady Thatcher, the Archbishop of Canterbury, Jonathan Aitken, Sir Brian Mawhinney, Sir John Hall, Nigel Havers and Barry Humphries. We had an enjoyable evening, but couldn't help feeling we were in over our heads!'

Edwards concluded his first day as world champion and owner of a new Mercedes C-class by returning to the athletes' village to attend chapel. 'There were only three or four of us; it was simple and very quiet. It was an important moment to thank God for what had happened, to put it into its rightful context.'

What had happened was that Edwards had confounded those intimately connected with athletics. He had struck a chord for the common man. He had shown that nice guys could come first. He had pushed back the frontiers of his sport without warning, as American coach Dick Booth acknowledges. 'He was a kind of journeyman jumper – and all of a sudden he goes from a 57-footer to a 60-footer. What's so neat – and I don't mean this to sound negative or racist – but he's a white guy who isn't perceived to be this astronomical athlete. He's not all muscled up, he looks like an 800 metres runner. He's the kid next door, running down the runway real fast.'

Booth has given much of his career to coaching the triple jump. Conley, Wellman and Romaine are graduates of his. Speaking at the outset of the summer of 1999, he says that hanging opposite his desk in his office at the University of Arkansas is a photograph of Edwards flanked by Wellman and Romaine. The picture was taken during the medal ceremony in Gothenburg. 'I have had the good fortune to coach several world-class athletes and to me the thing that separates them is class ... there is no arrogance, no pretence, there is just a guy who has worked very hard and nice things have happened to him and he has kept them in perspective. Jonathan is certainly one of those people. He is as humble and self-effacing as anybody you will ever meet. He is the type of guy that you're just totally happy for. When the guys came home from Gothenburg they had a certain respect for Jonathan. Let me tell you, nobody understands better than the guys who are trying to do it. If you had dedicated 10 or 15 years of your life pursuing the same thing, knowing how hard it is, you would really have a respect for it [the world record].'

To Booth, there is an intricacy to triple jumping that makes it far more complex than the other jumping events. 'You know, I can go to a schoolyard and I can have little kids line up and run down the runway and jump into a pit. They can run and jump. They can't triple jump. This is ugly, this isn't easy; there's a process here and if you don't do it right it can just beat you up. There have been studies made that show that the impact, the stresses you land on that single leg at the end of the hop phase, can be as much as seven times your body weight. You're not going to be perfect every time and it's the ugly jumps that hurt. It's those ugly ones, when you get just a little heavy, you feel the impact go through your body so that it shakes your teeth. Jonathan has earned everything he has got. It has been a year-after-year thing and he has stayed with it. He has persisted – and he became great.

'Jonathan is the person everybody wants to be, wants to emulate, and we have studied him on film so many times. We always talk about the principle of a skipping rock: the faster it goes across the lake, the flatter it stays, the less water it displaces and the further it goes. Jonathan does that great – he's the perfect skipping rock right now.'

On that August night in Gothenburg, Edwards had jumped as Booth so graphically describes. When he flew home 36 hours later, there was a reception party of approaching 1,000 people to greet him at Newcastle airport. His local newspaper, *The Journal*, presented Edwards with framed copies of its front and back pages recording his success in Gothenburg. The front page was headlined 'King Jon!'; the back page showed him cavorting with a Union flag under the headline 'Golden Boy'. Alison had brought their sons Sam (celebrating his second birthday) and Nathan with her to the airport. Sam sat on his father's shoulders and tried to eat his gold medal, while cameramen captured the endearing image for posterity.

Outside the Edwards family's small, neat flat in Heaton there were balloons, flags and a homemade banner reading 'Simply the Best'. Another note was pinned to the front door: 'Jonathan Edwards, 1740, Revivalist. Jonathan Edwards, 18:29, Triple Jumper.'

Predictably, some journalists were not content with soundbites from a news conference. Valerie Groves, a feature writer from *The Times*, arrived unannounced on Edwards' doorstep, as did a young woman reporter from the *Sunday Mirror*. 'She said I had agreed to see her and I was a bit naive and accommodating at that time. It was a case of, well, as they've made the effort, I'd better see them. The woman from the *Mirror* started asking questions about our relationship and sex life and Alison got very upset. Alison, in particular, endured several anxious days fearing what would be published. Anyway, the interview itself turned out fine.'

The article in *The Times*[10] was spread across two pages, with Ms Groves observing, 'Indoors, the telephone never

---

10 *The Times*, 11 August 1995.

stops, messages piling up, most insistently from *Hello!* magazine. If they had arrived with their cameras they would have found a small maisonette, and the sweet-faced wife Alison, daughter of an evangelist from the Hebrides, taking their two sons to the mothers and toddlers club.' This was merely a taste of the attention to follow.

Edwards had redefined the boundaries of his event, in the same way that Bob Beamon had revolutionized the long jump in the rarefied air of Mexico City 27 years earlier. It had been an exceptional journey. He had begun the year busking for car-parking space at stadiums; now promoters wanted to send limousines to chauffeur him to events. He won all 14 competitions he entered and earned over $400,000. 'It's been a remarkable time for an ordinary, skinny little guy who jumps into a sandpit for a living,' he said.

Sadly, not quite everyone revelled in Edwards' moment of triumph. Extraordinarily, his return to the gym at Gateshead was marred by an astonishing verbal assault from Carl Johnson. While the nation was showering Edwards with bouquets, applauding his talent, congratulating him on his Corinthian spirit and celebrating his spiritual integrity, Johnson asked Edwards to accompany him to the privacy of a small anteroom off the main gym.

'Carl was very upset. It took me completely by surprise,' explains Edwards. There were friends of Edwards listening in the gym who were on the brink of coming to intervene. Johnson was infuriated because, in his view and the view of his family, Edwards had not paid him enough credit in his post-Gothenburg interviews. 'I felt his criticism was completely unjustified,' says Edwards. 'I was acutely aware of the difficulties for Carl because my success had come, more or less, at the moment I distanced myself from him. It was an awkward time for Carl, I understood that. Those closest to him felt for him. However, when I made my breakthrough in Lille, the media rang Carl to speak to him and he refused to talk. After that, the media ignored him and he missed out on his rightful share of the glory and the credit. Yet by the same token, I bent over backwards in my interviews to mention that I had reasons to be grateful to Norman, Peter and Carl. My conscience is totally clear.'

Shortly after he had been harangued in the gym, and unbeknown to Johnson himself, Edwards received a letter from Johnson's wife Isabel, recounting their family's hurt. 'It upset me greatly, but it was a misunderstanding, no more than that. Still, I felt the need to go and see Isabel,' he says. He had to close the chapter in person.

Today, Edwards and Johnson have forgotten their differences and their paths often cross in the gym at Gateshead Stadium. Edwards' eyes had been opened, however. He was going to have to accept that he was now vulnerable in an unfamiliar world.

Chapter 7

Awards ... and Alison

*A life without love, without the presence of the beloved,
is nothing but a mere magic lantern show.*

GOETHE

The doors to a new world had been thrown open to Edwards. After his leap into history in Gothenburg, he was on the 'A list' of celebrities to be invited to all the end-of-year award dinners. Indeed, he was shortlisted, it seemed, for everything except the Nobel Prize. Des Lynam had provided an early clue to the demand that Edwards would experience when he closed his BBC interview with him in Sweden by saying, 'See you at the Sports Personality Awards.'

Edwards, clean cut, articulate, husband, father, devout Christian and world champion, had done more than capture a record. He had captivated the nation. When we met in Newcastle in late November 1995, the BBC were already running trailers inviting viewers to vote for their sports personality of the year. From the emphasis of the broadcasts, it was apparent that the poll would be reduced to a two-man duel between Edwards and Frank Bruno.

To Edwards this seemed an absurdity. Bruno had a catch-phrase ('Know what I mean, 'Arry?'); Bruno was a lovable pantomime entertainer; and now Bruno, at last, owned a version of the World Heavyweight Championship. 'To most people I'm just "that long jumper", aren't I?' said Edwards. 'Frank Bruno's more popular than the Queen, isn't he? He's a genuinely nice guy, and when people look for role models he's a pretty good example.'

Edwards had been to the awards just once before, as a young member of the British squad who won the team award in 1989. Bruno, it appeared, was pretty much part of the furnishings on the evening when the BBC awarded the famous trophy. He was interviewed year after year, and the same question would inevitably be fired at him: 'So, Frank, are you going to bring the World Championship back to Britain?' As 1995 was drawing to a close, the question had become redundant. Bruno had beaten Oliver McCall, to claim the WBC Heavyweight World Championship.

'When I was younger I was a big Bruno fan,' confided Edwards. 'I remember being devastated when he lost to Bonecrusher Smith. He may not be the most talented boxer ever to have stepped into the ring, yet through hard work, dedication and turning a deaf ear to those telling him he should quit, Frank's actually won a version of the world title. And the BBC Sports Award is not given simply for achievement; it's about personality, about having a place in the heart of the public. It's not something I could expect to have at this stage of my career, having had just one year of success. To my mind, it's ridiculous to think I could win.'

Edwards was seriously underestimating the impact he had made, by what degree he would discover later.

Meanwhile, the social whirl was about to engulf him. His first date was at Buckingham Palace, where he was named male athlete of the year in the BAF awards.

On 9 December he had to be in Monte Carlo for a black-tie gala awards dinner hosted by the International Amateur Athletics Federation (IAAF), the world governing body for athletics. He was unaccompanied at the Monte Carlo Country Club as his wife Alison was unwell, suffering from bouts of acute abdominal pain. Before the night was out, however, Edwards was to be shown to the table of Prince Albert of Monaco. The Englishman beat men of the calibre of Haile Gebreselassie, Moses Kiptanui, Michael Johnson and Noureddine Morceli to be named the IAAF's Athlete of the Year. 'I feel like I'm in an armchair and watching a film of someone else's life – someone who looks remarkably like me and answers to the same name. World Athlete of the Year! Incredible, really.'

Edwards brought more than the award home from Monte Carlo. He had found time to visit a jeweller's to buy a ruby ring for Alison. 'There's a verse in Proverbs (3:15) that says, "She is more precious than rubies; nothing you desire can compare with her."'

He had an early alarm call on the morning after the gala dinner, as he was booked on the first flight from Nice to London. Producers at the BBC were fearful of him being delayed by bad weather. He had to be in London for rehearsals for the Corporation's award show which was being broadcast from the Queen Elizabeth Centre that night. The show routinely involved sportsmen and women in some active, often amusing sideshow to break up the main event. When it was schemed to incorporate a standing jump competition in the programme, Edwards was a natural selection. So was Steve Ojomoh, an England rugby player but also the holder of the home triple jump record at West Buckland School. Steve Redgrave, the awesome Olympic oarsman, and Steve Backley, the javelin thrower, completed the cast list along with Denise Lewis and Martin Offiah.

Edwards was game for a laugh, still not believing for a second that he could win the main award. In London he was reunited with Alison, who felt well enough to travel from Newcastle to meet her husband. Editor of the show Brian Barwick took Edwards aside before the programme to warn him, 'I can tell you that you're in the top six. If you're third, you'll collect your award and stand to the left; if you're second, you'll go to the right; and if you win, you'll speak to the nation.'

For Edwards this whole evening was of unquestionable importance. 'This award is a fixture in the British sporting calendar as much as Wimbledon is,' he reasoned. 'It has a huge history and a national audience.' This was the stuff of *Boys' Own* legend for someone like Edwards, the son of a vicar who jumped into a sandpit. He was in contention for an award engraved with names like Bobby Moore, Henry Cooper, Mary Peters, Nick Faldo, Ian Botham, Sebastian Coe, Daley Thompson, Nigel Mansell, Damon Hill and Her Royal Highness Princess Anne.

After being a part of the amusing cabaret and finishing second in the standing jump (behind rugby league star Martin 'Chariots' Offiah) in the studio, Edwards was rushed backstage to change. Before he returned to the theatre, he was asked to put on a microphone. At face value, he interpreted this as an encouraging sign. 'When I got into the hall I looked to see who else might be wearing one.' He could see that Redgrave had a mike on, and so did Rob Andrew, who so memorably delivered the drop goal that enabled England to defeat Australia in the quarter finals of the Rugby World Cup during the summer. Bruno, too, was wired. So Edwards was back to square one again; still waiting, still hoping, but not for a second daring to dream.

As the evening progressed, hosts Des Lynam, Steve Rider and Sue Barker presented highlights of the sporting year in between speaking with the prominent sportsmen and women. Edwards was interviewed at some length, but this was nothing less than he had expected after Gothenburg. Bruno was also quizzed, along with a host of other fine performers. Finally, the moment arrived to unmask the winner of the 1995 BBC Sports Personality of the Year.

Edwards can remember the preamble '...and in second place, a man who has finally achieved his ambition...' There was a sharp intake of breath within the studio as the introduction could only have been for Bruno. Kelly Holmes nudged Edwards in the ribs. 'You've won!' she whispered. Edwards blanched.

Bernard Gallagher, captain of the victorious European Ryder Cup, who was making the presentations, never got much beyond his opening gambit in announcing the winner. 'A man who jumped—' He was immediately drowned out by a tidal wave of applause.

In a trance, Edwards rose to his feet. In another part of the auditorium, his still unwell wife smiled bravely, while nursing a secret fear. 'I was sitting there praying I wouldn't faint,' she says. 'I felt really light-headed.' Her husband was in a similar state for a vastly different reason. He began his acceptance speech to the wrong camera, as the floor manager tried desperately to correct him. Edwards told the audience how he had watched this particular award being presented since his schooldays, though he confessed that, as it was held on a Sunday, it had not been an especially good night for him! Of course, he tried to ensure in his speech that he thanked all the people closest to him – his wife, his parents, his coaches.

In truth, he was feeling hopelessly overwhelmed. 'It was almost too much for me to be there. I was a little boy in another world, thrust there through circumstances, but not really belonging. At least, that's how it seemed.' Brendan Foster, a much respected member of the BBC's commentary team for athletics, recalls, 'I have never seen anybody so excited about winning the BBC Sports Personality of the Year Award. Jonathan was genuinely moved.'

There were more awards to be collected before the year's end. Edwards was named sportsman of the year in the coveted poll of the Sports Writers' Association and he was voted sportsman of the year by *Daily Express* readers. To crown this dazzling, memorable year, Edwards was informed that he was to be made an MBE in the Queen's New Year's Honours list.

The Edwards family were living a fantasy, or so it seemed. Nonetheless, if Jonathan proved to be an accomplished yet humble recipient of so much silverware, so many lavish compliments, Alison was not entirely comfortable with life in the limelight. 'It's lovely to be the centre of attention, to get dressed up for a dinner or a party, but it's not really a natural lifestyle for us. I'm not belittling it, because we had lovely times, but we're not great party animals. We're just an ordinary couple, an ordinary family; that's what makes this all so bizarre.'

Throughout this whirlwind of celebration, Alison remained unwell, to the extent that she and her husband became steadily more anxious as Christmas came and went. With an imminent house move and a three-month training trip to Florida coming up, there was an urgent need to get to the bottom of the problem. 'I had been back to my GP on numerous occasions since November and had had a variety of investigations without conclusion. Eventually, I was referred to a gynaecologist who recommended keyhole surgery to look inside.' An appointment was made for Alison at the Royal Victoria Infirmary for 7 February 1996.

Edwards took his wife to the hospital at 8.00 a.m., then continued across the Tyne to train at Gateshead Stadium. After the training session, he filmed a segment for his appearance on the BBC television programme *Songs of Praise*. When he eventually returned home, there were the usual high number of messages left on his answerphone. One of them was from the hospital, requesting that he contact Alison's consultant immediately. Edwards was informed that his wife had undergone emergency abdominal surgery.

'I came round feeling like I'd been hit by a bus,' recalls Alison. 'I remember saying groggily to a nurse, "Is everything okay?"' Fortunately for her, it was now. To the surgeon's astonishment, Alison had an ectopic pregnancy. Without trying to sound overdramatic, the operation had saved her life. She had been at constant high risk from sudden collapse. 'You can bleed to death in an instant,' she says. 'We thought I might have been pregnant in November, but the test was negative. No one could believe I'd had this condition all that time.'

With his wife needing to rest, Edwards vowed to contribute more around the home, including getting up in the night to nurse their baby son Nathan. 'I will need to do much more about the house, but I'm not worried right now as all my thoughts are with Alison,' he wrote in his diary. 'But I know I will find it difficult and will feel that it is not helping my training. God knows, though, that I have the Olympics in six months. It is a relief, however, for us to have got to the bottom of Alison's health problems. That has been a great pressure.'

His wife came home after three days in hospital and her mother Anne, already down from Edinburgh to help look after the children, was there to greet her. To Alison's frustration, she was unable to participate as she would have wished in the family's house move from Heaton to Gosforth. 'I'm not the kind of person who can sit back and see things done. I'm like my Dad: I like to be up doing things.'

With the stress of convalescing from major surgery, combined with the strain of moving, it was little wonder that Alison wanted to tear up the family's air tickets to Florida. 'I really, really didn't want to go.' Yet three weeks after her operation, Alison flew with her family to Tallahassee, where her husband was to begin his countdown to the Olympic Games in Atlanta. She is Edwards' partner, in every sense.

'I liked Jonathan, but he was incredibly naive for a 22-year-old. At the same time, he was quite cocky and just a bit too sure of himself. He didn't strike me as someone who lived in the real world.'

Those were the thoughts of the young woman called Alison Briggs when she first came into contact with Jonathan Edwards in 1988. Alison, though born in Glasgow, spent her childhood on the Isle of Lewis in the Hebrides, where her father Ralph was a port missionary.

Religion was a central theme in Alison's life as she grew up with her two sisters, first in Stornoway, then in a more remote part of the island. It was a loving childhood, but she soon learned self-sufficiency, returning to the mainland to study physiotherapy when she was almost 18.

After his own idyllic childhood in North Devon, Edwards had made the Northeast his adopted home once he had graduated from Durham University. His chosen place of worship was Heaton Baptist Church, close to the city centre. By then, Alison Briggs had moved from Edinburgh to the Freeman Hospital in Newcastle. She also attended Heaton Baptist Church and was a member of the music group.

Edwards joined the group – and was infatuated with Alison from the beginning. 'Right away, I knew Alison was the girl for me,' he says. 'I saw her singing in the worship group and I thought she was very attractive and I wanted to get to know her.' Alison did not instantly sense she had found her Mr Right, however. She had recently ended a relationship and was not ready for another.

Edwards was a novice when it came to dating. He had just one real girlfriend before Alison. He identifies her only as Naomi and he went out with her for two years from the age of 16. 'We were part of the same social group in church, and it was generally known I liked her. I couldn't quite believe it when she liked me too. We went out for a couple of years, on and off. We got on great, but in the end it just fizzled out.'

He claims he was on the lookout for a girlfriend through his university days, but there was no one who met his exacting standards. 'The opportunities I had I never really wanted to take up. A few were non-Christians and I wasn't going to go out with somebody who didn't share my beliefs. I didn't date at all at Durham. It wasn't that I didn't want to, just that I'm choosy!'

As you would imagine from a man of high moral principles, sex before marriage was not an issue as far as Edwards was concerned. 'I was looking for someone to share my life with. I wasn't looking for a casual relationship. It wasn't quite as clinical as looking at a girl over coffee and thinking, "Is this the girl I'm going to spend the rest of my life with?" For sure, lots of girls I found attractive, but I was looking for more than that. I understand that sex is a big motivating factor in relationships; I was determined that was not going to be for me – before marriage.'

One girlfriend he did make at Durham University was Jo Harvey – now Mrs Jo Svarovsky. Jo befriended Edwards from the moment they met at the Christian Union. In those days, she liked to wear tartan minidresses and strong make-up and had bright, spiky hair, while Edwards was a shy, conservative teenager. 'I'd been brought up in a Christian home and I didn't want to turn my back on religion,' she explains. 'But nor was I convinced I wanted to be a fully badged member of the church parade. For some reason, I decided I wanted Jonathan to be my Christian friend. He wasn't the life and soul of the party, but I took an instant liking to him.'

During their time at university, Jo went to stay with Edwards' family in Ilfracombe and Edwards was a guest at her home in Northwood, Middlesex. Edwards says, 'I always remember Dad asking who "Jox" was, which was how she always signed herself on postcards. Of course, it was Jo with a kiss.' Jo recalls her mother quizzing her about Edwards. She had always wondered whether there was any romance bubbling under the surface. 'I had to tell her we were just good friends – and that isn't a euphemism for anything else.'

Jo accompanied Edwards to church throughout term-time at Durham, attending St Nicholas Church in the first year, then St Margaret's. 'Both were excellent churches that preached the gospel, and that's the important thing,' says Jo. 'I would say St Margaret's was more of an active style – and the congregation was smaller. Going with Jonathan was good for me, because I knew that if I ever felt I couldn't be bothered he would knock on the door to collect me.' Jo willingly accepts that Edwards, in her words, kept her 'on the rails'.

'Jonathan was amazing at university. I think he had a very big effect on a lot of people from a Christian perspective. Not because he went around preaching to people – Jonathan was not one to thrust religion down your throat – but even at this stage, when he was quite a young guy, his faith was utterly, utterly central to his life. His relationship with Jesus Christ, his love of the Lord, was at the core of what he did, who he was. People noticed that, people became aware of it. Hardened rugby players – very sweetly – would feel embarrassed swearing in front of him. Not that Jonathan complained; it was just that he had the respect of those guys because he was a lovely bloke and a talented sportsman.'

Edwards remains friends with Jo to this day. Along with her husband Eddie, he invited her to accompany him to Wembley when he was guest of honour on the day England played the Czech Republic in the autumn of 1998. 'Imagine, a car came to our house at Earlsfield to collect the three of us, and I was like a barrage balloon as I was pregnant,' she says. 'Eddie, who was a semi-professional footballer, was really thrilled as his family is from Czechoslovakia. Jonathan hadn't bothered to mention that he was being presented to the teams before the kick-off...' Their tickets were in the Royal Box.

If Edwards found friendship rather than love at university, he knew his fate was sealed when he met Alison Briggs. All he had to do was be patient; all he had to do was to change her impression of him. Over the ensuing months Alison noticed Edwards more and her attitude to him softened. 'I think Jonathan's character was starting to mature,' she says. Eventually, he persuaded her to be his guest at an athletics meeting he was competing in at Gateshead on the August Bank Holiday in 1989. 'I remember leaving the stadium hand in hand,' says Edwards. 'It was a moment I had waited, hoped and prayed for.'

As far as he was concerned, he had found the girl he was going to marry. It was just a matter of when. 'I don't think Alison was as sure as me to begin with, but I left her in no doubt about my feelings for her.' Alison adds, 'Initially I wanted to take things slowly, but I was soon head over heels in love.'

The following Easter Alison and Jonathan went to the Isle of Lewis to stay with Alison's parents. They took an instant liking to him; his manners were impeccable and, clearly, he was a man they would be happy for their daughter to marry. 'He treated me very well,' says Alison. She especially liked his chivalry. 'Jonathan was just a real gentleman, opening the car door and walking on the outside of the pavement, just all these little attentions to detail. I felt that he really cared. I'm quite an independent person and for once I felt I could rest, let someone else take control.'

Edwards admits now that he wishes he had proposed to Alison when they were on the island. There was one golden opportunity he especially regrets. They were visiting Carloway, a ruined fortress framed against wild and stunning seas. 'We had gone out sightseeing and there were breathtaking views of the island. I was on the verge of asking Alison to marry me, but decided not to let myself get carried away with the romantic environment. We laugh about it now – I was a real idiot!'

Instead, on the Monday morning after they had arrived back from the Hebrides, Edwards telephoned her at work – both of them were at the Royal Victoria Infirmary by then – and asked to meet for lunch. They met for a salad just down the road in the restaurant in the Newcastle Playhouse. 'Jonathan began with an apology,' says Alison. 'He said he should have asked me when we were away ... then he proposed. "Will you marry me?" he asked across the restaurant table.' Edwards, not easily embarrassed, and certainly not a hostage to his emotions, confesses, 'Given another chance, I would definitely propose differently!'

This was May 1990 and, once Edwards had formally asked Ralph Briggs for his daughter's hand in marriage, they arranged the wedding for 10 November. 'We didn't have much money at that point, so we split the cost of my engagement ring so that we could get the one I wanted,' explains Alison. She was sorely unamused when Jonathan disclosed to his mother the amount the ring had cost – around £500.

Edwards has always had a close, loving relationship with his family. They were unembarrassed with outward displays of affection. In particular, his mother Jill had been his point of reference, his anchor, from childhood. He concealed little from her, even now as a 25-year-old who was engaged to be married. 'Initially, I found that very difficult,' admits Alison. 'I'd think, "What are you telling your mother for? It's between us." I didn't really know his family and found the strength of their relationships a little intimidating. I had this idea of them being a bit formidable. I come from a close family and we got on fine, but we didn't have that kind of intensity.'

Alison had found independence early and she could not fathom how Edwards could still be so rooted inside his family, living so far away in Bournemouth. 'It was almost as if he hadn't quite pulled away. Yet Jonathan's Mum and Dad were lovely and treated me as one of the family from the beginning. I can remember going to see them after we had become engaged. The first thing Jonathan's Mum said was, "Well, let me have a look at the ring." She made a big effort, planning day trips out for us all; she put a sweet basket of dried flowers in my room. We had a great time, but I still found their closeness a bit daunting.

'It's not as though Jonathan was always on the phone to his Mum, but there were times when he had this tendency to want to refer any major decisions back home. It wasn't until I got to know them well that I could understand. Jonathan's Mum is a very wise lady. I have come to respect both her and Jonathan's Dad's opinions. It didn't take long – I suppose everyone has to get to know their in-laws. It took a while to get used to all the kissing! There's just this easiness between them and their love for each other was expressed in a very different way to what I was used to. Now I feel very much part of the family. We have a very good relationship with Jonathan's parents and, though we value their opinion and their advice, we come to our own decisions.'

Alison and Jonathan planned their entire wedding themselves during meetings over lunch at the Royal Victoria Infirmary and the local Kentucky Fried Chicken. Reverend Edwards performed the actual wedding ceremony. The guest list included athletes Kriss Akabusi, Barrington Williams, Vernon Samuels and Judy Simpson, and the wedding breakfast was held at Corbridge, some 15 miles from Newcastle. For the evening, Mr and Mrs Jonathan Edwards had organized a ceilidh. Akabusi, irreverent to the last, took Edwards to one side and asked, 'What is a sealid, anyway?' He had planned to stay for only a short time, as he had to return to his home in Portsmouth. 'Typically, Kriss was in the thick of it until midnight,' laughs Edwards.

Edwards and his wife split their honeymoon between a cottage in the Cotswolds and a chateau on the northwest coast of France. They returned to begin the task of making their first-floor, three-bedroom flat into their home. 'Jonathan's parents bought us a bed and my Mum and Dad bought us a washing machine for wedding presents,' says Alison. 'We borrowed a three-piece suite, we did some painting and wallpapering – all the things that you do when you're starting out and making a home together.'

From those humble roots, Edwards and his bride struck out to conquer the world together. They could hardly have supposed that within five years they would be the proud parents of two sons, Samuel and Nathan, and that Edwards would be deluged with invitations to be fêted at award ceremonies at home and abroad.

There is a great warmth to their relationship – their friendship is real and visible, their love for one another unmistakable. 'We're just an ordinary couple,' says Alison, but she knows that cannot be the unadulterated truth. Once her husband jumped out of the sandpit into history on a summer's evening in Gothenburg, their lives were catapulted into the public domain. Despite this, Alison's refusal to be seduced by their celebrity status and her husband's consistent dignity and grace under pressure have left them unspoiled by the experience. Their walk with God is being made together, hand in hand as Edwards had hoped the moment he caught sight of Alison Briggs in the music group at Heaton Baptist Church.

All the awards were undoubtedly flattering, a school-boy's fantasy made real. Nonetheless, with the resumption of training, and Alison finally convalescing after surgery, there was much for them to contemplate with anticipation and no little anxiety. For Edwards, the Olympic Games in Atlanta beckoned, promising further hymns of glory for the world record holder who jumped in praise of Jesus Christ. The question was, would he measure up?

Chapter 8

Money, Money, Money

Calvin: *'I'm a simple man, Hobbes.'*
Hobbes: *'You?? Yesterday you wanted a nuclear*
powered car that could turn into a jet with
laser-guided heat-seeking missiles!'
Calvin: *'I'm a simple man with complex tastes.'*

FROM THE CARTOON STRIP BY BILL WATTERSON

Athletically, the wind-down to the end of the 1995 season had been a rich, rewarding experience for Edwards. His itinerary included shopping in Italy for Armani-designed clothes with Michael Johnson after he had shared star-billing in Rieti with one of the most venerable athletes of the age. There was, however, to be a less rewarding exchange of differences with his principal sponsors, Puma.

Edwards was commencing his entrance into the hard world of commerce, a journey which in time would find him accused of being seduced by wealth. The Porsche 911 Targa sports car he briefly owned was deemed Exhibit A by his detractors. There were those who had foreseen such difficulties, like Willie Banks, his predecessor as world record holder. Banks replied to the note Edwards had sent him from Gothenburg with this message in response to the Englishman's leap into history: 'It will change your life, but don't let it change your soul.'

Edwards, despite such a thoughtful warning, could still not be expected to comprehend the scale of the challenge ahead. The first dealings with Puma might have provided an early clue. In those halcyon days of 1995, Edwards had been under the impression that his contract included a bonus for each time he broke the world record. Puma, however, thought they were obliged to pay just once. Edwards will admit that he was in terrain of which he had little experience, but he was sure of his ground. 'Dorothy Moulson was my main contact at Puma and we developed a very close relationship. She had realized midseason that there was a difference in interpretation of the contracted bonuses. She really worried about the whole affair. It played heavily on her mind.'

His contract with the company did not expire until the end of 1996, but Edwards felt that his new status warranted an overhaul of the original, quite modest deal. His mood was in common with any sportsman or woman finding themselves elevated into a new arena of performance. Through his jumping skills and his unspoiled charm, he had created the environment in Gothenburg to become Jonathan Edwards Inc. For Edwards, however, becoming heavily involved in high finance for the first time in his life was comparable to jumping into a sandpit after it had been mined.

As a Christian, a self-confessed servant of God, was he now going to be charged with worshipping Mammon? 'Without making money my god, I will try to maximize my earning potential,' he said during our first meeting in November 1995. 'I have a responsibility to my family.' There was a legitimacy to that ambition which, surely, no one could deny. Yet he invited me to inspect his new, leather-upholstered Mercedes – his prize for becoming world champion – with the enthusiasm of a showroom salesman. At £230, the personalized number plate J18 JDE was an irresistible extra, he said. He was the proverbial kid with a new toy. Again, this should surprise no one. The car was part of his reward for being a successful, professional athlete. Was he supposed to apologize for this? His circumstances had changed. What was to be gained from denying that he had moved into a new league – or, as Kriss Akabusi put it so succinctly, 'a new stratosphere'?

Edwards' dealings with Puma illustrated to him that he had to appoint an agent to explore the commercial avenues now opening to him. Even this was to prove fraught with difficulty, however. 'I was hugely keen to renegotiate a longer-term contract with Puma,' he says. 'At one stage I got quite upset when their initial offer fell below expectations. I suppose they thought that, as they still had me under contract for another year, there was no need for them to move at all. I think part of the problem was that I was dealing through a third party and the negotiations became confused. After a time, I called them direct to tell them I felt they hadn't given me adequate value. I informed them that I was looking at the possibility of finding another company who would be willing to buy me out of my contract. I didn't want to do that, but I felt there had to be a certain amount of fairness from those at Puma.'

Edwards' personal submission produced a positive response. 'The company came to an agreeable compromise on the bonuses, a goodwill gesture I appreciated.' They paid two-thirds of the disputed amount, which was around $100,000. Accordingly, he signed a new Puma contract, committing himself to them until the end of 1998 in a deal estimated to be worth £500,000. 'The fact that I was under contract certainly reduced my bargaining position, yet I was happy with the deal.'

He already had an accountant, a man called Martin Robbie, who had been looking after his finances since April 1992. It would be fair to report that Edwards' portfolio in those days did not require much management. He was hardly scraping together £5,000 a year as a part-time athlete, supplementing his income with his £8,000-a-year salary as a part-time laboratory assistant at the Royal Victoria Infirmary. As recently as 1993 – just two years before he became world champion – Edwards was finding the family finances stretched after the birth of their first son, Sam. His godmother Auntie Georgina – Georgina Mason – sent him a cheque for £1,000. 'We were never in that kind of dire straits, but we were touched by Georgina's kindness. Happily, we were able to send the cheque back by return.'

Robbie, in his capacity as a partner for Grant Thornton in Portsmouth, acted for other athletes like Linford Christie, Roger Black, Kriss Akabusi, Dalton Grant and Tony Jarrett. He was prepared to wait for Edwards to blossom. In common with other upcoming athletes and swimmers, Edwards was offered discounted fees. With commendable foresight, Robbie wrote in an internal office memo dated 7 April 1992:

Fortunate enough to pick up another athlete. His name is Jonathan Edwards, a triple jumper. He is also a devout Christian, who does not compete on Sundays, which means he did not compete in the World Championships last year. However, to give you some idea of his qualities, his personal best would have put him in fourth position in the World Championship competition. I therefore believe we have in Jonathan yet another potential Olympic medallist.

In the autumn of 1992, when some businessmen invited Edwards to speak to their guests on a boat trip on the River Tyne, he called Robbie to ask what to charge. 'That's simple – charge them £500,' said Robbie, by now a trusted friend.

Edwards was startled. 'Why would they pay me that?' he asked.

'Because you're Jonathan Edwards!' replied Robbie. 'But despite what I said,' he remembers, 'Jonathan knocked them down to £250.'

Robbie confirms that Edwards' box-office worth as an athlete pushed his earning power from the basement through the roof. 'Post-Gothenburg he was perfectly capable of earning well and truly into six figures,' he explains. That is a conservative estimate in the extreme. Edwards, who as a young, unknown athlete began jumping for $100 on an Andy Norman-organized trip to compete in Spain in 1986, could now command appearance fees as high as £25,000. 'Obviously, I think there was a bit of angst, being a Christian and suddenly having all this money,' says Robbie.

Had Edwards been able to have an extensive dialogue with Willie Banks, he would have been granted a graphic insight into the turmoil and trauma that the world record delivered uninvited into his life. Banks, a charismatic athlete, responsible for popularizing the triple jump, responsible for encouraging crowds to become emotionally involved, explains how he allowed himself to be a victim of his own success following his leap of 17.97 metres which brought him the world record in 1985.

'I think it blinds you when you realize you have enough money to do what you want to do,' he says. 'You start accumulating things rather than accumulating friends.'

Banks has now resettled in Carlsbad, Southern California after three years spent chasing business opportunities in Japan, where he has retained some commercial interests. He was candid in his revelations and charm personified when he spoke from his home in the autumn of 1999. 'I have very strong convictions when it comes to my Lord,' he said. 'I was blessed with the talent. Even when I broke the world record, my Lord spoke to me and told me that would happen at the time it happened. I didn't know how much it could affect you, but once you set the world record and you start getting all this fame and wealth, you start to lose track of where the blessings came from. You have to be really strong. One of the things I found the most difficult was that people look at you differently; and you have to constantly remind others, even more than you would normally, that you're the same guy. Otherwise they're going to remind you that you're somebody different.

'When you can lose track is when you get a lot of money – not as much as Jonathan or the guys like him now – but at that time, *bam*, it was a lot of money. Of course, I went out and I bought a car, I bought houses, I bought things. It was just fun to buy things. I no longer went to church.

'It wasn't like I was being bad or anything, I just didn't have the time to put into nourishing the things that were most important. I went through a divorce. I paid a huge price; I think I'm continuing to pay. Although I'm no longer in the spotlight, I'm paying the price for the things I did when I *was* in the spotlight. I didn't think I was that bad. I didn't shun people, I wasn't the type that said,

"Forget it, I'm not going to talk to the media." I wasn't the type who wasn't going to write people back. My problem was less the issue of not being accessible, but more an issue of finding things more valuable than people.'

Banks is quietly restructuring his life, attempting to be a father to the four children he has from his two marriages, and nowadays it is the soccer pitch, not the track, that draws him. He attends church on occasions, but prays on a daily basis. Ask him what got him back on the rails, and he says, 'Losing the income, I guess.' You suspect there is more than a half-truth behind this statement. So, yes, Banks sympathizes with Edwards, and respects him for remaining unscathed.

There has been genuine conflict for Edwards, no doubt. As the demands on him escalated, he understood that he not only needed an agent, but also secretarial support. Annette Collins became his PA, working out of Brendan Foster's offices, Nova International. Yet his reference points on life were still to be found in the Bible, rather than the *Financial Times*. His passion for high-powered, expensive cars is the one indulgence that Edwards has had to exorcise, at some pain and cost as will become clear. If his spending spree on cars turns out to be his only misguided action, he will consider that he did not betray his principles.

From the outset of his fame, Edwards tried to rationalize what pitfalls lay ahead, and within months of being showered with offers as the world champion and world record holder, he told Stuart Weir from Christians in Sport, 'The Bible talks about the love of money being the root of all kinds of evil. I am under no illusions. I have the same evil desires inside that everybody has. The difference is that I also have God's Holy Spirit inside to help me to overcome them. Nevertheless, there is that within me that recognizes the devil will certainly come and try to tempt me, try and take me away from my family, get my focus away from glorifying God, on being a star or being a celebrity. I certainly feel, having had disaster as well as incredible success, that success represents the biggest threat to my walk with God.'[1]

Yet there were pragmatic, businesslike decisions he had to address. The need for an agent was paramount, simply to deflect the avalanche of calls Edwards was now receiving. He had been contacted in the middle of the 1995 season by Jonathan Marks, a man whose central London-based company, MTC, represented Sally Gunnell and would later manage Denise Lewis, Steve Smith and young decathlete Dean Macey. Marks, 35, is sharp and loquacious, with a wealth of experience, and is involved in the entertainment industry as well as client management. Marks' MTC, for example, holds the intellectual rights to the Hammer House of Horror films and *Eurotrash*. But Marks had to wait to get Edwards on his books. 'I wrote to him three times in early 1995 and didn't get so much as a reply,' he says.

When Edwards came home from Gothenburg to be greeted by a deluge of offers, however, he realized that he had to appoint someone to sift and analyse, shop and sell, and he responded to the advice of Brendan Foster – the man, remember, whose grant had enabled him to become a full-time athlete. Foster encouraged him to be managed by an American called Brad Hunt. He looked after a stable of athletes, including Michael Johnson, who had won the 200 metres and 400 metres titles at the World Championships

---

1 From the video *More than Champions*, produced by Christians in Sport.

Jonathan, aged nine, pictured with his family in 1975…

…and in the summer of 1996 with his brother Tim and sister Rachel.

Celebrating in Budapest at the 1998 European Championships.
© *Mark Thompson/Allsport*

Overwhelmed and besieged by photographers after breaking the world record for the first time during the 1995 World Championships.
© *Clive Brunskill/ Allsport*

Jonathan, with legendary England cricketer Frank 'Typhoon' Tyson, at a Durham University function to honour the sporting achievements of the two alumni. © *North News and Pictures*

The 1983 West Buckland School basketball squad. Jonathan (no. 4) is seated next to former England prop, Victor Ubogu. Jonathan's P.E. master, Lawrence Whittal-Williams, is at the far right on the second row.

All smiles –
Jonathan and
Alison heading off
for their wedding
reception, 10
November 1990.

All smiles again –
this time at
the Palace for
Jonathan's MBE.
© *Sean Dempsey/*
PA News

Jonathan with Gwen Torrence in the official picture of the 1995 World Athletes of the Year. © *John Gichigi/ Allsport*

A happy family reunion at Newcastle airport following Jonathan's triumph in the 1995 World Championships.

Jonathan lands his first jump in the World Championships in 1995 – he likes it! © *John Giles/PA News*

Not the ending they had hoped for. (After the triple jump final in the Seville World Championships in 1999, where Jonathan finished a disappointing third.) © *Stu Forster/Allsport*

Jonathan prepares with Norman Anderson for another session at Gateshead International Stadium.

Jonathan wins the 1995 BBC TV Sports Personality of the Year Award.
© *Andrew Redington/ Allsport*

Kenny Harrison congratulates Jonathan on his silver medal during the presentation ceremony for the 1996 Olympic triple jump competition.
© *Tony Marshall/ Empics*

Sam and Nathan in Lanzarote during a warm-weather training trip, Easter 1998.

Jonathan soars out to the furthest triple jump of all time, albeit wind-assisted, while representing Great Britain in the 1995 European Cup in Lille.© *François Mori/AP Photos*

in Gothenburg and who, by midsummer four years later, would possess the world records in both events.

'It wasn't a great move for me to go with Brad,' confesses Edwards. 'I'm sure he's a great agent, but he's in America. From a commercial viewpoint I have no doubt that I missed out.' Edwards does not contradict the estimate that having the wrong commercial manager at a peak period of his career cost him at least £100,000 in missed opportunities.

'Brad is big, brash and American. I'm sure the film *Jerry McGuire* was made about him!' suggests Marks impishly. 'He's a larger-than-life character, good at his job, but sometimes when he talks he makes everything sound so glossy that you don't realize he's even talking about athletics. You need to understand that Jonathan Edwards is a very English product.'

Clearly, Edwards was not a man to hunt down every available pound and penny. Steadfastly, he rejected chances to cash in, simply because he was not prepared to associate himself with the wrong product. One contract he refused was offered by an energizing drinks company. 'I was offered £30,000 a year, a two- or three-year deal, but they had a horrible advertising campaign and I wanted nothing to do with it. I wasn't interested.'

His world had been upended. His diary became manic, his phone was ringing off the hook and he began screening all calls with an answerphone. Some of the more absurd requests to filter through to him included an invitation to abseil down the Tyne Bridge – for charity – and a plea for him to run the London Marathon. Akabusi, who had grown up in foster homes and then joined the Army before he realized he had a talent to run, had heard alarm bells clanging from the moment Edwards caught the plane home from Gothenburg.

'I'm thinking, how does the meek and mild, the quiet and self-effacing Jonathan Edwards deal with the real money?' says Akabusi, whose own conversion to Christianity never muddied his business plan on life. 'Was Jonathan strong enough to say, "That's going to cost you"? The real commercial world – how was he going to deal with that? I was a working man before I became a Christian; and I was a man of the world before I became a Christian; and I had learned the tricks of the trade before I became a Christian.

'Money had never been important to Jonathan. I think Jonathan had been brought up in a level of comfort that meant that money wasn't important to him. Whether that's 10 grand, 20 grand or 100 grand a year, they had enough money. And comfort is often in the mind. You can be contented on £10,000 a year. But it was more *where* he was coming from, where he was at. Whereas someone like myself, for example, I'd always been in what I'll call the discomfort zone! I couldn't have the latest shoes, the latest clothes; I couldn't go out to concerts. So when I had the opportunity, I worked hard to make money. My faith brought me a perspective, but money was still a factor in what I was working for. But I knew Jonathan was going to be put into an area of conflict. Who would watch out for him, God or Mammon? The question confronting him was, "How do I define that line between serving God through Mammon or serving Mammon as my God?" You're going to be pulled left, right and centre. You're going to have ethical choices, moral dilemmas.

'Every now and again, in his deepest moments, I think Jonathan has a little pang of guilt. He was brought up thinking that serving God has to be on a mission field and there he is, jumping into a sandpit. Sometimes when he competes, it's as if someone tells him, "You can win this, but you're not going to bother." Yet if you're in for the penny, you're in for the pound. If he's going to be in the pantheon of the gods, he has got to win the Olympics. He can win it. It's there for the taking – he's just got to take it. It's his.'

Roger Black, never quite world-champion class as a 400 metres runner, but a man of substantial class in the public domain, is another contemporary of Edwards who can comprehend the moral maze he had entered. 'I think you can control the intrusion into your life, certainly in athletics,' says Black. 'But what Jonathan didn't realize was that his stature was changing; the way he was perceived had altered. More people want a piece of you. Jonathan was never meant to be a superstar. Linford Christie was a superstar; Daley Thompson was a superstar; Sebastian Coe was a superstar. Jonathan Edwards – no. He was supposed to be one of the ones who was there or thereabouts.

'People deal with that new-found stature in one of two ways. They either love it or they retract from it. Some find it a burden. I remember when he won the BBC Sports Personality of the Year Award at the end of 1995 and he came out with that wonderful quote, "All I do is jump into a sandpit." This obviously isn't true, and I think he found that out, that he didn't just jump into a sandpit. He's far bigger than that.'

Black's opinion is valuable. He is an athlete who has crossed comfortably from the track to the television studio, his silver medal behind Michael Johnson in the Olympic Games in Atlanta the pinnacle of a career remorselessly ravaged by injury. While content in retirement, however, he remains restless and likes to extend himself. He seeks to explore 'the edge' by playing poker at casinos in London and Las Vegas. On a sunlit morning early in the summer of

1999, in the huge, high-ceilinged drawing room of his home amid the rolling hills outside Guildford, Surrey, he is still rebuking himself for folding his cards when he had a healthy hand. 'Bottled it!' he says, self-mockingly.

The inference is that he is not yet assertive at the tables, unsure of his purpose. Once he was like that as an athlete until the penny dropped. 'I have a belief that you cannot really fulfil your potential at something until you are very clear as to why you need to do it. For the first 10 years of my athletic career I was very good at running, but I never really had that deep understanding of what it really meant to me and why I was really doing it. Some athletes are instantly clear. Christie is absolutely clear what athletics means to him. It isn't an issue. Athletics was everything to Thompson; Akabusi was always clear. In the end I achieved. I did everything I could in Atlanta. I created the right environment for me to perform. For me, that was my moment.'

What about Edwards? 'Jonathan has to ask himself a question. Is Gothenburg that moment, or are the Olympic Games in Sydney going to be that moment? Jonathan is in conflict as to what his need is. Yes, it's only running, it's only money... No, it's not! Jonathan has his faith and his family and they are what matter most. But sport is not about money and it's not about fame. That's part of it, fine, but when you line up – I know other people felt this was important – when you're lining up for that Olympic final, you know this really matters, matters now. It's actually unimportant, you know that too. I was thinking that as I watched Manchester United play Juventus in the Champions' League while there was a war going on in Serbia. To those people in the football stadium, the war was irrelevant. But the war mattered, of course it mattered.

Sport in the grand scheme of things doesn't matter, and you can't intellectualize it and say it's the most important thing in the world, because to do that you're missing the point. But for the moment you're participating, for that instant, it *is* everything. I still wonder if it is for Jonathan.'

Alison Edwards, who has known her husband for 10 years, who shares the same deep Christian convictions, whose values have been unaltered by the onset of wealth, testifies that it is. 'I think sometimes I don't really appreciate the conflicts Jonathan has … I don't think many do really understand. From the outside, it looks a bit of a waste of time, no real purpose to it. We have good friends who are doctors and, in comparison to them, you wonder what Jonathan is doing. Here we are, moaning when Jonathan isn't jumping well. You think, come on, get a grip! Yet Jonathan's sport is very much part of our lives. I know it doesn't matter in the grand scale of things, but it does on a day-to-day basis. It matters an awful lot. When things aren't right it gets you down, it causes friction. When he's standing at the end of the runway, Jonathan cares.'

He does, he cares greatly. Yet he cannot always banish a tinge of guilt, the feeling that he should be making a difference. For example, in conversations with journalists in Helsinki for the European Championships in the summer of 1994, Edwards was reviewing his first full year as a professional athlete. He unhappily confessed, 'Sometimes I lie in bed at night and think, "I jump into a sandpit for a living. Am I doing anything worthwhile here?" The pointlessness of it. You see doctors in Rwanda and think, "They're making a difference, but I'm jumping into a sandpit. Who benefits from that?"'

Those thoughts pursue him even now, but there is a greater understanding that this is a temporary phase of his life and he can use his gift in the name of God. Edwards explains, 'If I'm honest with myself, when I'm competing it consumes me as much as it does everyone else. Whether I have the same level of need to win as other people is questionable, I would agree. It isn't the be-all and end-all.' The 1999 World Championships in Seville did not entirely consume him. What was it he said afterwards? 'On the night something in my heart was not touched by what I was doing. In my head, I wanted to be world champion. But in my heart, I don't know.'

These are the raging waters of uncertainty that Edwards must constantly try to navigate. 'As a Christian, God doesn't love me any less if I don't win. I could retire happily without an Olympic gold medal or another world record jump, yet that doesn't mean that I won't be attempting to win at the Sydney Games. The truth is, to a degree it's still a shock to me to have done what I've done. I don't see myself as being this mega-talented superstar that some people obviously perceive me to be. All I know is that I have a fabulous opportunity in Sydney and, I hope, by now there's not much that can take me by surprise!'

One man with whom Edwards has maintained a 14-year dialogue is John Crotty, once the national event coach for triple jump and an educationalist by profession. 'There are a number of people you look at in sport and think these are the ones you would want to bring sport into the next century,' he says. 'Jonathan Edwards is one.' Crotty has watched Edwards graduate from a student who would not train on a Sunday, when he came to national squad sessions at Crystal Palace, into a man who has jumped further than anyone in history. 'The image of sport has to be maintained and Jonathan is a great public speaker, a fantastic bloke, a really caring person.

Sometimes it's a bit difficult to be caring in the ruthless world he's in. I mean, it's cutthroat.' But listen to Crotty's postscript, and colour it with the validity which his long, ongoing relationship with Edwards warrants. 'If you're not selfish, you will be no good. In terms of triple jumping, Jonathan is selfish, self-centred, dedicated and totally focused. When he's on the run-up, there is nothing else. Even God takes a back seat.'

It can be assumed that Edwards would take exception to that bald statement. Yet that does not mean that he is entirely comfortable with the treasure he has unearthed in the sandpit. Over the years Martin Robbie has become someone in whom Edwards confides, as well as the man he entrusts to structure his finances. He has observed from close quarters as Edwards has fought to find a balance in his life. 'There is always going to be a conflict between what the human being wants and what the Christian thinks he ought to do,' he argues. 'I think he does face a dichotomy. He earns – he has earned – hopefully long may he continue to earn – a lot more than he feels comfortable with. Jonathan, though, hasn't chased the dollar. Not at all. So many people in his position would have moved to London or the Southeast, but Jonathan loves being where he is. There's a warmth in the people that is second to none. I went to the FA Cup Final as a neutral at the end of last season and Manchester United may have won the trophy, but the people from Newcastle won the contest between the fans.'

The Edwards family may not want to leave the Northeast, but after Gothenburg they alerted Robbie that they wished to acquire a new home. The flat they had bought in Heaton for £37,500 in 1990 – £3,000 on deposit, the rest borrowed on a mortgage – had become too small for their expanding family. Edwards, though, chose their next home with typical conservatism. Not for him the grand house on the hill that his burgeoning wealth could have bankrolled. He opted for a beautifully located, five-bedroom, semi-detached house in Gosforth, recognized as one of the more desirable suburbs of Newcastle.

'I told him to buy a bigger house, in the sense that it should be at least detached,' admits Robbie. 'He wouldn't do that. But I never saw Jonathan as someone who was going to chase property. He wanted a family house, he didn't want an investment. I understood, but still tried to get him to go for a detached house. It didn't need to be in huge grounds, just detached. For no other reason than that he has young kids and they can be noisy. You don't want to get a reputation that Jonathan Edwards and his family make a lot of noise!'

Edwards says that the house they purchased – and still live in – has all they need as a family. 'Martin assured us we could have afforded to spend another £50,000, but I liked the house we bought and still do.' The house is a monument to the couple's exemplary taste, with exposed wooden floors and classic furnishings. Their sons Sam and Nathan are well brought up and, though boisterous at playtime, they are never likely to be the cause of neighbours' complaints. On forays to London and the Southeast, Edwards cringes like a man taking a punch to the solar plexus when he surveys property pictured in the windows of estate agents. 'It's difficult to comprehend that a terraced house in the right part of London can sell for half a million, when you could buy a palatial home in Newcastle for that.'

Edwards' wealth is substantial and a gold medal at the Olympic Games in Sydney would be comparable to owning a ticket with a winning share in the Lottery – a million-pound share, that is. 'You'd have to be pretty stupid if an Olympic gold medal didn't make you a millionaire,' says Roger Black.

'What of the biblical text about a camel passing through the eye of a needle more easily than a rich man into the kingdom of heaven?' asked Brough Scott, in a profile on Edwards published in the *Sunday Telegraph* just before the World Championships in Gothenburg. Edwards was unequivocal in his response. 'Athletics is my job. It's my way of providing for my family. But it's also my talent, and my chance to bear witness to my faith in God. I believe Satan consumes the world and it is important to shine forth with the light.'[2]

Again, it is hard to argue with such sentiments. Alison Edwards still shops carefully, still wears jeans and a sweatshirt around the neighbourhood and can still take or leave those glitzy, showbiz-style evenings. Yet she suggests, plaintively, 'Why does Jonathan have to be this humble little boy who jumps for nothing? Why is it any different for Jonathan than it is for Tim Henman, who plays for £450,000 at Wimbledon? I think this is unfair, but then it's probably something Jonathan's created by being so open and honest about the whole money issue. Being a professional sportsman hasn't changed Jonathan's core values. He is a man of integrity, who strives to make good decisions. We all make mistakes, but he tries to do right by everybody. Sometimes you just can't win, can you? But I think, over recent times, he has become less worried about what people might think and has just got on with it.'

---

2 *Sunday Telegraph*, 23 July 1995.

Working on the advice of their accountant, Jonathan and Alison Edwards have secured their future across a multitude of sound investment plans, from mid-term to long-term. They have made provision for their sons' education. They are also alert to the possibility that Jonathan's parents, on the retirement of Reverend Andy Edwards, will need to buy or rent their own home after a lifetime spent living in property belonging to the Church. They have also made undisclosed contributions to charities, and have not been slow to assist both sides of the family when needs have arisen.

Tim Edwards, who was proclaimed during his schooldays as the likelier of the Edwards boys to make a career as a professional sportsman, says, 'You watched him buy the Porsche and realized it was not a good idea.' Tim, who – with his wife Anna's blessing – has invested his family savings in taking a postgraduate Masters at the Hebrew University in Jerusalem, adds, 'Jonathan always liked fast cars – and now seems to have got that out of his system. He has never given us anything money-wise, but this has not been an issue as we haven't needed it. The potential for great wealth was in place after Gothenburg, but he has said to me, "I have the same principles, the same faith; it's just the circumstances of my life that have changed. The core, what's real, is the same." I recognize what he has been through as a hard challenge; just as it would be tomorrow if they woke up and they had nothing. But I'm sure the core of his values would remain the same in those circumstances too.'

Anna Edwards, who has left her art business in Bath under management to raise three small daughters in Jerusalem while her husband completes his Masters, adds poignantly, 'The danger with giving lots of money away is

that you can end up being Lord Bountiful. It's a very fine
line and I sense you can't win. But to me, Jonathan seems
very balanced and, don't forget, Alison has had to meet
the challenge too. She has never changed, never made me
feel uncomfortable that she has gone into a new world.' As
they speak, there is an undisguisable sincerity in the voices
of both Tim and Anna.

Others have also understood that such dramatically
changing circumstances represent a huge cultural and spiritual shock. While worrying about how Edwards would survive in the commercial jungle, Akabusi tried to impart
some serious advice to the man who was such a valued
friend when they read the Bible in hotel rooms from
California to Barcelona. They shared some private time
when they were invited to record a joint appearance on
BBC television's *Songs of Praise*. 'We were together a couple
of times in the car and we ended up talking, as always,
about our faith and how it works in our lives,' explains
Akabusi. 'I remember telling Jonathan he had to be pragmatic in his demands. You have to identify someone in
athletics to deal with your athletics and someone in the
business field to do all your business. They're not the same;
don't throw it all at one person. You need to be – in
Christian parlance – as wise as a serpent, but as gentle as
a dove. I had no problems with him being as gentle as a
dove. No problems. It was the serpent I was worried about.'

Just after the Atlanta Olympic Games the following
summer, Edwards opted for Jonathan Marks to manage
his commercial affairs and since 1998 Marks has also been
responsible for his media relations. Marks has negotiated
solid contracts with Bausch & Lomb, now entering its
fourth year, with Edwards as an ambassador for their soft
contact lenses; there is a new deal with Rover Cars for

2000; a long-standing association with Scandinavian vitamin company Vitamex; and he was hopeful of landing a deal with a major watchmaker for Olympic year. 'As a company we are not pure sport, we have a broad base; we are in entertainment and entertainment rights,' says Marks, 'and within that is Jonathan Edwards.'

Marks has come to know Edwards' foibles. His reluctance to leave Newcastle to attend meetings in London is the source of much amusement in the MTC offices. 'There is a cheer when the staff hear we've got him to come down, because they know what an achievement that is,' says Marks. From an agent's perspective, there is another indisputable truth to be confronted. 'There is no doubt commercially, whether he likes it or not, and I don't think he minds, he would have achieved a lot more if he didn't have the religious card. It sounds terrible, and I'm not irreligious myself, maybe not the same religion, but I think sometimes he could have kept his feelings to himself. There are times when the PR agent, the ad manager or the brand manager are watching and they think, "Mr Edwards, the devout Christian" and not "Mr Edwards, the mean, lean jumping machine".

'They are noting that as well, but they are thinking, "Do I want my brand associated with that?" Most people get very scared by that. But it's not a problem to him whatsoever, and it's not a problem to me. That's the man. I'm not going to ring him up and say, "For goodness sake, do me a favour: next time you win, keep God to yourself." Jonathan is a pleasure to work with, but I can't say we've set the world alight. Put it this way, why do you think the Vinnie Joneses of this world get the commercial deals they get? Because they're the complete opposite to Jonathan, in terms of being irreverent and aggressive; much more attitude. People think this will sell more products than someone who is wholesome and has that clean, clean image. Bit perverse in a way, but it's a direct reflection on the way people's psyches are.'

Marks accepts that Edwards' gaze does not automatically fall to the bottom line. 'With Jonathan we have come to expect the unexpected.' He senses that Edwards is a natural communicator, and his future could lie in that direction should he so wish. 'I think Jonathan now feels that he deserves what he has achieved, and to a certain extent he enjoys his fame, whereas before he felt a bit uncomfortable. The more established he has become, the more comfortable he has become; and he is established. From our research, we estimate there is a 90 per cent recall on his name and that's high. Also, he's the most natural of speakers.' In the autumn of 1999 Marks' office took a call from the BBC. It was an enquiry to see if Edwards would consider appearing on *Question Time*. 'These are things Jonathan relishes – not the status side, but the opportunity, and he thrives on it. It's that boyish kind of enthusiasm that comes out. He gets more satisfaction from the recognition from that, let's say, than from other accolades.'

Edwards has never been less than his own man. Controversially, that independence has seen him retain Andy Norman to devise his competition schedule. Edwards' loyalty remained unshaken even after Norman had been removed from his seat of power in British athletics in the wake of a coroner's inquest into the suicide of journalist Cliff Temple. Norman, not a universally popular man within the sport, has been involved at all levels for years and watched Edwards' growth from gawky novice to world record holder. His theory is that Edwards is only beaten by himself. 'You know, you've got to have that killer instinct,' he says. 'If Jonathan was a steeplechaser and his biggest rival fell in the water jump, Jonathan would stop and make sure he didn't drown. Whereas he should be thinking, "I'll put you under." He's that sort of a guy, the old-fashioned English gentleman.

'Right now, if anyone wants to put on a triple jump in Western Europe, you've got to have Jonathan Edwards competing otherwise you don't have one. No Edwards, no appeal. Not that Jonathan will compete for the sake of competing. He won't. Some athletes just go and jump for the money and underperform. Jonathan's not like that. If he's not in shape, he won't go. I agree with that. Injuries have cost him a huge amount of money. The opportunities come at the end of the season and I'd say he must have lost a million dollars.'

Some would say that Edwards has introduced further and unnecessary conflict into his life by continuing to work in conjunction with Norman. Patrick Collins, chief sports writer and award-winning columnist for the *Mail on Sunday*, suggests, 'Whenever I think of Jonathan Edwards I think of Norman. I always think, "Jonathan, you could be better than that and you should be better than that." He set the standards and I think he is falling below them by that association and I think that's a huge pity.' Collins, as we shall see, is not a lone voice.

Chapter 9

Mr Athletics –
a Controversial Friend

*Here they have a man hanged and
then proceed to try him.*

MOLIÈRE

Andy Norman was a policeman. He was also Mr Athletics. He was a promoter, a matchmaker, an impresario of the track. Norman's influence stretched back to the days of Don Quarry and Hasely Crawford, sprinters from the Caribbean who won gold medals at the 1976 Olympics in Montreal. He brought track legends like Kenyan Mike Boyt and New Zealander John Walker to perform in England, and he had strong ties with American Willie Banks, the man who held the world triple jump record before Edwards. Norman was for years also a mentor for Steve Ovett, Olympic 800 metres champion in Moscow in 1980; likewise Scottish sprinter Allan Wells, the 100 metres champion at those same Games.

Norman was the man foreign athletes called when they wanted to run in Britain. He also exerted great leverage with overseas promoters. If Norman telephoned, people listened. In many respects he was a visionary, comprehending the need to make athletics telegenic. Norman understood that only the involvement of television companies could generate the finance necessary to popularize the sport outside Olympic competition. He was behind the initial blueprint to invent an athletics Grand Prix circuit. His plan was rejected, but later embraced in a barely disguised format.

For some years, Norman combined his passion for athletics and his entrepreneurial skills while still retaining his job within the police force. He successfully manoeuvred himself into a transfer to Bromley, where he was a desk sergeant. This was conveniently close to Crystal Palace, the premier athletics venue in the country. Norman's marketing plan was unconventional, to say the least. 'We used to sell out Crystal Palace before we decided the events or named who was going to run,' he says. Posters advertising the meeting used to appear at railway stations across the region, usually after a policeman had been seen patrolling the neighbourhood!

'There are three million people if you head down from Crystal Palace to Anerley Hill, out to Addiscombe, on round to Dartford,' says Norman. 'So filling 17,000 seats shouldn't be too difficult an exercise. Also, you would get core groups from Marlow, Aylesbury and Guildford. All gone now, sadly.'

Norman's first strategy was to ensure that a promotion did not clash with Crystal Palace Football Club staging a match at nearby Selhurst Park. 'It's just common sense, no secret.' His other recipe was to create an environment where the public could spend much of the afternoon watching British athletes win.

'As an organizer, you didn't set up a British athlete to get stuffed off the park. People want to see a British athlete in front, don't they? Jim Balding was an American quarter-mile hurdler in the days of Britain's Alan Pascoe. Back then, I was in the Crime Squad at Chelsea and I would come back into the office and be told there was a message for me from a man called Balding. He would tell me that he had raced three times that week and that he was on his way to England. Unless Balding had raced three times, Pascoe was never in the race! Lovely fella, Jim. He used to lead Pascoe into the last hurdle, then his legs would pack up. Pascoe would go past, the crowd would go bananas, and everybody was happy.

'Ovett, Seb Coe and Steve Cram could always be found someone like American Steve Scott to race. He was considered a good middle-distance runner, of course. Scott would meet Ovett somewhere on Monday night, Coe on Wednesday and Crammy on Friday. He'd get a day off, then meet Peter Elliott. By the end of the week, he was stuffed, gone. Of course, our athletes were all avoiding each other. Never twigged. You need to be Superman to handle that.'

Eventually, Norman resigned from the police force to become the most powerful voice in British athletics. What had begun as a hobby had become a full-time profession. Officially, at last, Norman was recognized as the supremo of track and field in the country. This was not an appointment that caused the bells to be rung across the nation, however.

Norman's power base should not be underestimated. You ran with him, or you ran against him at your peril, according to Kriss Akabusi. 'I've had conflicts with Andy on every single issue – money, race, all sorts,' he says. 'I've had the whole gambit. Andy Norman was a forthright, upfront, in your face type of guy. I liked him, inasmuch as you knew where you stood with him. He was very partial to his boys, and you were either for or against him.

'He had a great stable. Steve Ovett, Linford Christie, Colin Jackson, John Regis, Steve Backley, Sally Gunnell. Because he had them, Andy could say to a promoter, "You can have these guys, but Akabusi ain't running." So I would have to go to meetings where either Andy didn't have the influence, he wasn't involved in the organization, or the organization was so big, they could say, "No, Mr Norman, we'll have your boys *and* we'll have Akabusi." There weren't many who could do that.'

Roger Black, the 'golden boy' of British athletics, became ensnared in the same scenario. 'I'm guilty for that,' admits Akabusi. 'I took Roger under my wing, he listened, he was loyal to me and took my side. If Roger had stayed with Andy, he would have been a milllionaire. Andy would have seen to that. Roger was a white boy in a black event (400 metres). Roger was the Great White Hope – and he could have made a packet. I've got as much sin in my life as Andy Norman. It's just that I've handed mine over to God. So I'm not condemning him, but I have had personal battles with him.'

Akabusi and Black have both been confounded by the fact that Edwards remained loyal to Norman, particularly after *Sunday Times* journalist Cliff Temple committed suicide. Temple, a man devoted to athletics, a coach as well as a respected commentator, had begun to write more and more negatively about Norman. In essence, he felt Norman had been granted too much licence. Norman became increasingly agitated, privately and publicly. In the spring of 1994, Temple took his own life on a railway line. Not long afterwards, Norman was removed from office within British athletics.

Patrick Collins of the *Mail on Sunday* was a friend of Temple. 'I have a book with a most chilling quote, where

Neil Wilson [*Daily Mail* athletics writer] gives evidence to the BAF hearing into the circumstances surrounding the death of Cliff,' he says. 'Neil said he had spoken to Norman in Brussels, all very light-hearted. "Only when he asked me about Temple did the tone harden. I offered the opinion that Temple had enough on his plate, with his divorce and financial problems, without the unwarranted allegations that Norman had been putting round the athletics world about his coaching of female athletes. Time to lay off, I suggested." Norman's reply: "If there is anything I can do to push him over the edge, I will." I think that was evil.'

In award-winning columns over three decades, Collins has regularly declared his own affection for athletics. 'I knew Andy Norman a long time; in fact he had done me good turns. He made it possible for me to interview Steve Ovett when I was writing for the *Evening Standard* in 1978–9. It was a time when nobody else spoke to him. If anything, I had reasons to be grateful to him. But I had seen over the years how his influence had grown and I thought it was an increasingly malign influence. Certainly by the time Cliff Temple attempted to investigate the ramifications of his influence, it was a desperately damaging state of affairs for British athletics. Cliff wasn't really an investigative journalist, but he made honest attempts because he was concerned to delve into the influence Norman was exerting. The result was that he was turned on – totally false allegations made against him and intimidation and bullying.

'Cliff's suicide went to the Coroner's Court, Folkestone, April 1994. Norman didn't give evidence. The jury returned a verdict of suicide and identified as contributory factors "the break-up of Temple's marriage and the allegations which Norman had made against him". And the coroner said he felt "Norman's threats had tipped the balance". I think that is unforgivable.

'Jonathan Edwards will say nobody is unforgivable. Again, I totally understand that point of view. Maybe you have to forgive, but you don't have to make the man your personal manager. I lost a good deal of respect for him in light of that. I think that Norman is good at his job. If you want to make money, then Norman is probably your man. But I don't think you should necessarily want to make money through a man like that. Sounds pompous and pious, but I do believe it.

'The point I'd make is that Jonathan brought the moral dimension into it. If he said, "I don't give a stuff, Andy Norman is the best bloke out there to manage my affairs and the rest of you can all go and take a flying ..." that's fair enough. But I find it difficult – and he should find it difficult – to tread that line which occasionally smacks of hypocrisy. You say I want to adopt those attitudes, but at the same time I want Andy Norman, who is the man the coroner said tipped this decent man over the edge, I want him to be my man. I don't think you can have those two, but he does and that's his business.

'I'm not against him at all. He's a terrific sportsman and an admirable figure in many ways, Maybe he's making that mistake for the best reasons. Maybe he genuinely believes we should forgive. Of course you should forgive, but I don't think you should allow someone like that to take over important sections of your life.'

Colin Hart from the *Sun*, a man nearing retirement after a distinguished career, presents a contrary opinion to that of Collins. 'Cliff Temple was a good friend from the time I began writing about athletics in 1969, and I've known Andy all the years I've been covering the sport.

Cliff confided in me, like he confided in other friends, and told me about the allegations being made about him.

'I subsequently told Andy I thought it was terribly wrong, but some of my colleagues were hysterical. As for blaming Andy for the death of Cliff Temple, I thought that was outrageous. I think Cliff was a troubled man for many reasons, and I'm sure Andy didn't help. But, in my opinion, he was not responsible for what happened. It wasn't because of Andy Norman that Cliff ended his life. We were all horrified when we found out Cliff had committed suicide, but Andy was blamed without taking into consideration Cliff's domestic life, his financial position and his emotional state regarding his family. That was just totally disregarded.

'To me, there is no conflict in Jonathan Edwards using Andy to work out his schedule. If I was an athlete, I'd want Andy to do my scheduling, like I'd want Mickey Duff to look after me if I was a fighter. Look, I grew up in the East End of London where our motto was "All coppers are *******". Andy Norman thinks like a copper, he acts like a copper. He's street smart. I would trust him to look after my career.

'He was brilliant at what he did. His contacts were second to none; the athletes believed in him; they would run for him; he was a great promoter. Like I say, he was the Mickey Duff of athletics, and Mickey was arguably the greatest matchmaker in boxing this country has ever seen. Andy ended up the victim of a witch-hunt. He made a mistake – but that doesn't mean he should be condemned for the rest of his life.'

Akabusi's view of Edwards' ongoing relationship with Norman is this: 'I admit I didn't understand, but it's not something we discuss. Jonathan will have his reasons.'

Edwards' association with Norman puzzles Black too. 'Many people in the sport think it doesn't weigh up,' he says. 'Andy paid me pretty well, I got on well with him, but I was never one of his boys. It made sense to be with Andy if you wanted to get on. And then the Cliff Temple thing happened and it didn't make quite so much sense.

'If you want to get on in athletics, Andy Norman is the man you want. He's fantastic, he'll get things done, he'll protect you. I rate my athletics career as being a lot harder for not being with Norman. I was always involved with journalists, guys from television and newspapers; and those you're around influence you. I couldn't possibly deal with Norman when I knew the stories that were circulating. Morally, I just could not. And certainly, the way Norman was with Kriss Akabusi, it was impossible for me, absolutely impossible. He gave Kriss a terrible ride.

'But I respect Jonathan's judgement. Some might think it's like trading with the devil, but Jonathan could say he's being compassionate. He's a wonderfully nice man, a devout Christian, but I think there's more to him than that. I believe there's an edge to Jonathan and that is demonstrated in his Andy Norman situation.'

Edwards is not the least apologetic for his friendship with Norman, and it is a genuine friendship. He remembers that Norman was encouraging from the early days, when he was an unknown, trying to make a mark in an event that was not the most marketable part of the programme. He likes his economic way of making a point, his rasping humour. He likes his unshakeable loyalty to him. He has deep respect for his knowledge of the sport, his capacity to open doors, his organizational skills, his street wisdom. He was proud to be invited to speak at Norman's wedding to Fatima Whitbread, once a world champion in the javelin. He has occasion to be grateful for the manner in which Norman has looked after his wife, Alison, and his parents.

He could so easily have refused to discuss his involvement with Norman. He could have asked for his relationship with him to have been mentioned only in passing in this book. He did not. He wished for a range of opinion to be heard.

Edwards explains his position and responds to criticism like this: 'In no way do I condone what Andy said to Cliff Temple; I also know that Andy sincerely regrets the whole incident. He had no idea Cliff was about to do what he did. People will remember Andy's words to Neil Wilson, and on the face of it they seem very damning. But they were spoken during an athletics meeting when Andy would have had a million things going through his mind. I don't think that brief exchange and Andy's kneejerk reaction comments are trustworthy grounds for condemning him – we all say things as throwaway remarks that don't really reflect our true state of mind.

'There is no way Andy wanted Cliff to commit suicide and he has told me as much. Andy Norman is not the evil man that some writers would have us believe. A coroner says Andy tipped the balance. What does that actually mean? The tiniest weight can tip a balance.

'Large sections of the media would have us believe that Andy pushed Cliff from the platform. My own judgement is that Andy would never have followed through his threats; he was simply trying to scare Cliff to keep him from investigating some of the perceived "conflicting interests" in Andy's dealings. Such dealings, it must be said, were by no means limited to Andy, but he always was the fall guy for British athletics. He had broad shoulders and protected a lot of people in high places.

'Cliff's suicide and Andy's alleged part in it gave a proportion of the media a pretext for unleashing their prejudice towards him. Cliff was also a journalist; Andy didn't have a chance. It was disappointing that so few people stuck by Andy for fear of being pilloried by the press. That attitude persists today.

'I have a very high regard for Andy. He has been incredibly supportive of me all through my career. I regard him as a close and trusted friend. The implicit accusation by the likes of Roger Black and Patrick Collins that I stay with Andy for financial reasons is simply not true. In fact, Andy's interests are more in meeting promotion than athlete management. There is even an argument that I might have done better elsewhere. The reality is that appearance fees are fairly standard, regardless of who your representative is.

'Obviously, I thought very seriously about leaving Andy after the Cliff incident. It would have been the easier decision to make. As an outspoken Christian, I had a lot to lose by continuing to stay with Andy. But from speaking very openly to him about the situation, I didn't see sufficient reason to leave. It's interesting that none of the athletes Andy managed at this stage saw fit to do so either. Linford Christie and Colin Jackson only left him a year or so later, after they created their own management company. Andy made a mistake and knows that. I know he isn't perfect by any means – who is? I have a clear conscience in my continuing professional and personal relationship with him. He is probably one of the most respected and highly regarded figures in world athletics.'

Norman lives with Fatima Whitbread – his second wife – and their young son in Essex. His two grown-up children from his first marriage are not in his life. 'Athletics cost me the marriage,' he says. 'Plus the problems that came along – they're better off without me.'

He has not spoken publicly for almost six years, and he made it plain that he did not wish to involve Edwards in a regrettable episode of his life. 'In the end, they got what they wanted,' says Norman. 'They got rid of me from British athletics. Now, when I ignore some of the media they find that very difficult. People hate being ignored. It happened all my life as a policeman. You walked down the street and people didn't want to know. You can easily adopt that mode yourself. I won't say a great deal more, but a lot of people have shown themselves to be hypocrites.

'It's interesting that, when you have problems, those who come to support you are the least likely you'd think. Those you've been close with and done a lot for run for the hills. Seb Coe was very supportive, Daley Thompson too, and they had no reason to be like that. Some told me, "Andy, if I speak up for you, they'll bury me." I don't think the public realized that happened. Like when all the media went for Graham Taylor. The team hasn't played that much better since, have they? But it doesn't help when you attack a doyen of the media, as I did. That doesn't make you friends for life. If you play with fire, you'll get burnt. I got burnt.'

As well as Edwards, Norman still looks after the scheduling of javelin thrower Steve Backley, European 400 metres champion Iwan Thomas and middle-distance runner Kelly Holmes. In the summer of 1998, he was summoned as an eleventh-hour troubleshooter by the organizers of the European Championships in Budapest to rearrange the timetable to the satisfaction of athletes and broadcasters alike. He organizes second- and third-tier athletics meetings for the European Federation. 'I survive,' he says. 'Athletics isn't the be-all and end-all. There are other things in life.'

Norman is from the old school. He moved the sport and he moved athletes into a more profitable environment. He worked without recourse to lawyers. His methods would not be acceptable in the modern world, of course. 'I'm a dinosaur,' he smiles. Ex-hurdler Alan Pascoe's company is now responsible for the commercial funding and promotion of athletics in Britain. 'Alan never got involved in the politics. He's running a business, an empire. He's taking the risk, but he's a multimillionaire. Good luck to him.'

For Norman, there is always a plane to catch, a deal to be struck, but there is also an ongoing, affectionate affair with his sport. 'Jonathan Edwards is a gentleman. I don't have a contract with him, or any of the athletes I work with.' He has been a good friend as well as a bad enemy.

Brendan Foster, a close friend of Norman's and a man with a lifetime's experience in athletics, says by way of closing argument, 'Andy is a complete rascal, but he's Andy. I think he has helped Jonathan over the years and I think Jonathan simply recognizes that fact. Whatever else Andy has done, I'm not sure what crime he is guilty of. If it had been a real crime, he would have been in and out of prison by now, wouldn't he?'

Chapter 10

Georgia on his Mind

Yesterday is not ours to recover,
but tomorrow is ours to win or lose.

LYNDON B. JOHNSON

With the frenetic award season over and his newly donated dinner jacket returned to the wardrobe, Jonathan Edwards began to write a diary at the dawn of Olympic year, 1996. In small type above the lined opening page is a quotation from Psalm 118:24. 'This is the day the Lord has made; let us rejoice and be glad in it.' Immediately beneath, Edwards makes his first entry in black ink in a very legible hand.

1 Jan: What a difference a year makes! The question I posed myself this time last year is virtually the same as the one this year: 'Where do I go from here?' The only difference is that it comes from the opposite end of the emotional (psychological) achievement spectrum. My athletic goals for '95 were modest and with good reason and if you had told me that my worst recorded jump of the season (17.29 in Rieti) would be my season's best I would

have taken it there and then! (never mind ONE WHOLE METRE FURTHER!) So that brings me to this year – what are my goals? First to become focused on being an athlete again. So much has happened that has sent my head spinning and my first priority is to establish the same kind of routine that led to such success last year (easier said than done). Obviously I want to win the Olympics but that doesn't really become realistic until I get myself into good shape and jumping well again. As Norman [Anderson] would say: Today's session is what matters – the rest is history!

His year is shaped, his mood purposeful. Or is it? The very next day Edwards tells his diary:

2 Jan: Between Christmas and New Year I suffered a bit of a crisis of confidence. '95 was over and '96 was beginning. I was in all the reviews and the previews. One paper said that I was 1–4 to win the Olympics. I felt an overwhelming pressure and no ability to withstand it. Looking back it was because I hadn't really got my brain in gear, focused on the challenges that lie ahead and subsequently I didn't really have the framework in place to deal with the sudden rush of emotions that the end of my 'annus mirabilis' produced. Today felt much better. Training went pretty well and I feel I've got my teeth into the challenge. No doubt there will be a few more 'shaky moments' along the way but I'm excited about the prospects. One thing that would help no end though was if my youngest would sleep through the night! Also went to St James's Park for the football match (New 2 Arsenal 1). Pity athletics isn't as popular. Though they do seem to like me.

*   *   *

For Edwards the journey to the Olympics, still almost eight months away, was to be the kind of roller-coaster ride Mr Disney still has to design. Edwards was to find himself living on the cliff-edge of his emotions until the last stride of his final jump into the pit in Atlanta. This is how it is at the elite, sharp end of sport. The sweetness of success is always scented with the fear of failure.

Against the traumatic background of his wife Alison's illness, the turbulence of moving house and the sleepless nights induced by his infant son, Edwards was involved in a constant battle of wits – with himself. There was a natural uncertainty in his mind. He knew the record books said that he was the best in the world, but he knew also that it did not guarantee that he would produce the best jump in the Olympics. Looking back, he senses echoes of his childhood, when each new school year made him insecure to start with. Only now he was being observed; now he was the man who had won a viewers' poll to become BBC Sports Personality of the Year. 'The idea of being famous was a nice one, but it was all so new, it was hard to be natural. I wasn't wanting to feel pleased with myself. I was very aware of the thin line between being satisfied and being conceited.'

If Edwards himself could not comprehend what kind of athlete he was – freakishly talented or a man apart – those on the sidelines could be forgiven for not being able to tell either. 'Had I been jumping 18 metres all my life, I would have been fine! If you've done it for 10 years, you know you can do it in the eleventh. But I'd been jumping 17.10 metres and 17.20 metres for nine years, and then I do 18.29 metres. You have to ask yourself, "Which one is going to happen next?" There are few who are endowed with complete and utter self-belief.

I remember a conversation I had with Linford Christie after he had won the World Championships in Stuttgart. He admitted how scared he was beforehand – not that you would ever know.' Christie worked to a simple principle, and that involved imposing his personality on all those around him. Edwards could never create that kind of frenzy; or perhaps he was just not such a good actor.

The New Year was less than a week old when Edwards drove to Gateshead Stadium for training as usual one morning. Instead of turning into the entrance, however, he drove straight on. Some days you know when it is not worth getting out of the car, he explains. This is Edwards, master of his own universe, not an athlete governed by traditional convention. Later that same evening, Edwards finally caught up with the film *Chariots of Fire*. 'The depth of feeling it arouses leaves me with no doubt how important this year is to me,' he confided to his diary. 'I can almost feel the adrenaline coursing through my veins; the fear and the excitement.'

Yes, the Olympics were hovering on the horizon and there was much serious, hard work to be done. Yet for all his maturity – and Edwards would be 30 years old before the Olympic competition – he retains a boyish capacity to discover new fruits of life. To reward himself after a hard training session (and with a lovely, self-deprecating touch, he admits, 'I rarely set the stadium alight by my red-hot performances') he will soak in a hot bath and, on occasion, take a small glass of vintage port and a slice of Brie.

You would not generally mention that kind of indulgence in the company of those who use the lived-in gym at Gateshead Stadium, a community that has included 'faces' from the Newcastle underworld and nightclub doormen keeping themselves in trim for the weekend.

Edwards is accepted in their company, though there are moments when his naivety is exploited. One day a man with shoulders like a Welsh dresser and a nose that had been rearranged without anaesthetic told Edwards in the gym that he was also a jumper. Edwards politely enquired what type of jumping he did. 'Ah joomp over walls, like, to get awa' from the coppers!' he replied, to general amusement. There is more than a grain of truth in this kind of story. On another occasion, the stadium was blockaded by armed police hunting for a suspect in connection with a serious crime.

'You think: Jonathan and Newcastle – bad mix,' says John Hedley, smiling slowly. 'When I first met him he used to look like a Young Conservative on a canvassing trip. There are a lot of blokes in the gym you wouldn't want to cross, but they all give Jonathan a wave; they have a bit of a joke with him because they know he's a decent bloke.' Hedley had become Edwards' regular training partner at the gym shortly after the calamitous Barcelona Olympics in 1992. In those days Hedley worked for Gateshead Leisure Services while competing on the professional sprinting circuit in Scotland. 'We hit it off on a personal level straight away, which you might not have predicted,' says Hedley. 'I mean, Jonathan has his great Christian beliefs, and I'm a rather lapsed Catholic. I'm the quintessential Northeast guy, you know, I like to go out for a beer at the weekend. You think of Jonathan as this middle-class, Christian bloke – why does he choose to live in Newcastle? You can't quite understand some things!'

Edwards, in fact, has always felt comfortable in Newcastle. He likes the people and the city, their football team has become his football team, but he draws the line at defending the weather. With pride, he completed his collection of awards on 21 January 1996 when he was named the Northeast Sportsman of the Year, a title he felt might have been destined for Newcastle United striker Les Ferdinand. That night he wrote in his diary, 'I felt a genuine warmth from everyone and a heartfelt delight I'd won. I would dearly love to bring Olympic gold back to the region.'

Hedley, who later went to Scotland to study radiography, was by Edwards' own assessment the perfect foil for him in training. He was a dependable partner, flexible to Edwards' needs. He was competitive in the weight room and fast enough to keep him honest in track sessions. He was also entertaining. 'Jonathan would always ask on Mondays what my weekend was like – and he would laugh at some of the things I used to get up to. Just the normal sort of high jinks that come up when you're a young lad.'

That is not entirely true. On one weekend, Hedley went to Peterhead, north of Aberdeen, to drive a friend of the family back to her barracks. 'She was with the Military Police in the RAF, but had hurt her knee in a car crash, so her brother and I drove her to Scotland. We ended up getting separated and somehow I managed to end up drinking on a Russian fishing boat at two o'clock in the morning. The local constable took us in for the night...' For Edwards, stories like this were the lifeblood of training.

By 1996, Edwards and Hedley were doing their weight training under the supervision of Norman Anderson, whose very limited sight was not a handicap when it came to dispensing motivation and wisdom. Anderson is a native of the region, blunt but soft round the edges. 'It's funny,' says Hedley, 'but one of the few things we do at the gym to accommodate Jonathan is that, when we want to tell a rude joke, we go to the far side of the room. Norman and I really laugh and carry on, and Jonathan just looks and thinks, "Ah, telling jokes." In a lot of cases, it's not because we're scared of offending him, he just doesn't get them. His mind doesn't work the same way. I told him one the other day and he just looked at me, blank. You lose the power of the pun when you're trying to explain the punchline to him! Sometimes he's in a little world of his own.'

Behind those pictures of Edwards splashing triumphantly into the sand in Gothenburg, behind those images of Edwards resplendent in black tie, accepting award after award at the end of 1995, there is an unglamorous reality about his job. This was what I found on a wintry mid-February morning in 1996 when I paid a visit to Gateshead Stadium. Edwards was to be witnessed not in a dinner jacket, but in a tracksuit and a navy-blue bobble hat, trying to cheat a wind born in Siberia.

What little was visible of his face, sheltered by his hat and wraparound shades, was the colour of rare-cooked meat. His exhaled breath surrounded him like the smoke from a good Havana. The empty stands in the stadium exaggerated the bleakness of the landscape. Nonetheless, with Hedley as a companion, Edwards was sprinting through the cold – and even inside a heavy overcoat you knew this was a fatherless wind – with grim determination. He was running towards Atlanta and he knew it.

'I enjoy training here,' he said. 'There are hard edges everywhere; no televisions playing MTV, no girls in leotards doing aerobics. This is a serious, no-frills training environment. Perfect.' He talked of his excitement, of the anticipation already enveloping him. 'I don't probably fully appreciate the size of it yet, but there is a huge expectation on me. People want a track-and-field gold medal. I'm positive. I'm excited. But as well as being exciting, it's also scary. I'll be petrified...' Just how petrified would become apparent soon enough.

Edwards is now a fixture at the stadium, even though the staff have been more accustomed to outstanding athletes lapping the track, like Brendan Foster, Steve Cram, and Charlie Spedding. As president of Gateshead Harriers, Foster likes to joke that if a man walks into the club on Monday as a shot-putter, he will be running 5,000 metres by Friday. Running, you see, is the stuff of legend in the Northeast. Yet Hedley tells how the groundstaff will accommodate Edwards, the skinny bloke with the 'funny' accent. 'A lot of the guys who work at the stadium have been there for over 15 years and they're sort of institutionalized, they don't like things to be any different. They go in and get their eight-hour shift out of the road as painlessly as possible. There are times when Jonathan will say that he'll be in the next day, and ask if there is any chance they could get the sandpit ready for him. The sand in the pit gets compacted. It's hard work, it's backbreaking to turn the pit over. They'll have a moan. One of the lads, Simon, a huge, rugby-prop sort of a guy, said to him one day: "You had one good jump in your life and that's it, you're finished." Jonathan likes the way he's treated like everyone else.' Of course, the pit is always turned over for him.

In the early days of that titanic year, Edwards was planning a return to Florida for a long, training hibernation in the winter sun. He had rented a house so that he could take Alison, Sam and Nathan with him to the United States. He had also arranged to work again with Dennis Nobles, jumps coach at Florida State University in Tallahassee, with whom he had enjoyed training the previous year. This time the Edwards family would benefit from going to a place where they already had a network of friends from the congregation of the church they had attended 12 months earlier.

Then, of course, Alison was suddenly required to have surgery in early February 1996. Two weeks later, the family moved from Heaton to their new home in Gosforth. Reverend Andy Edwards and his wife Jill came north from Bournemouth to assist them. With his wife sorely incapacitated, Edwards was mightily grateful for the presence of his parents. 'We still loved the house and that was a relief,' said Edwards, sounding no different from anyone else consumed by anxiety on the eve of a house move. Yet at this point he just wanted to escape the stress. All he really longed for was to get on the flight to Florida. Rather against the odds, they did just that and, with Alison unable to carry children or luggage, the Edwards family were afforded VIP treatment for their multi-legged journey from Newcastle to Tallahassee.

Once in Florida, Edwards was in his element. At his disposal was a Jeep, a four-bedroom, three-bathroom dream house and the freedom to move around anonymously. Surprisingly enough, he was not a slave to a nutritionist's diet sheet – far from it. He tucked enthusiastically into fast food from Kentucky Fried Chicken, McDonald's or Taco Bell. A Jeep and fries to go: he was the authentic, all-American boy. He still wanted familiar faces around him, though. He had arranged for his friend and fellow triple jumper Rogel Nahum to join him in Tallahassee to train. Hedley was also flown from Newcastle at Edwards' expense to resume his role as regular sparring partner for a month. Edwards was to cherish the 10 weeks he spent in Florida.

Out in the States he was deaf to the speculation at home that continually branded him as the 'banker' to win a gold medal for Britain in Atlanta. He was also spared the disappointment of witnessing Newcastle United surrender their huge advantage at the top of the Premiership to Manchester United. Nonetheless, if Edwards was to come to relish his exile on the other side of the Atlantic, the early days in Florida were undeniably tough. Alison remained unwell, which was a constant source of worry. Also, he found it difficult to establish a training rhythm.

Even here, too, there was the occasional intrusion from the media. Edwards was to regret granting the NBC network permission to film him at the training ground at Florida State University. The television men arrived with a high-speed camera, bolted to a huge truck. The truck kept pace with him as he ran down the track. 'I was an idiot to do it,' he says. But Edwards was a slow learner. He wrote in his diary on 19 March:

> Today was a miserable day. I didn't feel well at all but felt obliged to jump because of *Sports Illustrated* being there. I felt heavy, lethargic and generally washed out. Add to that the cameraman and the fact that Rogel forgot his jumping spikes and the session was delayed 20 minutes and you can imagine the picture. It was also cold and the wind direction extremely variable. I didn't however jump too badly; 16.10 from 10 steps was really as good as last week when I felt great – every cloud has a silver lining – or so they say! I did feel awful afterwards and spent the rest of the day resting inside apart from a visit to KFC for tea! It is really frustrating feeling ill again – hope I feel well again soon.

Four days later, he flew to Atlanta as a guest of the *Mail on Sunday* for a unique photo shoot and a preview of the Olympic Stadium. His visit to jump at the track at Georgia Institute of Technology – which would become the heart of the athletes' village when the Olympics came to town – had taken a mere three months to arrange and could be accountable for the introduction of further grey hairs for those of us who were involved.

A man called Roger Kelly, sports editor of the *Mail on Sunday* at the time, was indirectly responsible. Four years earlier, wishing to show how far Steve Backley threw the javelin, his sports department had dreamed up a masterful stunt at Crystal Palace. Backley threw his javelin over a line of red, double-decker London buses and the flight path was traced by computer technology to give the newspaper's readers a graphic indication of the distance. 'So how do we illustrate how far Edwards jumps?' asked Kelly mischievously over a beer towards the end of 1995.

We hatched an idea for breathing three-dimensional life into the triple jump. The plan was to line up a row of cars, door handle to door handle, headlights facing the runway, until there were enough in place to cover the 18.29 metres Edwards had leapt in Gothenburg. Then, with the cars forming the backdrop down the runway, all we needed was for Edwards to jump, thus providing a visual impression of the distance of his phenomenal world record.

What could be simpler to organize, given an immediately positive response from the Ford Motor Company's Public Relations department at Brentwood, Essex? How about the fact that Edwards was going to be in Florida for the entire off season in the spring? We overcame that by offering Edwards a sneak, provisional look at the Olympic Stadium. He made himself available for a few hours in Atlanta, which is only a 40-minute flight from Tallahassee. One problem solved, two to go: all we needed were the cars and an athletics track. Simple? Wrong. How about the fact that, although Ford builds cars at a plant just outside Atlanta, those vehicles were already sold and could not be borrowed? Any cars we wanted would have to be brought from Detroit, a round trip of almost 1,500 miles. How about the fact that the track at Georgia Tech – the only suitable one in the neighbourhood – was being renovated for the Olympics?

After an unrecorded number of telephone calls and a flying visit from London to Atlanta, we were eventually able to gain access to the track at Georgia Tech in return for a modest fee; and the Ford Motor Company generously arranged for the cars we needed to be brought by transporter from Detroit free of charge. All we had to do was find a date suitable for Edwards.

On Saturday 23 March, he strode across the arrivals concourse at Atlanta airport on a day-return ticket from Tallahassee. In his hand was a holdall containing his kit and spikes. As Edwards changed out of his tracksuit after the drive across town to Georgia Tech, he watched in amazement as truck driver Tommy Dutton positioned the fleet of Ford Taurus cars alongside the runway of the track with the care of a choreographer rehearsing a Broadway musical. Edwards re-enacted his jump in stealthily planned phases, but the picture that ran across two pages of the newspaper provided unique testimony to the distance he had flown that night in Gothenburg. His jump carried him past nine cars. Mission accomplished.

As we stood under a cloudless sky, with the silent tower blocks framing the downtown Atlanta skyline that would become as familiar to television viewers as their own back garden, we garnered from Edwards a description of his taxing art.

At the head of the runway I do not have any particular mental preparation ... I focus quite naturally. I clap my hands as I like to get the crowd involved, to know they are watching. I rock back a couple of times on my heel, wait to see what the wind is doing, then tell myself, 'This is it, let's GO.'

Maybe, four or five strides out I will look at the take-off board. But then I am looking ahead. I don't even think about the board. Hopefully, it just happens to be underneath my foot at take-off. If you start thinking about the board it becomes a barrier. And if you are sprinting and looking down, it is going to affect your whole body position. The idea is to maintain speed all the way through the jump.

I take off on my left foot, land on that foot and take off again. Your feet have to be striking the ground very fast in order to lessen any braking effect. In transition from the hop to the step, you are moving so fast, that sometimes you get the feeling of flying through the air. I changed my arm action last year, driving through the jump with both arms moving upwards together. It's still not perfect, but I am at the stage where all the constituent parts of my technique are in place. Bio-mechanical analysis suggests that I transfer my speed very well. But, frankly, it's just the way I jump; it's simple and obvious theory, it's not something I have to analyse or practise.[1]

If perfected – and at take-off, remember, Edwards is travelling in excess of 25 miles an hour – this technique makes it possible to fly beyond the width of nine cars parked door handle to door handle.

1 *Mail on Sunday*, 7 July 1996.

On that day in Atlanta in late March, Edwards was relaxed and, as usual, exceedingly good natured. When he first saw the concrete and steel construction site in the downtown Olympic city, he caught his breath. 'Wow, so that's where it's going to happen!' he said. Those words will not instantly qualify him for an entry in the next edition of the Collins *Dictionary of Quotations*, but with that simple exclamation Edwards had taken his first look inside the Olympic Stadium, the theatre of his dreams.

In the grand measurement of time, the 1996 Olympic Games were merely a hop, step and jump away. 'To see the Olympic Stadium serves to firm up the strong resolve which already exists deep inside me. But, also, just standing here represents the unknown. I know I'm seen as the big Olympic hope in track and field. No, wrong, I'm seen as the certainty.' Sadly for him, he was not exaggerating. Perhaps no jumper since the late and lamented Red Rum has carried so much of the nation's expectation and goodwill as Edwards.

It was now lunchtime and the men in hard hats and worn denims were heading from the stadium in a constant relay to a grimy fast-food shack a block away. The unpretentious Mr Edwards voted we join them. He wanted deep-fried chicken pieces and fries, with some coleslaw on the side. He wanted to devour the gossip on Newcastle's faltering progress in the Premiership. When we had eaten – and this was not a salubrious neighbourhood – he volunteered to chase down a taxi, a vehicle we speculated that was as rare in this part of town as a Rolls-Royce Silver Cloud.

Edwards succeeded, however. 'Y'all comin' back for the Olympics?' enquired the driver. Edwards was, he was told – as a gold medal favourite hotter than a July day in

Georgia. 'You an athlete?' demanded the driver, who could not have been more surprised if he had just had a Colt .45 pressed in his ribs. 'Not eating that crap, you're not. You're kinda old to be the champ, anyway. Kinda too grey...' Edwards smiled benevolently.

He was six weeks away from his thirtieth birthday. 'Age is not an issue with me,' he commented. He was to utter a similar sentiment in Seville nearly three and a half years later. 'Like Linford, I came to my sport seriously late and there's much to be said for that.' He caught a late-afternoon flight back to Tallahassee to rejoin his family. He felt like he was going home, he said.

John Hedley understood as well as anyone why Edwards felt more content at this period being in the United States rather than in Newcastle. 'I think Jonathan didn't respond that well to becoming famous,' he says. 'He told me how Alison had wanted to go shopping one day at home and they went to the Metro Centre and he couldn't bring himself to get out of the car. He said he felt like he had three heads because everyone was pointing and staring at him. The pressures on him were huge. I think he was wanting to do well in Atlanta for the wrong reasons. He wasn't necessarily wanting to do it for himself; he wanted to do it because everyone expected him to do it.'

In Florida, Hedley was Edwards' barometer. He could judge all his work against him, just as he did in Gateshead. 'Jonathan has tremendous natural speed,' says Hedley. 'In training we've clocked him at 10.20 seconds over 100 metres.' Often Hedley's father Eddie might attend their training. 'Some days Dad asks us not to run flat out, but around nine-tenths, and keep everything relaxed. He wants us to power down the track without any tension. I feel like my arms and legs are going at 100 mph; then you watch Jonathan and he looks like he's running at half speed. Technically, everything is fantastic. And that's the same with the Olympic lifting that we do. I mean, to look at him, you'd think he couldn't punch himself out of a paper bag. The guy's like 11 stone wet through, but he's so phenomenally strong, it's unbelievable.'

To Hedley, living in Tallahassee among professional athletes was manna from heaven. The social scene was not without its moments either, and one night in particular springs to his mind. 'There was a reception for potential Olympic athletes in this fantastic Southern mansion that looked like it had come from *Gone with the Wind*,' he recalls. 'Long drive, the lot. Jonathan drove and there was myself, Denise Lewis, Michelle Griffiths, Mark Procter the shot-putter and his coach. In all, about eight or ten of us and the great and the good of Tallahassee society. Glasses of wine were being brought round and we were chatting to these people who were obviously helping to fund the British Olympic camp. I got a fit of the panics – *I* wasn't an Olympic athlete!'

Hedley, five years younger than Edwards, is not a man easily lost for words, however. Edwards was standing beside him when an American asked Hedley if he adhered to a special diet before big races. 'I try not to drink as much Guinness,' he replied, his accent as thick as fog on the Tyne. Hedley laughs at the memory. 'The poor American guy looked completely lost … and Jonathan, well, I thought he was going to keel over!'

Hedley has seen Edwards grow from fashion victim – 'Young Conservative on a canvassing trip' – to a man seeking, if not the cutting edge of the era, at least a semblance of street cred. Edwards has experimented with his hair, from razor short to slicked back with Brylcreem. He has had the sparsest of goatee beards. His clothes now tend to have a designer label. 'Jonathan's had this middle-class upbringing, with his Dad a vicar, but I think he went through a little rebellious stage,' chuckles Hedley. 'He even talked about getting his ear pierced. In Tallahassee, Jonathan had a stud clipped to his ear. I think it's because he had no rebellious streak in him at all – he never had any teenage tantrums. He gets them now – what age is he? Alison just shakes her head.' Edwards thinks the world of Hedley.

In the United States, Hedley wrote Edwards a letter to thank him for his hospitality and invited Jonathan and Alison to dinner as his guests. They went to an establishment called the Buckhead Brewery and ordered steaks. Hedley and Edwards both approve of American-sized portions. To Hedley's glee, they were serving a beer marketed as similar to Guinness. Edwards ordered a pint as well. 'I thought that was very bold,' suggests Hedley. 'When he ordered a second one I thought, "Something's going on here!" He had to give me the second pint to finish, though he swears to this day that he wasn't drunk. But, put it this way, his behaviour wasn't exactly rational for Jonathan. On the way home, Alison was driving the Jeep and Jonathan was nibbling her neck and saying he wanted to try for a daughter that night – and all the time I'm sitting on the back seat not quite sure where to put myself! He completely shocks you sometimes.

'I mean, the guy I first met in 1992 was the man who wouldn't jump on a Sunday. He had this insular lifestyle, where he was training and being with his family and church friends. I've seen a great change in him; he'll have a beer, a few glasses of wine; he's just a more outgoing bloke. For a while he was a boy racer with his cars, too.

I don't think it's a change for the worse. It's been a natural evolution of the way he has come on through his athletics.' Edwards would not dispute that potted biography of his metamorphosis.

He certainly liked the familiarity of having friends like Hedley and Nahum in his orbit during the months of preparation that year. Not that he was ever going to fall for the pre-Olympic propaganda surrounding him. He was taking his position as favourite as no more than an act of faith by the bookmaking fraternity. 'All my rivals think they will be jumping as far as me,' he predicted at the time. 'They feel I have opened a door and now they can walk through it. It might be true … but I know I have crossed the threshold. Yet that doesn't mean I don't feel vulnerable. It's a whole new experience to go from also-ran to favourite.'

For Edwards, the stay in America was an exceedingly welcome respite from the harshness of a Northeast winter and a time of peace to be shared with Alison and their two young sons. Yet there was the ever-present suspicion that his build-up was not progressing as it should have been. Again, his diary provides telltale evidence of his creeping anxiety. 'Perhaps I need a rest and that is what I plan to do next week,' he writes on 30 March.

Will the spark return? What if it goes away on the week that really matters? There are so many question marks and no certain answers. And as I write, it's not just me, it's not just my family and a few friends who are watching to find out the answers. It is at times like this that I am aware of the tightrope that every top athlete walks, the fragile thread from which things hang and yet one good session and those feelings are quickly gone like an early morning mist. And the funny thing is you never seem to learn from experience. Every low could be career threatening, yet in reality it rarely is, yet those feelings are as real every time.

His diary-keeping became more sporadic, but when he did reach for his pen it was clearly a cathartic exercise.

20 April: The last week or so since I wrote in the diary has been up and down. I have changed to a new weights regime and it has taken quite a lot out of me which has affected my ability to jump. I have generally felt heavy and fatigued. I hate feeling anything but sharp. Dennis says I need a competition and he's probably right. Viruses apart this is probably the longest time I have gone without a competition. It also coincides with a time when I have been more concerned with my level of performance than ever before – a volatile mix I can tell you! The last couple of sessions though have been good and I also jumped 17m feeling bad, so it's not all exactly bad news – excepting that I might be in a padded cell by July!! (only joking).

Edwards was in regular contact with Norman Anderson at his suburban home in Newcastle. Anderson was supportive at the time, but in the summer of 1999 he voiced for the first time his disenchantment with how things were unfolding in 1996. 'Jonathan introduces people on the scene like Dennis Nobles, unilaterally,' he says. 'He never discusses it, they just appear. At first I found that very hurtful, because at that time I was believing my own publicity from the work we did in 1995. He came back from America full of Dennis. "Dennis does this, Dennis does that." I was hurt, but I thought I had to try and be a bit adult.'

Anderson may be legally blind, but he likes to think he sees most of what is happening to Edwards. As he spoke to him from across the Atlantic, he knew Edwards was capable of leaving his rivals in his slipstream, leaving them choking on his exhaust fumes. He also suspected that he was vulnerable to beating himself. 'In my view, Jonathan's jumping is 95 per cent natural ability,' says Anderson. 'He can get his technique all wrong, but because he's so athletically gifted he can get a long way. Genetically, he's a beautiful athlete. He could have done all sorts of things. He finds acquiring new skills dead easy. He's frighteningly quick, his power-to-weight ratio is unbelievable. You could call him sparrow-legs and take the piss, but you watch him: he can power-clean 135 kilos, he can snatch 100 kilos. He's phenomenal. That's a frustration – do you see what I'm trying to say? I think his fault is self-belief. Now he doesn't accept that. He's got his God...'

These were not the sentiments, however, that he offered Edwards when he took his calls in the spring of 1996. After speaking to Anderson towards the end of April, Edwards opted to take a break from lifting. He had been lifting at a much greater intensity than the previous year – understandable when you consider that 12 months earlier he had still been feeling his way to fitness after the Epstein Barr Virus – but one of the secrets of high-calibre training is to know when it is time to rest.

Yet his unease remained detectable. On 29 April he told his diary, 'Spoke to Andy [Norman] on the phone this morning and now the summer feels closer than ever. Both Alison and I are feeling like it might all be too much. I'm sure it's just the anticipation and once the season has begun it won't be quite as bad as we feel it will be right at the moment.' That is the last entry Edwards made in his diary. The process had become too dispiriting, the exercise too repetitive.

Throughout his period in the United States, Edwards had been trying to get his technique grooved. In particular, he was trying to make his double arm shift become second nature. Instead, it became alien. 'I always felt the double arm movement was one of the main pieces of the jigsaw in 1995, but it didn't go that well in training. When I went to compete I inadvertently reverted to my old style, bringing my right arm over the top in my hop.' The disadvantage of this is that his arm tends to move his upper body too far forward, causing his centre of gravity to be too far forward and forcing him to over-rotate. Edwards fought a losing battle to rectify his technique before the Olympics.

His flaw was all too obvious when he went to Atlanta in mid-May to compete at a Grand Prix meeting, ostensibly designed to provide the Olympic Stadium staff with a dry run before the Games, as well as offering the athletes a feel of the arena. Before flying to Atlanta, he had escorted Alison, Sam, Nathan and their good friend Linda Donaldson to the airport to catch their flight home to England. There was a heaviness in his heart, and not just because his family was departing. He knew their restful preparation was at an end. From here on he had to be on a total business footing.

In Atlanta he had to confront Mike Conley, the defending Olympic champion, the man whose style Edwards most liked. There was a decent crowd for this trial workout, but nowhere near the 85,000 capacity that would make the stadium a wonderful cauldron throughout the Games themselves. For someone like Edwards, it was important to get acquainted with the track, with the heat and humidity. In truth, the time spent in Tallahassee had already enabled him to acclimatize for the Games. The humidity in Florida proved to be far greater than anything he experienced in Atlanta, although that was due to good fortune and not forward planning. To hold the Olympics in the dog days of summer in Atlanta was madness from the athletes' perspective, but the timing meant that the Games had little serious competition from other sports for airtime in the USA. Those nice people from Coca-Cola, major sponsors of the Olympics and with their company headquarters, coincidentally, sited in down-town Atlanta, thought this made a lot of sense. Commercially speaking, of course. Those who pay for the five-ringed circus get to call most of the tunes.

Edwards came, jumped, won, and cramped. Surprisingly, the triple jumpers were condemned to remain in the humid arena under a burning sun without a semblance of cover. 'I think it alerted me – and probably everybody else – to the problems of dehydration and the possibilities of cramping up and being unable to perform.' Nonetheless, Edwards claimed a morale-boosting win over Conley; and there would be sideless tents to give shade to the athletes during the Games themselves.

Deep down, however, Edwards left Atlanta fearing he was a stranger to his own prodigious talent. Not long afterwards, in Rome at the beginning of June, he would discover how fragile he was, mentally speaking. The triple jump competition in the Eternal City had been delayed for what seemed an eternity, an irritation that Edwards allowed to prey on his mind. 'I got extremely angry that the competition was taking place so late,' he said. He wished to be aboard a homeward-bound flight, not stuck on a runway in the Olympic Stadium in Rome as midnight approached. The distance he jumped was a respectable 17.55 metres, but the jump was immaterial compared to his mental state. 'Everything in me just wanted to walk away from the competition.' This was only too clear in the post-competition press conference. Reports filed home to the British newspapers in the aftermath of his performance intimated that Edwards was on the brink of meltdown.

Eleven days later, at home in Newcastle, Edwards was conscious that he was showing the symptoms of a psychiatric outpatient, not the characteristics of a man carrying with him to the Atlanta Games Britain's best chance of an Olympic gold in the track and field. 'I know now that I created a monster in my mind,' he admitted. There was a refreshing candour in his voice as we talked over dinner, no desire to offer a catalogue of trusted and plausible excuses as he explained why he had begun the most crucial summer of his career like a man attempting to jump in leg irons.

'I've frozen under the pressure, under the weight of expectation,' he said. 'I know that a silver medal in Atlanta is essentially a failure. In competition, I've become inhibited. Tense. Strained. We all have our doubts, our demons, our uncertainties. Because I admit to some fragility, there are those who think I'm in need of a psychiatrist's couch. I receive some knowing looks, and even some top promoters have said, "Relax, calm down, Jonathan." It's nice that they care, but I can assure you I'm not a suitable case for treatment. I'm just experiencing a normal, human, emotional response to a dramatic change in circumstances.

'Last year, after two rounds I was waving to the crowd. The competition was over. I was never challenged. It was Jonathan Edwards against the tape. But I have to leave that behind. It's great, it's wonderful, I can get out the medal, look at the video – but, for me right now, it counts for nothing. At the moment, it's excess baggage and it's not helping. I need to start afresh. My rivals have had all winter to think about improving, to plot my downfall. People keep telling me I have a target on my back, and I've made what I've done look so achievable because I'm so ordinary.'

Edwards is not ordinary, though. He is a warrior in running spikes. In Rome, he had been a Christian thrown to meet his fate. He had trailed Cuban Yoelbi Quesada until the moment he improved his mark from 17.20 metres to 17.55 metres with his final jump, just before the witching hour. His pride, his resolve, had maintained his unbeaten record stretching over the past 18 months. 'I'd resigned myself to losing,' he said, 'but I produced a great jump when everything was on the line. The next challenge is to manage myself throughout a competition. I feel able to do that now. We'll find out soon enough if it's false courage.'

It is rare for any athlete, let alone a world-class one, to bare their naked soul in such a manner. Edwards has never been an exponent of self-delusion, however. He has always bled in public. Looking back now, he says, 'I could have given the impression I was taking it all in my stride, but that's not my way. I'm an open, heart-on-the-sleeve kind of guy. I've felt loneliness because not that many people experience extreme success like I did. I went from being a nobody to one of the main players and nothing prepares you for that. With hindsight, maybe I should have kept my feelings to myself and presented a strong image to the media. Maybe I should have been monosyllabic at press conferences, then dealt with my emotions in the privacy of my own back room with Alison and my friends. Maybe that would have been a better way of doing it. I didn't do it like that, did I?'

Like the man said, that's not his way, nor probably ever will be. Yet on that night in Newcastle, when other diners politely nodded in his direction and then returned to their own company, Edwards sensed he had resumed control. 'I have perhaps been trying to defend my No 1 position, my unbeaten record, rather than writing the next chapter. I believe I can go out with the butterflies, the excitement, the sickness of wishing I was somewhere else, but, in fact, not wanting to be anywhere else. That's the challenge.'

Once that had also been the challenge for Willie Banks, the American whose charisma and athleticism brought him more than just the world record. It made him the first triple jumper crowds actually came to watch. 'I like to think that might be a reflection of who I am,' he says quietly. 'I'm the type of person, I guess, who was ebullient and extrovert when I was out there. The support of the people was an important part of my jumping. But, you know, I didn't start it. It was synergistic. I was in Stockholm in 1981. At the time there were a few drunk people in the stands. I started my usual warm-up, which was clapping three times, concentrating and running. Well, I clapped three times and they mimicked me. They thought it was funny. I'd mimic them, they'd mimic me back. I ran down, jumped pretty well. They'd clap. I clapped. Each time I got up, people would join in. Really weird, but from then on it followed me everywhere.'

Banks could comprehend better than most how claustrophobic Edwards was starting to feel, surrounded by such high expectation. When the Olympic Games had last been held in the United States, Banks had been the overwhelming favourite to win gold in Los Angeles. 'I was expected to win in 1984,' he admits. 'I got a lot of publicity, then I injured myself. I remember thinking at the time, "Maybe it would be better to die now as a hero than to live on and not win the gold medal." Those were the thoughts going through my mind, silly as it may seem now. But at the time you are built up so much, that's how it gets to you.' Banks never did win the medal his talent merited.

Edwards, of course, was not alone in his quest to conquer the world in Atlanta. He had sterling support – from Alison, from Norman Anderson, from Peter Stanley, from Brendan Foster, a man bearing his own medals and scars from the track, and from the men in the unpretentious gym at Gateshead Stadium. 'See, you're still jumping rubbish, Jonathan, man!' The comments were delivered without malice and Edwards liked the honesty. He argued most convincingly to himself that he had his head wrapped around the job ahead. 'In Barcelona four years ago,' he said, 'I was a medal hope in my own mind and never even made the Olympic final. My dreams were shattered. I felt I was no good, I had no talent. Now I understand how to keep things in perspective. The build-up to the Olympics is important, but it doesn't need to be the beast I've created. I'm in a much happier state of mind, I understand the challenge ahead and I will be able to give of my best come the day.'

How those closest to him wanted to believe him. Alison Edwards had articulated her fears on camera for a BBC documentary to be screened before the Atlanta Olympics. 'Everyone who spoke made Jonathan a dead cert for the gold medal,' she says. 'But I thought, "This is sport, this is the triple jump, this is a technical event – no one can say that." I felt so bad because I was the only one who voiced any sort of doubt.' She was ironing as the camera filmed her, she recalls with embarrassment. 'We'll have to wait and see, there are no guarantees,' she counselled then, wisely. Later she would say, 'The pressure on Jonathan was absolutely enormous. I don't think he could bear it, really. To carry the hopes and expectations of a nation is a big job.'

Edwards cancelled an intended trip to compete in Madrid later in June, but otherwise he kept to the Grand Prix schedule he had devised with Andy Norman: Helsinki, Oslo, Gateshead, Crystal Palace and Stockholm. He was delighted with his form (17.82 metres) on a cold evening in Helsinki; more than satisfied with 17.68 metres in Oslo; content, if not ecstatic, with his performances in England; but then downcast about his poor jumping in Stockholm. He had his eye on the stadium record of 17.93 metres, set by American Kenny Harrison. Edwards' best effort was 17.20 metres. 'In Oslo, I remember feeling I'd got this game cracked,' he says. 'Then came Stockholm. Awful, just awful.'

By then Edwards had seen the results from the Olympic trials to determine the United States team. Harrison had jumped 18.01 metres, albeit wind assisted and therefore not legally registered. The man who had won the 1991 World Championships in Tokyo, only to succumb to injury and an unwillingness to compete much outside the United States, was back in business – big time. Conley and Quesada, Wellman and Romaine would all present a challenge, but Edwards suspected Harrison was going to be the most troublesome in Atlanta. He had been quiet for too long, and he had been overlooked, but not by Edwards.

When the moment arrived for Edwards to begin his final, serious countdown to the Games, he returned to

Tallahassee, now like a second home. The British Olympic Association had established their holding camp in the city for some 18 months and other athletes were also beginning to gather in Florida. 'It was all very relaxing,' says Edwards. 'My mind was very sharp. My chess was excellent, I can remember that. I invariably beat Roger Black. Out of sight a few times...'

He was just as aggressive on the track. At Florida State University, he participated in some track sessions with awesome sprinters like Linford Christie, Frankie Fredericks and sprint hurdler Colin Jackson. He went against the clock with them, though never head to head on the track. Over 10 metres, it turned out, he had been travelling quickest of all; over 30 metres, only Fredericks had a fractional edge over him. He is *that* fast. 'I think everybody was pretty flabbergasted. To be honest, so was I. I was absolutely flying. I knew then I was ready.'

On his final visit to Grace Church and the congregation who had welcomed him in the sleepy state capital of Florida, Edwards gave an address that was heard by team-mates Richard Nerurkar and Phyllis Smith. Edwards relived the experience of his last visit to the Olympic Games. He had been an anonymous figure then, distraught and dejected at the precise hour of Linford Christie's anointment as the world's fastest man. Edwards shared those memories, without doubting his ability to be the author of a different script in Atlanta. 'I learned from what happened to me in Barcelona and they were very important lessons for me as a Christian,' he said. 'From the devastation of losing, I had to place my trust in God. I had to understand some of the selfish motives I had.' Even as he was speaking, Edwards felt a totally different man to the one who had gone to Spain four years before. 'Coming to Atlanta, I felt completely prepared for what I had to do.'

For all that, he was still exceedingly nervous. He knew that the nation expected him to find gold in the Olympic Stadium sandpit, but for him this was never a cut-and-dried exercise. Sport is not like that. All he could do was place his trust in God, as ever. He boarded the plane for the short flight from Tallahassee to Atlanta desperate to succeed, afraid of the enormity of the challenge. This was it: let the Games begin.

Chapter 11

Silver Lining

The toughest thing about success is that you've got to keep on being a success.

IRVING BERLIN

Roger Black arrived in Atlanta at much the same time as Jonathan Edwards. Black's route to an Olympic medal in the 400 metres looked especially hazardous, given that American Michael Johnson had created an aura of invincibility around himself and world record holder Butch Reynolds was still a force in the event. Black, then, appreciated the continuation of his duel with Edwards across a chessboard.

'We played a lot in a coffee shop,' remembers Black. 'Jonathan whipped me there as well!' Black and Edwards have always had a good camaraderie, having arrived in athletics from similar backgrounds. They explore and analyse their performance, rather than accept the bald statistics of the stopwatch or the tape.

In the broadest context, Black says, 'We're all wrapped in our own stuff, but Jonathan is a very supportive person. Fundamentally, he's just an incredibly nice bloke, isn't he?' But there is a subtext, as Black explains. 'For 99 per cent of the year, if I see Jonathan he's fine, like most of us are. Yet I was privileged to see him under circumstances of pressure, that 1 per cent of the year when the real stuff comes. I thought the signs in Atlanta were good.' Even those with insight and natural intelligence can misread the signs, it seems.

Ultimately, the evening of Friday 26 July would be remembered for an event of more significance, something more shocking than the qualifying rounds of the triple jump. A bomb was detonated in the heart of Atlanta's Centennial Park, accounting for the loss of one life and staining the Olympics in bloodshed yet again. The bomber also blew wide open the hope that these Olympic Games were so heavily protected that they had been rendered impregnable, by terrorist or psychopath. Suddenly, in the dark of the night, there was fear and loathing on the streets of Atlanta; there was a constant screeching of sirens as police and medics went about their business; and there was anger that our ideals had been so senselessly betrayed.

The bomber did not strike until past midnight, and it would be crass to compare such an act of wanton terror with what had happened in the Olympic Stadium. Yet it is fair and accurate to suggest that, from an athletic perspective, Edwards was threatening to self-destruct much earlier in the evening. For the qualifying rounds there were two pits in use, laid parallel to one another on the far side of the stadium from the principal grandstand. The fates conspired to send Jonathan Edwards and Kenny Harrison to make their first jumps at virtually the same moment. Harrison went to his mark and the crowd went crazy. If Edwards had not known what to expect on the American's home turf, he did now.

Harrison responded by leaping 17.58 metres, which brought frenzied applause from the stands. His work for the night was done – he was in the final. Edwards jumped just 16.95 metres. The alarm bells were already ringing as Harrison walked past him on his way off the premises. Edwards waited impatiently for his next turn. When he was called, he bolted down the runway like a scalded cat. Unfortunately, he jumped like one too. He cleared only 16.97 metres – 'pathetic', as he would later describe it.

Still, he correctly figured that, though the automatic qualifying mark was 17 metres, there were not going to be 12 men who would outjump him. He had no wish to make a third and final attempt, his second-round effort qualifying him with something to spare. This was of no consolation as he left the field. 'I was completely demoralized and felt absolutely dreadful.' Edwards felt lost and confused, his hard-won confidence shattered.

His mood would not have been lightened when the new day – the day of the triple jump final – dawned with television and newspaper stories providing graphic accounts of the injuries caused by the bomb during the night. By good fortune and the grace of God, the murderous mayhem that the bomber intended had not occurred. The Games had been preserved from crippling tragedy by the amateurism of the explosive device that had been planted in a wastebin.

With admirable swiftness and commendable judgement, the organizers of the Olympics insisted that the Games should proceed. The Games could not, would not, be taken hostage and, fortunately, this had not become an atrocity on the scale of the massacre of 11 Israeli athletes at the 1972 Olympics in Munich.

The Israelis have taken responsibility for their own security ever since. Edwards' friend Rogel Nahum was accompanied everywhere in Atlanta by a man from the Israeli secret service. He was even with him in the warm-up arena and trackside in the stadium. 'We are still at risk from terrorist organizations,' says Nahum. 'Munich is our heritage. I think every athlete in Israel is looking differently on life. In Atlanta we had many security guys of our own from Mossad, as well as many from the local authorities. Ask Jonathan. We also had our own floor as a team in the Olympic village.' This was security on a level that would have put an international airport to shame.

The conflict in the Middle East is all too personal an experience for the Nahum family. Rogel's father, David 'Splint' Nahum, had been shot in the Yom Kippur War, the year after the Israeli athletes were murdered in Munich. 'I feel very lucky he lived,' says Rogel. Nahum is clearly held in high regard at home. He was chosen by the Israeli Olympic Committee to represent Israeli athletes when a memorial ceremony was held in Munich on the twentieth anniversary of the massacre. By the time the Atlanta bomb went off, however, the 1996 Olympics were already at an end for Nahum. He had failed by five centimetres to make the final. Voluntarily, he redirected his energies to becoming part of Edwards' support team. No one could have envisaged how huge a task that would be.

By lunchtime on the day of the Olympic final, Edwards was a mental wreck. He went to eat with Roger Black, Jon Ridgeon and Sven Nylander in the restaurant in the athletes' village. His agitation was evident, trapped on the inside seat against a wall on a table for four. 'I felt claustrophobic; I just wanted to get out,' says Edwards. 'I wasn't thinking about winning a gold medal, I was thinking I couldn't jump.'

He took sanctuary in his room. 'All of us had been given a copy of the New Testament with a verse on the front cover from the first book of Peter, chapter 1, verse 7. Of course, I had noticed it before, but this time it jumped out at me: "...so that your faith – of greater worth than gold, which perishes even though refined by fire – may be proved genuine and may result in praise, glory and honour when Jesus Christ is revealed." It put my predicament into perspective and was a great comfort to me, a reassurance. I was still in a state, but it was a very special moment. It brought back memories of 1992 and Barcelona and reaffirmed that this wasn't about me being successful. This was about my walk with God. If I win, I win; and if I don't, I don't.'

Included in his post on the table in his room was something from Alison and his sons, as well as something from his Mum. Edwards found himself in floods of tears. He called his wife, who was just as anxious all those thousands of miles away. 'Just come home,' pleaded Alison tearfully. 'Don't put yourself through it, it's not worth it.' As Edwards fretted, there was a knock on the door. Outside stood British team manager Malcolm Arnold. He was calling to offer his own support. 'It was unexpected, but I was appreciative of his effort. What on earth he made of me, red-eyed with an Olympic final only hours ahead, I can't imagine!'

Edwards would willingly have spirited himself onto a plane at that point, if he could have done. 'I thought what Alison was saying was a jolly good idea. I didn't want to go through with it.' Nonetheless, against the background of this emotional turmoil, Edwards headed not for the departure lounge, but for the warm-up track. Surprisingly, his concentration was interrupted by a man who should have known better. Innocent Egbunike, a former accomplished 400 metres runner, now working for a Christian organization, asked Edwards to have photographs taken with him just as he was about to go to the stadium to report for the final. 'It really annoyed me,' says Edwards. 'I remember posing and smiling and thinking, "I don't want to do this." That day was the most important of my career and I was furious inside. But I did it anyway.' Edwards had still not learned the art of being able to say no.

Once in the Olympic Stadium, he had to acquire his focus in a hurry. He was drawn to jump No 2 out of the 12 finalists. Harrison was jumping tenth, with Conley last. 'Some athletes like to go early, set a mark,' says Edwards. 'I know Steve Backley prefers to throw early: bang, follow that. I don't. I like to see what everybody else has done, then respond. I can take heart from the fact that everyone has jumped poorly, or I can be stimulated by the fact that somebody's jumped well.'

In the circumstances, all he could do was try to intimidate from the front. When he was introduced as the man to jump next, he caught his first glimpse of a group of British supporters whose allegiance was unmissable. Each one of them had a letter on the front of their T-shirt and when they stood up in a line, their message read, 'K-I-N-G E-D-W-A-R-D-S'. He smiled appreciatively. All he had to do now was live up to yet more expectation. He was unbeaten in his previous 22 competitions over the past 20 months. He owned the four longest jumps in history. He was the man. Surely, those were thoughts to sustain him as he sprinted down the runway for his first jump.

His leap was impressive – he suspects around 17.70 metres – but that was all academic when a red flag was raised to show that he had fouled. Edwards looked wryly at the replay on the giant scoreboard, rising way above the stands not far from where the Olympic flame was flickering towards the night sky. He had been betrayed by his big toe crossing the take-off board. 'I think it would have been a completely different competition had that jump gone in,' he said later. 'It would have set my stall out: Jonathan's back in business. I was in great shape, and I would have relaxed, knowing I had five more jumps to really get out there.'

Edwards had blundered by the tiniest margin, and Harrison went for his jugular. With his first jump, he cleared 17.99 metres, a new Olympic record. The crowd screamed like they do for a touchdown in gridiron football. All around the sandpit, flags were waving as if it was a Fourth of July parade. Edwards was now competing not just against Harrison, but against a nation.

Harrison is how the Americans like their sporting heroes: rough, tough and ready to rumble. In Atlanta he had rings in both ears and wore a goatee beard. Remarkably, he was competing in his first Olympics at the age of 31. Since winning the World Championships in Tokyo in 1991, his career had been blighted by injury and inconsistent form. He was habitually absent from the scene for long stretches; he was an enigma. Yet there was no doubting the menace he posed to Edwards that night. From the moment Harrison hit the board, there was a sense that he was in a dazzling flight pattern. When he landed, he pumped his arms. He was a prizefighter and Edwards was on the canvas.

The Englishman understood his predicament even better as he produced a second no-jump. This time he overstepped the board by an even greater margin. An error on his next jump and Edwards, the favourite for the gold medal, would be out of the competition.

If the suspense in the stadium was becoming unbearable, for Alison Edwards at home in Gosforth there was a feeling of acute desperation. She was not watching at this stage – she could not bear that. As it was past 1.00 a.m., she was upstairs, but she was getting a running commentary from her close friend Linda Donaldson, who was monitoring the television in the lounge. 'It was agonizing,' says Alison.

A few miles away, Norman Anderson was listening to the commentators and blanching for Edwards. His blindness does not allow him to see the television properly, but he can build the images in his mind. Anderson knew precisely where Edwards stood at this moment. 'Like Marlon Brando's character in *On the Waterfront*, Jonathan was on a one-way ticket to Palookaville.' As Edwards contemplated his critical third jump, Anderson was feeling frustrated. 'Jonathan has the talent to have wiped the floor with Harrison.' That frustration would turn to pride, but he did not know that just yet.

In the stadium in Atlanta another man, apart from Edwards, was also overwrought with a feeling of helplessness. Willie Banks had met the Englishman before the Games began. There was an instant rapport between the two record-breaking triple jumpers and Banks felt he had the key to make Edwards technically unassailable. 'Right before the Games, we had a chance to talk,' explains Banks. 'We talked triple jump for an hour or so. One of the things I showed him was his take-off arm – he needed to shorten the lever. This gets a little technical, but he needed to shorten the lever so that he wouldn't take off forward of the board. Instead, he came off the board and he was continuing to go forward rather than straightening up off the board and being able to hold the jump. What happens is, he makes it through the first and second phase, but by the time he gets to the third phase, he's too far forward. You can see it. He goes *bam*, *bam*, then *bump* into the dirt.

'We never had a chance to go outside and work on it. If I could have worked on it, he would have that Olympic gold medal. And he would have jumped 18.40 metres, I guarantee you. It was so minor an adjustment, I just wished I could run across to the other side of the stadium to tell him, "Cut that stinking arm." In my mind, that one flaw was what separated him from the gold medal. He was a better athlete that day than Kenny [Harrison]. He just wasn't able to get that arm right.'

At trackside, Edwards was not short of encouragement, even if Banks could not get his message across. Andy Norman was pacing up and down behind the fence separating the crowd from the athletes. Rogel Nahum was trying to keep Edwards' mind together for him. Brian Wellman, his rival from Bermuda, the man Edwards had so graciously assisted in the midst of the bedlam of Gothenburg a year earlier, was trying to repay the Englishman for his generosity. 'Poor guy,' said Wellman later. 'Jonathan had looked terrible in qualifying. He was struggling to jump 17 metres, which, I mean, any time last year he could have tripped and fallen that far. I told him out there in the field, "Jonathan, you gotta lighten up. Can't you tell some kind of jokes or something"?' Like Edwards, Wellman is a devout Christian. 'In this sport you gotta have a good relationship with God,' he suggests.

Edwards, however, has always treated competition with the seriousness of a barrister at work in the law courts. 'It was nice of Brian, but I couldn't lighten up just like that. Brian's always tried to be encouraging in different situations. I appreciate the effort and I think it's well meant, but it probably doesn't help a great deal. I do go into my own little world. I come out of it for something specific, for something I see, or if I need a bit of advice from someone around me. Yet it's something I would prefer to seek out rather than something I invite.'

Edwards' objective in this steaming cauldron was so difficult, yet so simple that it could have been explained to the nursery class his oldest son Sam attended on Tyneside. He had to produce a leap that would place him in the top eight of the competition, or else he would qualify for inclusion in the Great British Losers hall of fame.

He stalked along the side of the runway in sweatshirt and track pants. He was staring ahead, seeing nothing. 'I was down and the referee had reached nine ... I was praying madly. I was fighting for my survival.' When his action is at its smoothest, he never thinks about hitting the take-off board. It just appears beneath his feet at the point of his maximum speed, he says. How he needed to rediscover that rhythm at this moment of truth! When his turn in the third round arrived, the track announcer said blithely, 'On the runway, world record holder Jonathan Edwards.' He omitted to add that Edwards had one foot over the precipice and if he perpetrated one more tiny mistake, he was history. The crowd knew anyway.

Edwards had brought his run-up back, to try to ensure that he would not foul on the board. 'In '95 my run-up was perfect, I hardly ever fouled. My rhythm was beautiful. But I think that the tension, the element of striving, just changed things. I didn't have the accuracy.' Contemplating that third jump, Edwards somehow managed to calm himself. He was thinking clearly, he was breathing deeply, slowly. He was ready.

As usual, Edwards rocked on his heels. Again, then once, twice more. He stared down the track long and hard, as though he was trying to bore a hole in the stadium. He placed his hands over his head, as Willie Banks had done that night in Stockholm in 1981 when a few drunks had responded by clapping back. Those in the stand closest to the pit took Edwards' lead and created a symphony of rhythmic applause to accompany him down the runway. He hit the board, his face drawn and tight, and his rhythm was good. He landed beyond the 17 metre mark, the white flag was raised and Edwards emerged from the sand to punch his fist. He had opted for conservatism, to ensure that his flight was legal, and his distance was measured at only 17.13 metres. It was enough to elevate him into the bronze medal position, however, and – most importantly – he had qualified for the final series of three jumps.

He had torn up the ticket to Palookaville and replaced it with a ticket to enter the Olympics proper. With his fourth-round jump, Edwards soared to something approaching his potential. He jumped 17.88 metres. Harrison must have felt his rival's breath on the back of his neck. 'I don't know where I got 17.88 metres from. Suddenly, bang! It didn't even feel great, but the competition began for me then.'

As Edwards patrolled an area near the runway, he was no longer a figure of desperation. His mood was vibrant. He was rising to the challenge and could do no more than that. His courage had not been found wanting. Those still watching on television in Britain would know that he had dug deep within himself. He had a silver medal assured now, but his eyes were fixed firmly on the gold. He was the best and he was endeavouring to prove it.

In the midst of the crowd was Dick Booth, the coach from the University of Arkansas, the man behind Mike

Conley and Brian Wellman. He heard a burst of disgruntled voices, their accents unmistakably English. 'They were very much Jonathan fans, that's the reason they were there,' he says. 'But they started grumbling when he wasn't beating everybody. They kind of got down on him. "What's wrong with him?" they demanded. He's competing against the very best people in the world in this event and he's right there in second place, and they're asking what's wrong! I told them they should have some more people in the top two in the world. I felt that was so sad, that the expectations had gotten so high that you almost couldn't succeed. You know, anything short of a world record and winning, and he was considered to have had an off day. You've got to let these guys be human.'

On this evening, Edwards was having to defer to Harrison. His response to the Englishman's fourth-round revival was spectacular. The American's next jump was 18.09 metres, smashing his own Olympic record. The crowd went ballistic. Edwards was unperturbed. He had two jumps left. Overstepping the board spoiled the first one, but far from discouraging him, he took heart from that effort. 'My transition into the take-off was brilliant. I had discovered what I was doing wrong. I had found a rhythm. I had one jump left and I really thought I could win it. I thought, "I can jump 18.20 metres here, no problem."'

His concentration was marginally distracted as it became apparent that there was a commotion going on at the other side of the stadium. The start of the men's 100 metres was creating pandemonium – and central to the drama was Linford Christie. There was a roar of disbelief from 80,000 people as for a third time the starter fired his recall gun. To Christie's fury, he was the culprit. This was the second time he had been judged to have anticipated the start, and the rules decreed that he had to be disqualified. Christie was in a daze. He disputed the call and stripped down to his Lycra shorts. He did not leave the track until referee John Chaplin was summoned.

Across the stadium, Edwards tried to comprehend what was happening. His mind was swirling, and he was rewinding the calendar four years to Barcelona. Had Christie not been acclaimed as the fastest man in the world at those Olympic Games, at the precise moment when Edwards had failed to qualify for his final? Had Edwards' misery not been compounded by the sight of Christie joyously celebrating his gold – not because he did not want Christie to win, but because his triumph merely served to exacerbate his own sense of failure? 'I was thinking, "The opposite is going to happen here and now,"' says Edwards. 'It seemed God's plan and purpose. I thought, "This could be it!" The symmetry was right there. It was one of those spine-tingling moments, so tangible that I believed the competition was mine to take.'

Edwards could not have felt more positive. He was waiting to jump into Olympic history. He careered down the runway, took off and felt exhilarated. When he landed, he sensed the jump was around 18.20 metres, but as he turned round he saw the judge's red flag raised. He had fouled. 'I was that much from the gold,' he would say later, holding his thumb and index finger a fraction apart. 'Suddenly, I was running hard at the board and jumping like I did all last year. It was an incredible feeling.'

Harrison had one last jump still to make and Edwards, instinctively, went to the side of the runway to clap for him. 'Whatever I had jumped in my last round, the form Kenny was in, he could have come out and broken my world record.' In fact, Harrison fouled and Edwards was there to greet him as he clambered from the sand-pit. Harrison did a somersault. He had double reason to celebrate because, only a short time before, his live-in girl-friend Gail Devers had successfully defended her 100 metres Olympic title.

As Edwards embraced the man who had taken the gold medal which the British public had imagined was already engraved with the Englishman's name, Harrison confided in his ear, 'I would have been happy to come second.' Edwards laughs now – and only wishes he had known that beforehand. 'I was convinced he was going to jump far,' he says. Edwards took a lap of honour that evening and the crowd did not begrudge him. 'I had won silver, not gold, but I could have gone away with nothing. It was a lovely lap of honour.'

Unknown to Edwards, his wife was deflated, angry even, at home in Gosforth. In the early hours of the morning, she exchanged consoling words with Edwards' parents. 'I know Jonathan did everything but win,' says Alison. 'He was under enormous pressure and, but for a tiny foul, his last jump was brilliant. Yet I felt absolutely devastated. I couldn't come to terms with it at all. It probably sounds silly, but I just felt that God had let us down. I felt we had been through so much in the past year and God had brought us to a place where Jonathan was jumping so well, and yet the competition was such a struggle. Part of me feels that was his time. Looking back, if he was going to win the Olympics, it should have been then.'

In the stadium, one of the first to reach Edwards was Brendan Foster, his friend from the Northeast, wanting to interview him for BBC television. Edwards recalls their meeting like this: 'I was kind of exhilarated, but I thought I was met with a flat response from Brendan. I hadn't won the gold and I think everyone was flat. I was met with just nothing. You give so much, put so much on the line, and then there's this dismissal of the achievement. I thought that was grossly unfair. I resented that response, not so much from Brendan, but in general. It was gold or nothing. Everybody just assumed I would win. Part of it, I think, was that people just didn't know how to respond. I was delighted with my performance and my medal – and it was a genuine delight, I wasn't just putting on a brave face.'

Foster refutes the suggestion that he was the slightest bit dismissive. On the contrary, he suspects these Games were close to being Edwards' finest hour. Foster is worth hearing from in detail on this. 'I think Jonathan's performance in Atlanta was one of the great athletic performances of his life. When you're jumping as fast as he was in '95 and as strong as he was in '95 and as brilliantly as he was in '95, then jumping out of the pit in the World Championships is the culmination of your season; that's what you do. And as he's a great competitor, that's what he did.

'The next year he was up against it; he had a hell of a tough year. He had difficulty coping with the interest in him, his training had been haphazard, he was down, and these things affected him. He actually battled his way through and when he got into the Olympic arena, he performed brilliantly. He nearly won. I honestly believe that was as good an athletic performance as his previous thing [Gothenburg]. He was carrying all that baggage, all those burdens, and he came through.

'In sport and athletics, when you're asked to test yourself, it's not when everything is going for you. When you're suddenly faster, suddenly stronger, suddenly better, the wind is blowing in the right direction, you win every competition. Boof, all of a sudden the sun is shining on his back in Gothenburg and he jumps out of the pit. That's a great athletic performance, but a greater test of him as an athlete, and a greater test of his competitive ability, took place in Atlanta. He could easily have cracked. If you go into the Olympic arena and you get humiliated, you might never pick yourself up again.'

Foster is talking from experience. He had been Sebastian Coe's room-mate in Moscow and he recalls training with him the day after Steve Ovett had beaten him to take the gold medal in the 800 metres. 'We were out running – and this was in the days before the tabloid press took a huge interest in athletics – and a great lorry came along and a photographer took pictures from the back. Coe said to me afterwards, "If I don't win the 1500 metres, I'm off. I can't take this any more." I believe, if he had lost that race, he would have had two crushing blows and he would have been humiliated in public once too often. So the first thing I actually said to Jonathan in Atlanta was, "Congratulations!" He said, "It was all right, wasn't it?" and I said, "It was great."'

Faced with the suggestion that this was not the automatic response at home in Britain, where Edwards had been the shortest-priced odds-on favourite to return to Newcastle festooned in gold, Foster says robustly, 'Who cares? I finished third in the 10,000 metres at the Montreal Olympics in 1976 and everybody was expecting me to win. People were expecting me to win because they had been told that I was going to win. But the people who expected you to win didn't get up at 7 o'clock in the morning and run 10 miles, did they? Even so, I was feeling terrible after the race in Montreal when I met Cliff Temple, the late athletics correspondent of the *Sunday Times*. Cliff said,

"You know, the thing is this: as soon as your race was over, Morecambe and Wise came on the television. So people watch the athletics, and they go, 'Hard luck, lad, good effort,' and then settle down to watch Morecambe and Wise." Cliff was saying that you can't carry the burden of others, it's too big and at the end of the day they don't care. I've said to loads of athletes, "Who else is losing sleep tonight after the Olympics final apart from you? Your very close associates, two, three, at most a dozen people. Those are the ones you need to worry about, not the other 50-odd million."'

At home in Newcastle, Norman Anderson was trying to evaluate Edwards' silver medal in Atlanta. 'It was a failure, but it was a success,' he suggests. 'It was a failure in the sense that I think the strong competitive man would have wiped the floor with Harrison. That sounds an arrogant statement, but I know about competition. I've worked with Crammy [middle-distance runner Steve Cram], been to World Championships with him. I know the pressures. I've worked with Daley Thompson, not a lot, but he let everyone know that he thought he was the best. That's Daley: "You've got to kill me to beat me," and he's still the same now. He's still arrogant. I'm not saying you have to like him, but he believed he was the best. Now, I thought Jonathan was like that, but he's not. So he let it get to him. So that was the failure. The success was getting back into the competition. But Jonathan has the ability to have put the triple jump out of sight.'

To Edwards, that is an oversimplification. In his mind, he begins each competition having to prove himself. It was like that in Atlanta, despite everyone else making him out to be a banker to win gold, in the way that Steve Redgrave and Matthew Pinsent were expected to win gold in the coxless pairs. On the morning of 27 July, less than 10 hours after the bomb had exploded in Centennial Park, Redgrave and Pinsent duly obliged on Lake Lanier, a 90-minute drive from Atlanta.

Unfortunately, Edwards came up one colour light on the same day. Nonetheless, he understood the value of that medal; he knew how close he had been to leaving town empty handed. He went to receive his silver at the medal presentation in the stadium the next day and there was a smile of genuine accomplishment on his face.

Three days later he went to Hexham, some 20 miles west of Newcastle, to run in a 100 metres race and an enthusiastic crowd engulfed him. Sometimes, medals other than those coloured gold really do have a silver lining.

Chapter 12

Bumps and Bruises

Real friendship is shown in times of trouble;
prosperity is full of friends.

EURIPIDES

After the Olympics, life quietened down for Edwards, although the final weeks of the summer proved to be a financial boom. He won $200,000 in prize money from the lucrative Grand Prix circuit. Yet once the Olympic flame had been extinguished in Atlanta, the sports pages of the British newspapers were dominated with the onset of the new football campaign. Edwards concluded his own season in relative anonymity.

In common with all frontline athletes, Edwards' emphasis for the summer of 1997 was centred on the World Championships in Athens. He had a title to defend, of course – the title that had made his name. If, however, he hoped that a new year would deliver better championship fortune, he was in for a rude awakening.

In only his second competition of the 1997 season, while he was jumping in the European Cup on a rainy day in Munich, Edwards sustained an injury to his left heel.

He had long since jumped with heel pads inserted into his spikes to cushion his feet on impact. As a legacy of an old injury, the pad in his left shoe was slightly larger than the other one, to afford that heel greater support. On that day in Munich, he had swapped them over. 'My right foot was a bit sore and I felt it needed more protection.'

Unfortunately, Edwards suspects that the pad in his left shoe was not sufficiently snug to contain his heel. On the hop phase of his second jump, he felt a twinge of discomfort in his left foot. After all these years, he is sensitive to every tweak in his body. As any athlete would have done in the circumstances, he went to a physiotherapist to have the heel iced. His experience told him over the next week that the injury was not healing as hoped. Despite that, he kept a commitment to jump at Sheffield, where he competed in larger heel pads borrowed from jump coach Dennis Nobles, visiting Edwards on a vacation from Florida State University. Nobles wore the pads in his ordinary street shoes as a kind of shock absorber to protect his abnormally short Achilles tendons.

Still fearful of damaging his heel, Edwards began tentatively in Sheffield. He aborted his first jump. At the second attempt, he took a deep breath and – hang the consequences – hopped, stepped and jumped deep into the sandpit. He had easily jumped 17.54 metres, casting Olympic champion Kenny Harrison into the shade. Harrison could not match that distance. 'Had I been completely fit, I would have jumped 18 metres,' said Edwards. Instead, he pulled out. His calendar was dominated by the World Championships in Athens and this was no place to risk making the injury worse. A bruised heel to Edwards is like a bruised hand to Lennox Lewis, a point of contact that cannot be avoided. Not a gambler by nature, he would prefer to arrive in Athens devoid of competition rather than eliminate himself on the road to Greece. They do not award any medals in Sheffield.

For six weeks Edwards declined to compete, a decision which threatened to undermine his relationship with Norman Anderson. Anderson was his weights coach at Gateshead Stadium, an experienced physiotherapist and, for Edwards, much more besides. Anderson was a confidant, a motivator and an amateur psychologist.

'We had a difficult time,' admits Edwards. 'I felt Norman dismissed my problem as a minor injury and yet I felt competing on it was too big a risk. I had a physical problem. I wasn't making anything up.' Edwards pauses briefly, then taps his temple with a finger. 'Norman was more concerned with what was going on here than what was going on with my physical condition. When I need a physio, I just need a physio. Sometimes, our closeness confused that issue and I think this was a case in point.'

Outside Gateshead Stadium, the wind is stiff and icebox cold, as you would expect on this March morning in 1999. Inside, the air is warmed by the Geordie accent of Norman Anderson, a man of indeterminable age, with sons of 34 and 31. He is part of the fixtures and fittings of the gym.

Edwards is doing a set of lifting, snatching the bar above his head before releasing the weights to the floor in a crescendo of noise. It sounds as if the roof is falling in, but Anderson is oblivious as he enthuses over Edwards' effort. A mobile phone rings and Anderson reaches for his bag close by. 'I've told you not to ring when I'm working,' he says into the phone. 'These young girls will *not* stop bothering me!' Others around laugh quietly, as they know Anderson is speaking to an imaginary caller. It is a standard joke within the gym: Anderson's cellular phone never rings. The call was for Edwards, but he lets the phone ring unanswered. He is busy with his next snatch.

Anderson is not tall, but his square shoulders have been defined by years of lifting weights. He is a power-lifter, a past competitor in the World Championships in his age and weight category. The gym is his domain. He trades in the latest jokes with the other men, while never forgetting that to him this is a place of work. Anderson intuitively encourages Edwards to scale the heights of his own potential. There is an obvious chemistry at work, a mutual affection.

Nonetheless, Anderson admits that their relationship, built at the gym near the banks of the Tyne, has not always flowed smoothly. 'Jonathan and I have had our ups and downs,' he says, by way of an opening gambit. Three months have elapsed since that cold, spring morning in the gym. We are now in the lounge of his spotlessly tidy semi-detached house, a five-minute drive from Edwards' own home in Gosforth. Anderson negotiates a coffee table in the middle of the room to take a seat in his favourite armchair with such dexterity that for a moment it is easy to forget that he is registered as legally blind.

Denis Kapustin had beaten Edwards the day before, on a rain-washed afternoon at his home stadium in Gateshead, the first track-and-field meeting since CGU had announced a four-year, £10-million contract with UK Athletics. This was the second weekend in succession that the Englishman had fallen to the Russian. Edwards was at a low ebb when he rang Anderson that evening. 'If he had been a drinking man, I'd have told him to get drunk,' says Anderson.

They arranged to meet the next afternoon. 'Jonathan's said to me in the past that he's a good competitor, that there's nothing wrong with his competitiveness. Clearly there is. Now, nobody expects him to jump a world record every time, but you expect him to bomb out the Russian guys, don't you? This Kapustin had come to Gateshead to take Jonathan on in front of his own crowd. Jonathan should have wiped the floor with him. Have you seen him? He's a big horse. But he's got a rock-hard backbone. He didn't give two monkeys about being in front of Jonathan's crowd.'

Anderson is a man of diverse talent, who has been involved with athletes dating back to Jimmy Alder, who won the marathon at the Commonwealth Games in 1966. Brendan Foster tells a story which he believes encapsulates the essence of the man who began to go blind when he was a 12-year-old growing up in Byker, a hard, working-class neighbourhood of back-to-back houses in Newcastle. Foster had planned an attempt on the world two-mile record at Crystal Palace in 1973, only to get injured the week before the scheduled race.

This is Foster's account of what followed: 'I began to have treatment and I asked Norman what he felt I could do to keep my training on track. He instructed me to jog two miles on grass, then see him, before jogging another two miles the next day. I was expected to run a 1500 metres race for Great Britain at Crystal Palace on the Saturday, and make the two-mile world record attempt on the Monday. I left Newcastle on Friday to go to London and Norman assured me my leg was healed. But he told me that after the 1500 metres race I would be sore as hell the next day. I was not to worry, though – the soreness would be caused by the scar tissue round the injury. I equalled the British record for 1500 metres, and the next day I was as sore as Norman said I would be.

'I rang Norman and he said I was not to be concerned. He also told me that I would be sore when I warmed up on Monday for the two-mile race. He was right again, and when I set off in the race I remember thinking, "What's going on here?" Well, I broke the world record that afternoon – and, to be honest, if he hadn't told me how I was going to feel, I would never have done it. I would have thought my leg was too sore to think about running. That was the skill of the man. He knew what to do to keep me from getting down: like making me jog a couple of miles on grass; like telling me I was going to be sore. He's a great psychologist.

'It was not only me he helped. Steve Cram was like a thoroughbred, always on the brink of injury. Crammy broke world records as a middle-distance runner after Norman had had to repair the pieces. Norman actually gave Steve his own ultrasound machine to use on himself. I honestly believe Jonathan would not have been the athlete he is without Norman. He influenced him and made him a stronger man; once he was stronger, Jonathan jumped further. Jonathan's power-to-weight ratio is unbelievable.'

Anderson's contribution to athletes in the Northeast is even more remarkable given his impaired sight, which grants him only peripheral vision. He has also had to overcome another, even more calamitous condition. Anderson had a nervous breakdown and he was diagnosed as clinically depressed. 'You never recover from depression, of course. It's an ongoing illness,' he says. 'You learn to live with it and adapt. It's ironic that, rightly or wrongly, I'm credited with providing this mental support. I used to say to people like Steve Cram, "You do the running, I'll do the worrying."'

His illness coincided with a bad car crash that happened in 1984. He was running in those days and he was returning from a veterans' 10,000 metres race in Wiltshire when the car his wife Oriel was driving was involved in a head-on collision. Anderson sustained crushed vertebrae in the accident. 'I went into deep depression shortly afterwards,' he explains. 'I couldn't go out. I'd just sit in the dining room and cry.'

For almost three years he was imprisoned by the four walls of his own house. 'My life seemed to stop. I reached the stage where I felt so suicidal and I felt as though people didn't appreciate how ill I was.' Anderson admitted himself to hospital. 'My mother had died of cancer when I was 16, and the old man hanged himself when I was 23. Those are things that are bound to impact on you. I had a long period of psychiatric help which, without knocking the people who did it, I didn't find particularly helpful. I had cognitive therapy, all sorts, but the therapists would usually end up saying that, as I had a very good insight, there was nothing more they could do. I asked a lot of questions, you see, so how could I be depressed?

'It becomes very frustrating and after a while you realize what you should have realized straight from the start: it's down to you. The best advice I ever got – and I only realized it much later – was from a consultant psychiatrist, who told me take the pills, sit still and let time pass. Honestly, I think that's what you do. Having said that, that's not a cure. You then have to look at your life and organize it differently – which is what I did, and this is very relevant to my relationship with Jonathan.'

Anderson is a complex man. He studied to become a physiotherapist, because he discovered that this was a subject that was taught to people with impaired vision. 'I was born to be a shipyard worker or a miner. Instead I found myself in a woman's profession. I didn't know what physiotherapy was, but I didn't care. I didn't know how much sight I had left. At 14, I was told I would be blind within a year.' That Doomsday scenario did not materialize, but Anderson's sight slowly deteriorated. 'I look at you and I can't see you at all. I'm totally blind looking straight down the middle. I see round the sides. People think I can see more than I can because I've had 50 years to get used to it, but it's worse than ever now.'

As a student, Anderson sailed through the three-year physiotherapy course. He was already beginning to become sceptical about physiotherapy, however, and his first jobs in hospitals in the Northeast reinforced the doubts that were taking seed in his mind. 'The physiotherapy I saw was appalling, a waste of time.' His most pleasurable appointment was at a miners' rehabilitation centre, but after three years he felt he needed a new challenge and he went back to college to qualify as a teacher. His wife is also a physiotherapist, but given Anderson's deep mistrust for the profession, they no longer discuss the topic at home.

He was teaching at a local polytechnic when he had the nervous breakdown. He was pensioned off with a phrase that cut him to the core: 'unfit to practise'. 'It sounds so hurtful. I'll always remember that.' Anderson was also operating a private physiotherapy practice with his wife, but felt unable to continue. 'I lost faith in physiotherapy. I still get nightmares.' Local athletes were among his clientele, although Edwards was not one of them, but Anderson became aware of him at Gateshead Stadium. As part of his rehabilitation, Anderson had drifted into the gym and began to experiment with weight training. 'With depression, physical activity usually helps. It produces a chemical release in the brain. For me, the most therapeutic thing of all is ironing!'

Anderson recalls of those days, 'We used to train on one side of the gym and the athletes, as they called themselves, would train on the other side. There was a group of them, young men and women, and there was a lot of chatting and giggling. There seemed to be a lot of lying on the mat and lounging around. We started to take the mickey. "What are you doing?" I used to ask. "I see you're doing six sets of lying down and five sets of laughing." I've always trained very hard, you see. The next thing I knew, I was talking about lifting and injuries with Jonathan; it wasn't something that was planned. Now, technically he was very, very good. I think Carl Johnson has to take some credit for that. Jonathan is an Olympic lifter, doing clean lifts, which is something I couldn't do to save my life. But my feeling was that he was wasting his time, and we began to talk about the amount of weight he should be lifting, the number of sets, the quality. That's how we got involved.'

Edwards has been something of an odd man out in this gym, full of men who earn money from their muscle, sometimes overstepping the law. 'One guy used to come in with a bullet-proof vest and armed,' says Anderson. 'Not that anyone ever caused a problem in the gym – we were no threat to them. There were guys who offered to protect Jonathan.' From what, was never made clear.

These two men have been drawn together from alien worlds: Edwards, the privately educated son of a vicar, a Christian and world-class athlete; Anderson, a fatherly figure hewn from a harsh, working-class environment, an atheist, registered blind and fearful of slipping back into depression. Yet they have taken strength from each other, and their lives might have been fundamentally different had they not come into one another's orbit.

To Edwards, Anderson is a sounding board as well as a trusted instructor in the weight room. 'He seems nearly always to understand what's going through my head. I know why Brendan used to visit him even when his legs weren't hurting: he just had to hear what Norman had to say.'

To Anderson, what Edwards supplies is a therapeutic insurance against the depression that constantly stalks him. 'Jonathan has been a vehicle for my rehabilitation; he still is. I feel useful, I feel as though I've been helpful to Jonathan, but I disagree with those who say I made him. Jonathan Edwards made Jonathan Edwards. He has achieved what he has, no one else. But I like to think that, if there were a balance sheet drawn up of his career, I would come out on the plus side. Having said that, he's been a big plus to me. He helped me restore some of my self-belief. I can't exaggerate how much he has helped me. Without him, I would have begun to get better, but it would have been a lot more difficult. That's why I bother. If you want it in simple terms, it gives me something to do. Depressives quite easily get up and think there's nothing for them but to sit around all day. There's a strong self-motivation in what I do.'

Inevitably, there have been moments when they have not seen eye to eye. Anderson has never properly under-stood Edwards' motivation for acquiring assistance in his professional life from outside sources. Given Anderson's own cynicism towards physiotherapy, Edwards has on occasion felt the need to seek another opinion. 'Norman's influence is crucial and we will always be inextricably linked, but I never realized he would react so negatively to outside intervention from other people I have seen, like Raimo my masseur or Jan Pospisil.'

Anderson admits to feeling disappointed when Edwards employed Finn Raimo Suikkanen as his masseur and embraced the ideology of Pospisil, a brilliant coach steeped in the knowledge of the old Czechoslovakian Communist regime. For a time, Edwards wore roller blades at the gym. He also stretched out to a new programme of exercises, some of which made him look as if he was auditioning for a part in a remake of Monty Python's 'Silly Walk' sketch. 'We took the mick. He looked ridiculous,' says Anderson.

'A lot of what Pospisil suggested is useful, but not new. Does it make any difference? No. Does it keep him happy? Yes. I watched him running with his arms over his head and then above his backside and everybody at the stadium was wetting themselves laughing. But is it doing any harm? No, of course not. So let him do it. That's how I rationalize it. The big problem is Jonathan's technique. The obvious schedule is to keep yourself strong and quick with weights and running and so on. Then you practise your technique, so that you can apply it. But do you know what happens? Jonathan has a pain in his foot. End of conversation.'

There is no question that their relationship came under increasing strain through 1997. Edwards knew he was injured – and he was handicapped by a hamstring injury as well as a bruised heel – but Anderson was sceptical. 'In 1997, I told him to confront the real problem; and I told him his foot was not the real problem,' says Anderson. 'Perhaps I did go over the top. My attitude was that the pain was an irrelevance. Well, by the end of that season everything came to a head. We had a total blow-up. He became so emotional and it made me feel terrible. I felt really bad. I backed away from confrontation, because I think it would have had a really detrimental effect on me if I'd taken it full on. I even suggested to Jonathan that, if he thought it was in his best interests, I would not continue to work with him.'

Anderson has also harboured reservations in recent times that Edwards' religious convictions could have been detrimental to his athletic ambition. 'I can't see how Jonathan's religious fervour and belief in Christ has helped him at all in his athletics. It seems to have been a barrier. Perhaps I'm naive in what I think religion is. To someone like Jonathan, God cannot lose. If a plane crashes and everybody escapes, it's a miracle; if kids in Kosovo get torn to bits and you ask, "Where was God, then?" you're told that you don't understand God's work. If anything good happens, give God the praise; if anything bad happens, it's not his fault.' Anderson pauses for a moment before he adds with a smile, 'But then, Jonathan thinks I'm doomed!'

Edwards responds, 'In some ways my faith has complicated the issue, but I think, from recent conversations I've had, that Norman sees things in a different light. Just because you're a Christian, it doesn't mean you don't have an emotional response to traumatic experiences in your life. Even though he knew God was in control, Jesus wept before he went on the cross; and he was weeping over the death of his friend Lazarus, whom he knew he was miraculously and imminently going to raise from the dead.

'The understanding that if you're a Christian, you're supposed to go through life smiling is simply wrong. The truth is, the pain of watching someone extremely close to you dying is as real for us as a family as it is for anyone. To admit that doesn't preclude the fact that God is right there in it with us. I think Norman would accept that.

'As for my injuries, I wasn't afraid of competing in the summer of 1997; I was just unfit to compete. For a triple jumper, a heel injury is a cause for great concern. One false landing and there would have been no World Championships for me. Believe me, I would have jumped if I could.'

All this created a festering undercurrent between Edwards and Anderson. For a period, their peculiar bond was not as strong as it had been. Slowly, however, their relationship has been re-established since then. They have invested too much together – celebrated and commiserated, laughed and cried – not to be able to withstand a slight chop in the water of life. 'At times Jonathan is so vulnerable,' says Anderson.

Their work towards the Sydney Olympics began in earnest as the days got colder and shorter in November 1999. As usual, Edwards drove from his home to Anderson's house to collect him. In the gym, the banter was light and punctuated with laughter. Anderson's cell phone remained silent, of course.

'I really want to help Jonathan,' he says. 'I think the world of him. I also happen to think his wife and kids are marvellous; they're like surrogate grandchildren.'

Chapter 13

A Modern Greek Tragedy

*Don't aim at success – the more you aim at it and
make it a target, the more you are going to miss it.
For success, like happiness, cannot be pursued;
it must ensue … as the by-product of one's
surrender to a person other than oneself.*

VICTOR E. FRANKL

While Edwards was protecting his injured heel after that early season jump in 1997, he saw Dr Steve Calvert, a GP from near Gateshead and once a member of the British Olympic Association's medical team. Calvert has treated Edwards down the ages, yet Edwards was not prepared for one of the directions in which Calvert drove the conversation during this consultation. He asked Edwards to consider visiting a sports psychologist. Again, Edwards argued that his ailment was physical, not mental. 'Norman was there as well; it was all a bit tense,' he says. 'But I was injured, not cracking up.' All he wanted was an opinion on whether Dr Calvert believed a cortisone injection would be valuable.

Edwards is an athlete willing to explore new methods of training, but he will not be persuaded into opening his mind to a sports psychologist. This is a road down which he will not walk, no matter that psychologists are embraced across the spectrum of sport, in the same way that nutritionists and physiologists are integrated into support teams. 'I find my psychological framework with reference to my faith and my trust in God,' he says. 'I concede the obvious benefits to which many athletes testify, but for me it's not the way forward. In some areas, I feel there would be a conflict with my faith. In performance I want my focus to be directed towards God, not myself. I'm not saying I don't have psychological challenges in competing at the top level, I just choose to deal with them in a different way.' For Edwards, psychology would be nothing less than an intrusion.

At the meeting with his doctor, Edwards formulated a strategy to ensure that he travelled to Athens fit. He withdrew from all competitions and kept himself ticking over in training. Even so, this was hugely disruptive to his preparation for the World Championships. When he arrived in Athens he had not jumped for six weeks. He would have to survive on memory, trusting that his technique would not crumble in the cauldron of a competition second only to the Olympics.

Still uncertain of his fitness, imagine his relief when he cleared 17.28 metres in the first round of qualifying. It was an effortless jump, especially when compared to the trauma he had endured at Atlanta the previous summer. The final was to prove more nerve-wracking, however.

In every final, Edwards always competes in a brand-new pair of spikes. He has tried them for size, but otherwise they are straight out of the box. Another peculiarity is that he must have his shoes laced to the point of strangulation. 'I like that tight feeling so the shoes are part of me.' He had taken the precaution of getting new, cotton laces, yet when he came to tie his shoes just prior to his first jump, a lace snapped. 'I was in a complete and utter flap. I tried to thread the frayed end, only for it to snap again. It was hardly what I needed, after six weeks without a competition.'

Fortunately, Edwards always gives himself time to spare in his preparation. As the athlete ahead of him lines up on the runway, he is practically ready to move into position behind him. In Athens, the man immediately before him was Kenny Harrison, the American who took the gold medal at the Atlanta Olympic Games which the British public had felt was hallmarked with Edwards' name. As Edwards scrambled for his second pair of spikes, Harrison hit the runway. His jump proved to be of poor quality.

This was of little consolation to Edwards. To compound his concerns, he was troubled by a slight tightness in his left hamstring. 'Mentally, I was at sixes and sevens. All my mental preparation was ruined.' He began with a jump of 17.33 metres, ordinary by his own high expectations. Yoelbi Quesada from Cuba cleared 17.60 metres with his opening round. 'Like in Atlanta, had I opened with 17.70 metres – which I was eminently capable of producing – it automatically becomes a different competition. I ran through my next jump and Quesada jumped 17.85 metres. I was the one having to play catch-up.' Edwards never did recover.

Quesada had benefited from a breeze off his back of +0.9 metres per second, while Edwards jumped 17.66 metres into a –0.6 wind in the following round. 'I was a bit unlucky. A 1.5 metres per second advantage is a big difference.' Brian Wellman, the silver medal winner at Gothenburg two years earlier, the man who had pushed Edwards to achieve a greater distance in Atlanta, was again pressing the Englishman to produce some urgency in his performance. Edwards was unimpressed. 'I didn't want him in my face, though I knew he was trying to help. The truth was, he wasn't helping me at all. I'm the sort of person people think they can come up to and say these things to. No one would dream of doing the same to Harrison or Conley if they were in a hole.'

In the last round, Edwards made a fractional improvement, securing the silver medal position with 17.69 metres. Unlike in Atlanta, however, he felt no pride in that achievement. On the contrary, he was enveloped by a wave of depression. He broke down as he left the track, dissolving into tears in the company of the BBC trackside reporter Paul Dickinson, an ex-international athlete. 'I felt empty. I was inconsolable, crying for five minutes, ten minutes, who knows how long? I was shattered. The medal meant nothing.'

With the benefit of hindsight – never less than 20/20, as everyone knows – Wellman wonders aloud a couple of summers later in 1999, 'I was trying to get Jonathan to relax because, if you know anything about pressure, it can make you tighten. I'll give you a great analogy. Greg Norman held a six-shot lead going into the last round of the 1996 US Masters – and lost. It's called pressure. It's about internalizing the situation and thinking about everything else but what you need to do next. I think Jonathan's a great competitor – but perhaps only when it's not for all the marbles.

'We're talking about a guy who has the capability of winning every time; not someone who has the capability, if they do their best on the day and everything falls into place, then they can win. We're talking about this guy who has been somewhere that nobody else has been before. If you're not hurt, or not having a major terrible day, you have to ask yourself: "Why can't you produce?" He has let the big ones get away from him.'

Edwards rejects to this day any suggestion that he lacks a com-petitive edge. 'I would stand in a dock and swear that's absolute nonsense,' he says. Yet, revealingly, he adds, 'Whether I have the same need to win as other people is questionable, I would agree. We also have to take into account the world record factor. The fact is, I've jumped further than anyone in history and sometimes that has a demotivating effect, in the sense that I've done it. I've noticed that trait in other areas of my life. Sometimes, the winning or losing is immaterial. It's enough for me to prove that I can do something to a high standard, and that can manifest itself in a friendly game of tennis or golf. If I'm honest, perhaps the main competition is against myself.' In Edwards' own mind, he has proved himself beyond question the best in his event. The downside of that achievement, when you listen to him speaking as he does here, is that he has run into a brick wall.

He needed to know the purpose of his profession, more profoundly than ever. That much was evident to those around him after he had failed to defend his World Championship title in Athens. At the press conference, he heard in translation that Quesada had predicted that three Cubans would stand on the rostrum at the Olympic Games in Sydney 2000. His rivals were beginning to sense that his reign was over.

Edwards' mood on returning with his silver medal to the room he shared with Roger Black was dark and intro-spective. Black recalls, 'Jonathan threw his medal across the room. He was absolutely dejected. He was so angry, so upset with himself. Such anger! It was clear there was an accumulation of a lot of pressure. He thought he could come back [from the Olympic Games] and he could win the gold medal and that would exorcise the demons, or whatever. It hadn't happened yet again. It was two years since he set the world record and I think he started to doubt himself.' Black's own observation was that at least his anger, his disappointment, was a positive reaction. 'When you're a world record holder like Jonathan, there's only one medal that you feel can be rightly yours,' he says.

'I always say that for the first 10 years of my career, I was very good at running, but I never really had that deep understanding of what it really meant to me and why I was really doing it. I think, when you line up for the big one, that's what comes through – if you are totally at one with what this means to you and what this is about and why you have to run faster or jump a long way, then I think that can be expressed. You are at peace to do that, which is how I felt before my 400 metres final at the Atlanta Olympics.

'The problem with athletics is that you can do so well on natural talent. You come into it young and just do it – you don't understand what it really means to you because you're just good at it. When you get up against the best in the world, they're all very good. Often what separates us at that level is the ability truly to understand *why* we're doing this. It's not just jumping into a sandpit; it's not just running round a track. It's far more than that. It's about knowing you have to fulfil your potential.'

Edwards' sullenness that evening in Athens was deepened by the minutest detail. At the buffet, the sight of chocolate cakes and other confectionery reminded him of the sacrifices he had made with his diet for the past year. What had been the point? That question had a deeper relevance. He was not truthfully bemoaning the absence of the odd cake or two from his tea plate. The real question in his mind was this: 'Where am I in my life?'

For Edwards, there has to be a connection between his role as an athlete and his faith. Otherwise there is a pointlessness about his jumping. 'It had all become joyless and hard work,' he explains. 'I'd got to a level of disappointment that I thought I wouldn't experience again after Barcelona. Something was fundamentally wrong and I began a period of soul-searching. I read a lot in Ecclesiastes, a book which talks about the meaningless cycles of life. It echoed my feelings.'

Perhaps it was a little like looking in a mirror and seeing yourself begin to age? 'All sorts of things,' he says. 'I thought hard about what direction I was going in, why I was feeling like this. Where was the enjoyment and sense of purpose? I had lost a lot of my motivation.' During that spring, Edwards had read a book by Viktor Frankl, a psychoanalyst and a survivor of the Holocaust. His theme struck a chord. 'His theory is that man's primary need is to have a sense of meaning in life. He was fond of quoting Nietzsche: "He who has a WHY to live can bear with almost any HOW."'

Edwards concluded that he had wandered into a wilderness of his own creation. 'I'd lost sight of what I was doing, where I was supposed to be going with my athletics. I'd focused too much on HOW – how was I going to get my arms to work, how many weights should I lift?' These would be the responses of most athletes, of course, especially those competing in as technical an event as Edwards. But to him, this was of secondary importance in the grand scheme of his life. Jumping for jumping's sake was not enough. 'As an individual, I was dry spiritually.'

At around this time, Edwards received a letter from the Church of Scotland. Once, the Church had worked closely with Eric Liddell. He used to compete at an athletics meeting, then preach and share the gospel at a rally afterwards. 'His athletics and evangelism were tied together. I liked that,' says Edwards. Deliberately imitating that precedent, the Church of Scotland extended an invitation to Edwards to become involved in some evangelistic work in schools in Scotland. 'I was happy to make the commitment.' This was precisely the direct connection he sought between his sport and his faith. He found great pleasure in the visits he made to Scotland in 1998 and 1999, meeting children and staff, sharing his experiences and his faith.

Edwards regards himself as 'born again', a prerequisite, he believes, for any true Christian. 'I think the phrase has become pejorative, synonymous with fanaticism. It actually originates with Jesus himself. Nicodemus, a Jewish religious leader, came to Jesus to question him. In his reply, Jesus said that no man could see the Kingdom of God unless he was born again. Jesus was talking about a spiritual birth, a spiritual renewal. Later in the same conversation, Jesus gave the basis for this spiritual birth, perhaps the most famous words in the Bible, given in John 3:16–18: "For God so loved the world that he gave his one and only Son, that whoever believes in him shall not perish but have eternal life. For God did not send his Son into the world to condemn the world, but to save the world through him. Whoever believes in him is not condemned, but whoever does not believe stands condemned already because he has not believed in the name of God's one and only Son."

'Jesus makes clear that the born-again experience is essential for a relationship with God. For me, it was a natural progression from the upbringing I had. This is a reality at the heart of my being. I believe people must be prepared for the final judgement. God is loving, but he is also just. It's easy to emphasize his loving side, but God is also holy and he cannot be associated with sin.'

Edwards had been confirmed when he was 13 years old, but was later baptized by full immersion at Heaton Baptist Church. This is an area of some dispute between Edwards and his father. 'I really thought I should be baptized as a believer. My parents believe in infant baptism for the children of believers and that's the source of some interesting and animated theological discussions between us. But we can disagree and not fall out.'

In the autumn of 1997, Edwards was not only unhappy and confused in his workplace, he was also profoundly disaffected with his church. This was a situation that had been building over a long period. 'During the time of greatest pressure, we hadn't been functioning as part of a church, particularly me. Over the previous couple of years, I'd become quite isolated spiritually. I'd lost the vitality of my relationship with God and that resulted in an emptiness in what I was doing.' He had resisted leaving Heaton Baptist Church, mostly because Alison still felt part of the community there. She had been heavily involved with a mothers' Bible study group, as well as a parent and toddler group. He did not wish to disrupt her life. He knew how much she disliked change.

For a time, Edwards had been exceedingly happy in the church at Heaton. He and Alison shared the fellowship of good friends, and they were an integral part of the congregation. Edwards played guitar in the worship group, and Alison sang. Some friends moved away, but then there was an inevitability about that. Perhaps he could have sustained the loss of friends, but the root of his dilemma went deeper.

He felt spiritually adrift at Heaton. 'As a family I felt we were square pegs in a round hole. If you're going to function as a Christian, you cannot function in isolation. Full stop.' Edwards had long resisted the idea of resigning from the church, both on the principle of loyalty and the pragmatic fact of Alison's contentment. 'But, suddenly, something snapped and I knew we had to change. For too long I had assumed I was fine spiritually. The reality was different. I believe I have a God-given responsibility to be the head of our household and I wasn't leading, not in the spiritual sense. I was letting Alison and the boys down.'

Alison's situation could not shield her from her husband's increasing loneliness within the church. 'I could ring up six or seven women, full-time mums, and suggest we go to the park or pop round for a coffee. We really encouraged one another and I felt really supported. I knew Jonathan was unhappy, but this was the church we belonged to and it's not something that you change lightly. I had lots of friends, but as a couple we were lonely. Jonathan was particularly isolated. I don't know if people felt differently towards him since he had become famous, although that shouldn't have been the case. We had been at the church for over 10 years. We were still just Jonathan and Alison.

'Sometimes we would hear other couples – our contemporaries – planning to get together and we weren't included. I don't know whether that was because they thought we were too busy, or whether it was because they didn't like us! The problem became more apparent after our stay in Tallahassee. While we were there we quickly became involved with Grace Church and suddenly realized how barren our church experience at home was. We were being invited to other families' homes for dinner, for barbecues, for games of softball, and we had this great sense of belonging.'

Alison and her husband have always preferred a worship style with a strong element of involvement. 'I'm not a raving charismatic, but we like to be involved,' she says. Edwards made a reconnaissance of several churches before the family committed to Holy Trinity in Jesmond. 'We were bowled over by the warmth of the people, and it had nothing to do with Jonathan being a successful athlete. It was just a lovely, genuine feeling of being welcomed.'

Edwards also felt immediately at home. Apart from attending services, the couple have also become regular participants in a home study group which meets on Wednesdays. Their circle of friends has been enlarged. 'This has been a real boost to me, having lost a couple of close friends who moved away,' explains Edwards.

Two of these friends are Richard and Georgia Gilbertson, whose daughter Hope befriended Sam Edwards in nursery school. Sam demanded that his parents meet Hope's Mummy. Edwards and Richard Gilbertson meet regularly to pray, study the Bible and simply share friendship. 'Richard was a great friend to me through these troubled days and helped me to think through a lot of the issues I was struggling with,' Edwards says.

Two years had passed since Edwards had burst into the headlines that night in Gothenburg and he was still coming to terms with the changes that had taken place in his life. The primary issue was the connection, or lack of it, between his sport and his faith, but there was more – what might aptly be called the $64,000 question. 'As a

Christian, what is a legitimate enjoyment from what God has given us, and what is self-indulgence? Where do you draw the line? Unfortunately there's no manual. Every decision, every purchase, is a matter of conscience and prayerful consideration.'

Edwards bought a Porsche 911 Targa in May 1997, a car with a showroom price of £65,950. He had not intended to do this. His original plan was to swap the family's Toyota people-carrier for a Chrysler model. Circumstances ambushed him, however. Edwards was taken out to lunch by a friend, who arrived in his sister's Porsche. 'I got in the car and I was besotted.' The people-carrier now had as much appeal as Del Boy's Reliant Robin.

At this stage, there was no still plan to buy anything other than the Chrysler he had in mind. After lunch they drove to the Chrysler showroom, which also happened to be the local Porsche franchise. Edwards never did look at a people-carrier. He went for a test drive in a bright red Carrera. He was wrestling with his conscience but he was, by his own confession, a soft target. He was given the car for the weekend. 'I'm probably not very rational in these moments,' he admits. He could easily afford a Porsche, after all.

By chance, chef and restaurateur Albert Roux had placed an order with Porsche for two 911 Targas and now wanted only one of them. Edwards decided to take the spare order. Coincidentally, Sue Mott from the *Daily Telegraph* came to interview Edwards that July, ostensibly to check that the athlete with the boy-next-door freshness had not been contaminated by success or pharmaceuticals. Edwards chuckles at the small deception innocently created when he collected her from the station. Sue Mott wrote in her article, 'If this man, a world triple jump champion, life-long Christian, father of two small sons and driver of a D-reg Volvo, isn't the genuine article untouched by Boot's the chemist then nobody is.'[1]

His Porsche was already awaiting him in the show-room. He had deliberately stalled delivery until after the World Championships – although he did take the car for a swift spin on 1 August before departing for Athens. Of course, when he took ownership of the car on his return, Edwards was at a spiritual crossroads. 'I was selective where I took the car, firstly because I was afraid it was going to get scratched and secondly because I felt uncom-fortable. I was always fighting that, everyone notices you if you're driving a 911!'

John Hedley, his erstwhile training partner at Gateshead, often rode in Edwards' gleaming sports car. 'It's one of the things you wouldn't expect of Jonathan, but he's a boy racer at heart,' he says. 'He was absolutely enthralled for a time by this Porsche. Fantastic, it was, but he was acutely aware of it as well. One day we were out and he had the roof down and the CD player on, but as soon as we got to Bedlington, where I live, he turned the music down and put the roof up. He didn't want people to stare.

'Another time, I went to York with him for a day. He did a radio interview at a priest's house and then he did a question-and-answer session at a large hall. A few hun-dred people had turned up to listen to Jonathan talking about his faith. Of course, as we left that night, people were still coming out of the hall as we pulled away in a silver Porsche – and Jonathan had been talking with them

1 *Daily Telegraph*, 19 July 1997.

about the need for humility. He told me that night that this didn't feel right…'

The end of Edwards' Porsche-owning days occurred after he had driven to Southport to support his friend Phil Wall's charity, Hope 10/10. The charity seeks to provide critical funds for two orphanages which are home to 100 AIDS-infected children in South Africa. Wall, a communicator and trainer with the Salvation Army, tried unsuccessfully with his wife to adopt one of the children. 'When we weren't able to do that, we thought we would adopt the whole lot financially,' he says. 'We promised each other and promised God we would do that.' Edwards accepted the role of patron and says with heavy irony, 'There I was at the launch of this charity at a big Salvation Army conference. I was champion of the poor … driving a Porsche.'

After the conference, he drove from Southport to Whitehaven to visit his parents in their new parish before driving home to Gosforth. On the A595, he let the engine have its legs. 'I'd look at the speedometer and think, "Am I going that fast?" Some Christians believe the angels leave you at 70 mph – I was on my own. But as I wove in and out of the traffic, on a day that was made for driving a Porsche, I realized the contradiction of this car in my life. Nobody would have guessed that the plonker driving the Porsche was a person committed to serving God. I arrived back home and told Alison, "This car has to go."'

Edwards spent an hour and a half with the garage owner and a salesman, debating the pros and cons of the Porsche. His mind was made up, however. The car was history. Instead, he bought a Subaru Impreza, 0–60mph in the blink of an eye. 'A bad move,' he confesses. 'It was probably faster than the Porsche, but not as eye catching.

I rightly got my fingers burnt, losing a lot of money buying and selling that car.' His boy racer days were over. He tried driving a Jeep for a brief period, but by the autumn of 1999 could be seen at the wheel of a sponsored Rover 45.

Phil Wall, a man from the East End of London and a one-time boxer, which provides a handy metaphor as he is not renowned for pulling his verbal punches, watched Edwards enduring this burst of self-indulgence. As a friend, he felt compelled to ask Edwards what most represented 1995. 'Jonathan told me, "That thing," and pointed to the BBC Sports Personality Award,' recalls Wall. 'During that conversation, I offered to take the trophy to my house and let him have it back when things had regained some perspective. What Jonathan did was to move the award from the lounge to the utility room, placing it on top of the washing machine.

'To me, the trophy was synonymous with Jonathan being catapulted into a whole new stratosphere. From the beginning, there was Jonathan and his Christian faith. He nailed his colours firmly to the mast. He was always happy to live with those expectations, but because of the nature of our society, that always puts you a little bit on the fringe. People are kind of gracious, even patronizing at times. They respected him for his beliefs, but at same time it was no doubt seen as a little quirky.

'Then, of course, came two further factors. The expectation of success, and that massive expectation at the Atlanta Olympics, became one of his greatest burdens. At the same time, there was massive expectation in terms of him being perceived as a statesman for sport, a role model. Suddenly the things that were implicit – this is who I am, I'm a Christian, blah, blah – suddenly became massively explicit in front of a few million people.

'There was the Jonathan and Alison they were, then there was the Jonathan and Alison they became and thought they had to be, trying to live under the weight of this expectation. For a lot of people, that catapulting impact sends them off the end; they never come back. The problem of being an athlete is that you become incredibly selfish – your diet, your timetables, everything is focused on you. When people start throwing money at you and saying nice things, you actually start to believe it's true. It's a little like returning to your childhood. I have a 12-month-old daughter who believes she is the centre of the universe. In three or four years' time she'll accept demigodship.

'Jonathan went through that kind of experience. When he bought the Porsche, I didn't know what to say, what with my values from my upbringing, what with my commitment to the poor. Jonathan told me the car made him feel guilty. I said, "Good." Jonathan had been thrust into that world; and that's not me making a big statement and saying you can't be a Christian and own a Porsche. His options had massively increased. The questions kept arising: "What should I do?" and "What can I do?" Of course, that's every Christian's challenge, but millions were watching for Jonathan's answers.

'He told me that he had become so selfish because as an athlete you have to be. The antithesis of selfishness is the Christian faith, or at least you hope it to be. That is the core of the angst Jonathan has been through. By definition, to achieve what he needs to achieve, he needs to be incredibly selfish.

'You hunger for authentic affirmation, as opposed to what a BBC poll tells you, and what people might write. I feel I may have let him down. I've been too distant.

I haven't taken into account that he's working in an affirmation deficit. Your family affirms you because they love you; the media affirm you because that's their job. But what about people who can't get anything from you? Jonathan and Alison remain who they have always been.'

Wall has pledged to be there for Edwards along every mile of the road to Sydney. Incidentally, Edwards called Wall to tell him he had sold his Porsche. His friend, of course, was not in the least surprised.

Chapter 14
Back on Track

I came through and I shall return.

DOUGLAS MACARTHUR

His name was Pappa Nelson. He was one year old, but weighed the same as a newborn baby. Jonathan Edwards cradled him in his arms, as he would his own sons Sam and Nathan. Only Pappa was little more than a bundle of skin and bones.

Edwards was in an orphanage in an African township not far from Johannesburg in March 1998, as part of his commitment to the Hope 10/10 charity. Phil Wall felt that involving Edwards in the charity would not only be good for his project. He believed it would be beneficial to Edwards as well, providing him with a meaningful focus to assist his athletic rehabilitation after the disillusion he had expressed in the wake of the World Championships in Athens. 'Phil reasoned that the further I jumped, the more I could highlight the desperate plight of these orphans. He encouraged me to remember Pappa Nelson at the end of the runway every time I jumped.'

For Edwards, the visit to this corner of Africa omitted from the guidebooks was a step into the unknown. 'I had never come face to face with Third World deprivation and I was uncertain how I would respond,' he says. 'You hear stories of people breaking down.' Edwards did not, yet he was overwhelmed by the manner in which all the children craved to be loved. 'In my experience with my boys, they love to be cuddled by me or Alison, but when somebody new comes into their world, they become tentative. All these kids just wanted to be picked up and loved. Every single one of them seemed starved of love and affection. You were engulfed with these lovely little kids just wanting a cuddle; it was lovely, and also very sad.'

The children – and there were almost 40 of them, no more than two years old – were caringly catered for, but Edwards says, 'Seeing those toddlers wandering around without a mum or dad was probably the hardest part. An orphanage is no place to grow up.' One of the two orphanages that Wall is trying to fund is called Ethembeni, which in the Zulu language means 'place of hope'. For some of the children, however, there is no hope at all. All these children are HIV positive.

Edwards, accompanied by Wall and a local Salvation Army officer called Timothy, later drove into Kliptown, a particularly poor and notorious township unaccustomed to visitors from outside their realm. A community like this is outside the jurisdiction of law and order, but Timothy assured them they would not be harmed. The odour inside the township was stomach churning for Edwards, but he was afforded a warm welcome. 'One home we went into sold meat,' he says. 'There were strips hanging down, as if they were on a clothes line, and the meat, if you could call it that, was covered in flies. Desperately sad. In another home, no more than a shack, five kids lived in one tiny room and their father didn't have a job. We asked the mother, a Christian, how they lived. She replied, "The Lord provides for us." That was a huge challenge for me as a believer. But she lived with incredible dignity and self-respect. Her home was immaculate, the yard outside was immaculate. They hadn't given up on life in any way. This was where they were at and they trusted God.'

Two days after Edwards left the country, Pappa Nelson died from AIDS.

Edwards' 1998 season was already underway before he went to South Africa, as he had tried to exorcise the gloom of the previous year by competing indoors over the winter for the first time in some years. 'As the 1997 outdoor season had been so miserable, I thought I should have a short-term goal.'

He had trained hard and felt in great condition when he went to Jarrow for a jumping session with his technical coach Peter Stanley to tune up for his first competition. Unfortunately, Edwards' good intentions went pear shaped as the session had to be halted when he bruised his right ankle. The injury was to be a handicap through-out the indoor season, in places as diverse as Norway, Finland, Birmingham and Japan. Yet he still established a new British indoor record of 17.64 metres in Birmingham to beat Yoelbi Quesada, the Cuban who had taken the gold medal at the World Championships in Athens the previous summer. He also took gold at the European Indoor Championships in Valencia.

Edwards' subsequent entrance to outdoor competition was unimpressive. In June, he decided to have a week at a training camp in Estonia with his Israeli friend Rogel

Nahum. Once ensconced in the camp, Edwards took a leap forward, physically hitting his stride in training. 'It struck me how much stimulus is crucial to me,' he says now. In the space of three days, he went from lifting average weights to lifting incredibly well. His performance in the weight room has always been the barometer by which he measures his expectation on the runway. If he is lifting close to his personal best, he supposes he will jump close to his potential. 'Before going to Estonia, I was struggling to lift 130 kilos, but once there I nearly made 140 kilos, which would have been an all-time personal best.' The presence of Nahum and the experience of training with someone like-minded had provided the motivation that on occasions he finds lacking in Gateshead.

Clearly, Edwards made an impression on his hosts at the Hotel Pirita, near Tallinn. They named a suite in his honour. 'I can go and stay there any time I like for the rest of my life!' he smiles. The week had been just the success, just the tonic he needed.

Edwards returned to the competitive arena to win the European Cup event at St Petersburg – but not without a price. Just when his right ankle seemed to have healed, so he began to experience problems with his left one. How serious this would become was not immediately evident, but remember how Brian Wellman described the triple jump event. 'It feels like going to the second storey of your apartment and jumping off the porch,' he said. 'And you do that six times in a competition, without taking into account the times you do it in practice. So, yes, it's like mini car wrecks, I would say.'

In this summer of 1998, Edwards was a strong candidate to challenge for the big prizes in the Golden League. Any athlete who could win his or her event in Oslo, Rome,

Monaco, Zurich, Brussels and Berlin would be eligible for a share in the $1-million jackpot. Given the demands of that schedule, only a handful of athletes could be considered as true combatants for the money. Edwards was most definitely one of them.

The first destination was Norway, and the knowledgeable crowd in the Bislett Stadium, Oslo. There is a great athletic tradition in this northerly outpost; indeed, there is a great passion for sport in general. Who could forget the delirious commentator who broke into English on the day Norway defeated England in a World Cup football match? His monologue went something along these lines: 'Lord Nelson ... Winston Churchill ... Maggie Thatcher ... your boys took a hell of a beating!' Extravagant commentating even by David Coleman's standards, you'll agree, but wonderful, eccentric stuff. The Norwegians had also proved to be exceptional hosts for the 1994 Winter Olympics in Lillehammer. The volunteers at all the venues had been helpful and polite, with not a Jobsworth in sight.

Edwards is precisely the kind of athlete the Norwegians appreciate – dedicated, gutsy and a winner. Edwards jumped into a lead that night in Oslo, and he was not under the remotest threat until the last round, when Kapustin stole in front by 22 centimetres with a leap of 17.65 metres. The Englishman had one jump left and the crowd took up the cudgels with him. Clap, clap, clap, clap, clap, clap, clap... Edwards rocked on his heel, again and again, then he was off, his arms moving like pistons, his head still. He hit the board and became airborne. He maintained his speed as he wanted, touching the ground only fleetingly until he landed in the sand. He knew the jump was good – and the board soon flashed the distance around the stadium: 18.01 metres, the first time he had passed that magic milestone since 1995. The man was back with a vengeance.

He won again in Rome – 17.60 metres – with a competition in Sheffield planned next. Once again, however, Edwards jumped appallingly at the South Yorkshire stadium. Steve Backley would later confide that Andy Norman was less than impressed. 'Edwards looks like he's on holiday,' Norman had said to him. Nevertheless, he did enough to win. But now his left ankle had swollen and there was a niggling problem with his heel. At home in the Northeast, Norman Anderson attempted to treat the injuries, but there was little that could be done before Edwards flew to the IAAF Grand Prix event in Stockholm.

After being forced to take a prolonged rest in the previous summer, Edwards was keen to compete in Sweden. He needed to find out the extent of his injuries under the stress of competition. Certainly, he was not of a mind to be idle until the European Championships in Budapest later in the year. And, yes, the Golden League was a consideration. As a professional athlete, he was more than entitled to think about keeping his prospects alive for a share of the million-dollar jackpot.

In Sweden, he was apprehensive during his warm-up routine. He was afraid to place weight on his damaged ankle. Edwards felt no more confident once the competition began. Extraordinarily, he ran through the first five rounds of the six-round event. In the last round, he actually landed a jump and his distance of 16.99 metres enabled him to emerge the victor by just one centimetre.

Later, Edwards was interviewed by Christina Boxer, another former athlete now working for the BBC team. She told him that Brendan Foster and Linford Christie had expressed dismay in the television studio that he had been jumping while injured. 'Brendan later said that he hadn't been giving me stick, he was merely concerned,' comments Edwards. Even so, friends felt he had been unjustifiably criticized that night. The reality was that Edwards felt the ankle had reacted to stress much better than he had dared hope. He reported just this to one athletics writer on a national newspaper, after the journalist had tracked him down to the physiotherapist's room in the stadium in Stockholm.

Edwards had declared himself fit to go to Monte Carlo to participate in the third round of the Golden League. Six other athletes were still in the hunt for the jackpot: Marion Jones, Haile Gebreselassie, Hicham El Guerrouj, Bryan Bronson, Svetlana Masterkova and Frankie Fredericks. When he arrived at Monte Carlo, Edwards picked up the newspaper by chance. He was deeply disturbed to find him-self portrayed as someone placing money ahead of glory. The inference was that Edwards was continuing to chase the Golden League jackpot, notwithstanding the fact that he could render himself lame before the European Championships in Budapest, when he would be competing in a British vest.

'It was a cheap shot, not representative of the conversation we'd had in Stockholm. I felt betrayed, especially as the athletics writers and athletes have a very amicable relationship. It was not a fair reflection of what had happened in Sweden, which to my mind had been a necessary and useful exercise. I was particularly upset because it reflected badly on my Christian faith. How I represent God, my witness, is of great importance to me.' At home, Edwards' family and friends were also hurt by the insinuation that he was consumed by a desire to make money at the expense of all else.

On the night of the competition in Monte Carlo, in the vast, ultra-modern stadium where the Monaco football team play during the winter, close to the apartment blocks where Grand Prix drivers such as David Coulthard and Johnny Herbert live as tax exiles, Edwards felt little pain from his injuries. He jumped far, yet his timing was fractionally adrift and he fouled his first three attempts to be excluded from the event. He was no longer a contender for the jackpot.

'I have to confess, I was relieved,' he says. 'I could see that the longer I remained in contention for the Golden League it would get worse and worse. If I'd gone on, all people would have been writing about was the million dollars.' Masterkova and Fredericks were also beaten and the three of them shared convivial conversation at the post-event banquet. 'We were out of the jackpot, but we had a really good evening!'

The next European whistle stop was Zurich, and for Edwards the event was the prelude to the European Championships in Budapest. A Belorussian called Alexander Glavatskiy, a long jumper who has converted to the triple jump, produced a high-quality third round from nowhere. While everybody else had been finding it impossible to break the 17 metres barrier, Glavatskiy suddenly leapt 17.53 metres. 'Until then, I wasn't at the races,' admits Edwards. With the adrenaline now running, however, he found a response. In his final two rounds, he jumped 17.73 metres and 17.63 metres. He could go to Budapest fortified with the knowledge that he could find his form when it was most needed.

Throughout this period, ominously, Edwards had been taking anti-inflammatory tablets to mask the pain and try to keep the swelling in his ankle under control. He flew to

Budapest a couple of days before he was due to compete, towards the end of the Championships. There was enormous anticipation within the British team, with athletes like Iwan Thomas, Colin Jackson, Steve Backley and Denise Lewis all arriving in peak condition. Edwards was also such a favourite that it was assumed he had only to catch the right bus to the stadium to collect a gold medal.

Once again, however, his equilibrium was disturbed by the nagging thought that his body might betray him. During warm-up for the qualifying rounds, Edwards was doing a routine exercise, loosening up with a small jump, when he felt discomfort in his ankle. 'That spooked me.' When he came to take his first jump, it was raining and he never struck his stride pattern with any conviction. He was aborting the jump in mid-stride when he landed on the long jump board, which had not been properly secured. In all honesty, by landing where he did, Edwards knew that he was going nowhere with that jump, but the organizers invited him to have another turn as they felt a responsibility for not having secured the board. 'My initial thought was that I hadn't been affected, I'd just made a bad jump. But then I caught myself and I thought, "It's raining, this is qualifying for a major championships – take the jump, stupid!"'

Edwards bettered the qualifying mark of 16.95 metres by two centimetres. 'In qualifying you can only lose, especially if you're favourite for a gold medal. Although you tell yourself to go out and jump as far as you can, you're just kidding yourself. Qualifying isn't the real thing; it's no-man's-land.'

He was especially nervous, too. Khristo Markov, the Bulgarian who had won the gold medal in the triple jump at the Seoul Olympics in 1988, bumped into Edwards in the hotel on the morning of the final. 'It's okay for you, so easy,' said Markov unthinkingly. Edwards knew that was a commonly held, if unrealistic, belief. It made him more uneasy than ever. He knew that he dare not lose. 'I think for the first time it played on my mind that I'd got two silver medals in a row. What would happen if I didn't get a gold here?' As ever, he began to imagine the distances that his rivals might be capable of jumping. Andy Norman's theory springs to mind once more. 'The only man who can beat Jonathan Edwards,' says Norman, 'is Jonathan Edwards.'

Not on this night. The stadium was bristling with energy, the crowd rising to appreciate the final day's competition. With relief, Edwards landed a first-round jump of 17.84 metres. Like any athlete, Edwards feeds on his own adrenaline, but in such a technical event, it is impossible to predict how you will fare from the outset. As in Athens the previous summer, he had arrived at a major championship plagued by the fear of injury. This time, however, he had managed to make a flying start, and nobody was to get within touching distance of such a marker. Once again, he was the man.

Edwards watched the javelin competition unfold as he passed on three rounds of the triple jump. There was a wonderful English sweep of gold and silver for Steve Backley and Mick Hill respectively. Unbeknown to those British fans watching the javelin, Backley and Hill had experienced a mild drama that had delayed their arrival in Budapest. The two friends had prepared for the Championships in Nymburk in the Czech Republic, working under the eye of coach Jan Pospisil, a man later to enter Edwards' world. On their last night in town there was a party, and so they were rather bleary eyed as they checked out of their rooms. The fact that they had left without their passports did not emerge until they tried to drive from the Czech Republic into Hungary. 'We did have a bit of a skinful,' Backley confided later. 'The people put on a barrel of beer and roasted a pig. Good party. It's true, Mick and I did have to wait for our passports to get to us at the border. But a few days later we won the gold and the silver, so how bad was that?'

'A different breed, these men who throw for a living,' grins Edwards, a good friend of Backley. On that night in Budapest, he forced himself to remain on guard as he observed the javelin competition. He could not relax until the last of his rivals, Denis Kapustin, had completed his six jumps. Only then would he accept that he was European champion.

After Kapustin failed to overhaul him, the Englishman had one jump left – one jump which was to be the final act of these European Championships. All eyes were on Edwards as he took his position on the runway. He did not expect much of himself as he took off. When he landed in the sand, his first instinct was that the jump had been technically flawed. As he climbed to his feet, his ankle was sore because he had driven himself hard across the ground. He looked around and heard the crowd cheering wildly: 17.99 metres was on the board. Jubilant, Edwards joined the celebrations already underway between Backley, Hill and the British 400 metres relay team of Mark Richardson, Iwan Thomas, Jamie Baulch and Mark Hylton. His summer had climaxed as he had wished.

This was just as well, as it transpired. Apart from a painful attempt to compete in Lausanne, Edwards' year was over. He did try to warm up to jump at the following event in Brussels, but the injury was impossible to deny any longer. After an examination in Brussels, Edwards made arrangements to visit the Swiss clinic of Dr Roland Biedert to have surgery on his troublesome ankle. Biedert, a man held in high esteem, has successfully treated a catalogue of athletes, including Roger Black and Sally Gunnell.

An operation in Zurich was planned for September. Regrettably, on the day the surgery was scheduled, heavy air traffic caused Edwards to miss his connecting flight in Amsterdam, after the plane he was on from Newcastle was placed in the holding pattern over The Netherlands. Edwards ended up making it to Berne at 9.00 p.m., and Biedert personally came to collect him from the airport. The operation was rebooked for the next day and Edwards slept in a bed at the clinic.

He had harboured a notion that after the surgery he would be able to resume jumping in four weeks. It was only when he was about to have a pre-op epidural that the gravity of the situation struck home. 'I'd been looking at all this through rose-coloured glasses,' he admits. When he awoke after the arthroscopic surgery, the ankle was swollen and bruised black and blue. Now, for the first time, he had to confront a terrible truth: his career was on the line.

Edwards returned home after the surgery, but hopes of being able to have a complete rest were dashed by a commitment he had made to continue with his evangelistic work in schools for the Church of Scotland. He went to Scotland on crutches rather than let anyone down. This may have been commendable – and typical of the man – but there was also a degree of foolhardiness about his action. The wound continued to weep, and Edwards was all too aware of the danger of it becoming infected. 'It was my worst nightmare,' he says. 'I had been warned by the surgeon that if the wound got infected there was a chance that infection could track into the joint itself. If that happened, that would be game over as a triple jumper.'

He later came to appreciate that he had paid insufficient attention to post-operative care. 'Just how much a risk I had taken I'll never know, but while I was in Scotland the wound was such a mess that I needed to make an emergency appointment with Alison's parents' doctor.' Edwards was prescribed a course of antibiotics, but he confesses to making a series of fretful telephone calls to Biedert's clinic in Switzerland. The post-operative trauma was far worse than he had imagined. Every day for weeks on end, Edwards would get up and wonder how the ankle was going to feel. Would he get to the 1999 World Championships in Seville, never mind the Sydney Olympics in 2000?

His relief, then, was tangible when he was given clearance to travel to a winter training camp in Sierra Nevada, which was being co-ordinated by the Czech coach Jan Pospisil. Steve Backley had introduced Edwards to Pospisil at the end of the summer in Lausanne, when the English athlete knew that he would require urgent treatment. Backley sensed from his own experience that the Czech's methods would be beneficial to Edwards once he was fit to resume training. 'Jonathan's open to ideas, and he got on well with Pospisil from the start,' reports the javelin thrower. 'Pospisil has that Eastern European background; he's at the cutting edge of the science of physical conditioning.'

Pospisil had worked for years with javelin thrower Jan Zelezny, the double Olympic champion and world record holder, and Backley's principal rival. 'Jan had thrown 98 metres – and if someone throws that far ahead of you, you've got to ask, "What are they doing different?"' reasons Backley. 'My need was to get a physical conditioning coach. I hadn't improved for a number of years.' The British athlete was not remotely surprised that Zelezny and Pospisil invited him to join them in training at the end of 1997. 'I've always been friends with Jan,' he says. 'He's not a man of a thousand words, but you can tell he's one of the good guys.'

Edwards is always receptive to expanding the frontiers of his athletic knowledge, and Pospisil entered his life at the right moment. From the beginning, the Czech's ideology struck a chord, and Edwards understood that here was a man who had once been at the core of the Communist plan to dominate world sport. 'I could only benefit, and lose nothing,' he says.

In Sierra Nevada, at a purpose-built athletic centre in a ski resort, some two and a half hours by road from Malaga, Edwards marvelled at his new-found working environment. 'Sometimes we were above the cloud base, surrounded by snow-capped mountains,' he recalls. If the scenery was beautiful, there was no little brutality about the work schedule. 'At 8.00 a.m. each morning, Pospisil had us running up 150 metal steps, two at a time. We would run down on our toes, then run up again, this time taking three steps in our stride. That's one eye-popping start to a new day!' Pospisil organized twice-daily sessions, as Edwards, Backley, Zelezny and one or two others absorbed the advantages of training at high altitude, 2,500 metres above sea level.

One day, however, their schedule was unexpectedly interrupted when a man and a woman arrived to see them without warning. They had not come to reconnoitre the facilities on offer for a skiing vacation. The two strangers had arrived to conduct random drug tests.

Chapter 15

Drug Busters

The spirit of the world, the great calm presence of the Creator, comes not forth to the sorceries of opium or of wine.

RALPH WALDO EMERSON

In common with all world-ranked athletes, at the beginning of each year Edwards must complete a form outlining in detail his planned movements over the course of the next 12 months. This information is collated by the IAAF for a sole purpose: random drug testing. The arrival of the drug testers in Sierra Nevada was part of the sport's ongoing and, some would argue, losing war against drug abuse. 'I wasn't actually one of those tested in Spain,' says Edwards. He did not have long to wait before it was his turn.

Not long into the New Year of 1999, the doorbell rang at Edwards' home as he was having tea with his family. On the doorstep was a man called Ken, carrying a small case. As usual, Ken had arrived unannounced, but Edwards invited him in, as he has done in the past.

Ken had come to collect a sample of Edwards' urine. The sample was then sent to a laboratory for analysis.

A few weeks later, Edwards received a letter telling him that his urine had tested negative for banned substances. This is how the authorities – UK Athletics in this country – try to police the sport. Ken and an army of men and women volunteers like him, working only for expenses, are given a briefing as to whom to visit. These random checks are designed to help the drug busters as they try to stay on the trail of the cheats. 'I think here in Britain we are serious about winning the war against drugs,' says Edwards.

Even so, he suspects that on a worldwide scale this is a forlorn hope, as he believes unscrupulous chemists will always be one step ahead of the scientists working for the governing bodies in athletics. 'That has to be the case, by definition,' he explains. 'The governing bodies send out to athletes a list of banned substances – and the chemists look for something that is not on the list. The scientists in the drugs laboratories are working on investigating the stuff that's being taken at the moment, not what's coming next.'

The sport is awash with riddles where drugs are concerned. What is a permissible nutritional aid, and what is a banned substance? When is a positive test negative? These questions have arisen most pressingly in British athletics in recent times. Diane Modahl tested positive before the Commonwealth Games in Canada in 1994, only to prove successfully that the testing procedure had been flawed. Modahl endured years of anguish. Her action to clear her name cost her a small fortune in legal fees and reduced to rubble the old British Athletics Federation. Modahl became embroiled in further, expensive litigation as she fought for compensation.

'Diane's case taught our governing body a lot in terms of how not to deal with something,' says Edwards. 'Her test should never have been announced the way it was. As it turned out, she was a genuine false-positive. But then, false-positives weren't something people considered. Now there seems to be an attitude to protect the sport from drug taking, yet at the same time a desire to protect the athlete as well.'

An even greater, potentially more damaging scandal broke in August 1999. Newspapers and television stations across the nation reported that Olympic hero Linford Christie was suspended from competition, having tested positive for the banned steroid nandrolone. 'SAY IT ISN'T SO' screamed the front page of the *Daily Mirror*.[1]

Christie, 39, had failed a drugs test after taking part in an indoor meeting in Dortmund, Germany, five months earlier. Professor Wilhelm Schanzer from the Cologne drug-testing laboratory was reported as saying, 'The result was 100 times greater than the permitted level of nandrolone. It was a clear, clear result.' Unsurprisingly, Christie, a fierce anti-drugs campaigner, insisted, 'I will prove my innocence. I did no wrong.'

Christie's case was examined by UK Athletics, as was the case of Scottish sprinter Doug Walker. The Scot had tested positive for metabolites of nandrolone in December 1998. Seven months later, UK Athletics cleared him of wrongdoing. David Moorcroft, the chief executive of UK Athletics, claimed afterwards that the present system of adjudication has to be reviewed. 'If the government is really determined to win the doping war, it should fund an independent agency,' he argued.

Walker's freedom to continue his career was short-lived. Almost as soon as UK Athletics gave him the green light,

1 *Daily Mirror*, 5 August 1999.

the IAAF suspended Walker pending its own enquiry. Christie was similarly cleared by UK Athletics in September 1999. A statement from UK Athletics said, 'It could not be proven beyond reasonable doubt that the substance present in the sample was derived from a prohibited substance.' Yet at the IAAF headquarters in Monaco, the Christie case remained an ongoing investigation. The IAAF rules on doping are based on the principle of liability, making an athlete responsible for what is in his or her urine sample.

As the Christie storm raged on, Tom Knight, athletics correspondent for the *Daily Telegraph*, reported Moorcroft as saying, 'I think the International Amateur Athletic Federation is very good at detecting substances. What it is quite poor at is explaining why the substances got there. I think, very often, the people from the IAAF haven't been careful. The system should be about protecting innocent athletes. It's in danger of becoming about protecting an imperfect system. We're answerable to English law and we have to prove beyond reasonable doubt that the athlete has to be innocent until proven otherwise.'[2]

Walker and Christie are just two of a number of athletes worldwide to have tested positive for metabolites of nandrolone. 'This spate of positive tests obviously undermines the public's confidence in the sport,' says Edwards. 'More fundamentally, it strikes a near-fatal blow to the belief that the governing bodies are capable of protecting the innocent and prosecuting the guilty. The disciplinary process has to be drastically rationalized and no athlete should be named until it has been proved beyond reasonable doubt that they are guilty.'

---

2 *Daily Telegraph*, 7 September 1999.

Edwards' view is that the protection of the athlete should begin at a much earlier stage. He suggests that there should be an expert employed within UK Athletics who could informatively advise athletes on what is legal to take and what is not. This would reduce the risk of an athlete moving outside the law. 'Ironically, it's a system I've seen at work in the Czech Republic.'

He argues vehemently, 'I would say most athletes would be willing to go right to the limit of legality in order to perform better. I'd include myself in that, health considerations withstanding. I wouldn't countenance cheating – but I would look at every possibility of improving my performance within the laws of the sport.'

Edwards began taking creatine at the beginning of 1995, the year he broke the world record. Carl Johnson, his coach at the time, explains, 'We had both by this time accepted the British Olympic Association's general advice that there was some value in creatine supplementation, having resisted for almost two years.' Edwards recalls, 'It certainly made a big difference in my weight training – and my story is one that any number of athletes will endorse.'

Creatine is widely used by sportsmen and women, including footballers and tennis players. It is a power-enhancing supplement. Edwards takes it at certain times of the year, when his training schedule is at its heaviest. One feared side effect of overuse is liver damage. 'I don't take massive amounts, nor would I on account of the possible health risk,' he explains. 'It definitely has a positive effect, and is performance enhancing. The recent condemnation of creatine has been hysterical. It has even been called a drug. If taking creatine is equivalent to taking drugs, so is eating food. Creatine appears naturally in meat and fish; true, only in smaller amounts, but then, you have to remember that the demands that athletes make on their bodies are hardly normal.'

Edwards has a contract with a Scandinavian vitamin company, Vitamex. On a daily basis he takes anti-oxidants, minerals, co-enzyme Q10 and Omega-3 fish oils, all available over the counter at a chemist's. 'I some-times wonder whether the general public have this idea that an athlete who is clean doesn't take anything at all,' he says. 'There isn't an athlete like that in the world. Athletes make such demands on their bodies that you'd break down if you didn't supplement in some way. The real question is, where do you draw the line? For exam-ple, Norman [Anderson] wonders what the difference is between training like a madman, breaking down and getting a cortisone steroid injection to compete, or stick-ing steroids in at the beginning, training like a madman and not breaking down? The sport says one protocol is legal and the other isn't. Ethically, it's a minefield. The only way I think you can approach it is this: the sport lays down a law and, rightly or wrongly, that is the line you don't cross.'

If you do cross the line and get caught, what then? Edwards is unequivocal in his response. 'For a first offence, I think an athlete should be banned for four years, missing a complete Olympic cycle. For a second offence, a life ban.' At present, an athlete proven to have taken Category A drugs (steroids) is banned for just two years. Quite clearly, this is a decision pre-empted by the fear of litigation. Edwards agrees, explaining, 'The IAAF never wanted to reduce the ban, but it was forced to by the legal situation in various countries, particularly America. It's a tragedy that a worldwide sport isn't free to police itself. Instead, we're at the mercy of the civil legal system, which is enabling the cheat to prosper.'

By coincidence, Edwards was randomly chosen for drug testing at the CGU British Grand Prix at Crystal Palace two days after the news of Christie's positive result had been published. Michelle Veroken, head of drug testing for the Sports Council, was present at the meeting. After the outbreak of positive tests for nandrolone – and these included Olympic sprint medallist Merlene Ottey, one-time training partner of Christie – Veroken moved quietly among the athletes at Crystal Palace, trying to assess their feelings. 'She wanted our impressions on the present system of testing. She wanted to know what we felt about the possibilities for false-positive results,' said Edwards.

After his event, he had a maximum of an hour to report to the testing room. He went immediately. In the room there were sealed drinks bottles to enable an athlete to rehydrate. Someone is assigned to watch the athlete pass urine into a container. 'You pour your specimen into two separate and uniquely numbered phials, marked A and B,' says Edwards. 'They are then placed in a polystyrene container. You seal it yourself.' At an approved laboratory, the A sample is analysed first. If it is clear, the B sample is poured down the sink. If, however, there is an adverse finding in the A sample – as the official jargon put it – the athlete in question has the right to be present when the B sample is tested. This allows the athlete to confirm that the seal he or she applied has not been tampered with.

Edwards has to assume that is what happens with the B sample, as he has not had the experience. As award-winning sportswriter Sue Mott wrote in the *Daily Telegraph* after meeting Edwards, 'If you take drugs, the sport of athletics might as well fold the tents and die ... When it gets to the stage that you suspect the starter is on beta-blockers to keep his trigger finger loose, the sport is in serious trouble. Edwards is the antidote to all that.'[3]

He most definitely is. Yet Edwards knows that the playing field is far from even. 'There is no doubt in my mind that there are people beating the system, there are cheats. How widespread, I don't know. Yet I do think it is often overstated. There are reasons for that. First, there is a mindset which says that you have to have drugs to perform. That's a legacy from the days of domination by the old Soviet bloc, which we now know ran state-funded drugs programmes. The second factor is that athletes themselves have an innate sense of jealousy or, if you prefer, a finely tuned self-defence mechanism. Whenever they're beaten, it's easier for an athlete to come to terms with defeat if they tell themselves that the person who won is a cheat.'

At the dawn of a new millennium, Edwards arrives at a sad, but undeniable truth. 'It's difficult to see how we can ever be certain that athletics is clean. Blood testing offers great hope, but its implementation is fraught with difficulty. In the end, it comes down to the integrity of the individual athlete.'

After yet another British athlete, Mark Richardson, revealed in February 2000 that he had tested positive for nandrolone, Edwards decided to take his own precautions and seek medical analysis of the supplements that he includes as part of his daily routine. Richardson had failed a drugs test in October 1999 and chose to tell a select gathering of the media, rather than wait for the news to leak. The talented 400m athlete explained how he took food

3 *Daily Telegraph*, 19 July 1999.

supplements. He vigorously denied taking any form of anabolic steroids, or any other kind of performance-enhancing drugs. Suddenly, in the year of the Olympics, he found his future in the hands of an IAAF arbitration panel.

When this bombshell exploded, Edwards opted to submit his supplements for independent analysis. 'In the end, it's my career and reputation on the line,' he says. 'It seems a matter of common sense to ensure that I am not taking anything which could unwittingly contravene the doping regulations.'

Edwards' training in Sierra Nevada had shown him he was capable of returning to competition at the beginning of 1999, a year when he intended to conquer the world again by taking victory in the World Championships in Seville. He opted to begin his year by escaping the misery of the British winter and flying to South Africa to participate in a few low-key events.

On the advice of his surgeon Roland Biedert, Edwards had asked his shoe company, Asics, to have some orthotic inserts manufactured by an outside source. Biedert reasoned that Edwards would benefit from extra support in his shoes. Critically, this theory was to be disproved in practice. 'I was injured in my last competition in Cape Town,' he says. Initially, Edwards was uncertain about the cause of his latest mishap.

It was soon to become apparent. Edwards' second competition back in Europe was in Paris and once again he came up lame. Now he began to look at the orthotics. 'It seems most likely they were to blame. Sometimes they work miracles, sometimes they don't. In my case, they didn't.'

Again, Edwards was having to prepare for a major competition while struggling to get himself properly fit. Yet he felt a strong, motivating force from his association with Jan Pospisil. In early May, three and a half months before the World Championships, Edwards went to stay with Steve Backley at his home in the Kent commuter belt, so that he might train under Pospisil's guidance once more.

Unprompted, Pospisil told Edwards that the moment had arrived for him to dedicate himself totally, selfishly, to his sport for a final assault on the twin peaks beckoning, in Seville and Sydney. 'Jan told me I needed to train in a better climate, with better training partners. What he said crystallized my own thinking.' Edwards talked aloud about the need to become a bachelor within his own household for the next 16 months of his life. 'I'm constantly aware and challenged by the difficulty of being a full-time athlete and trying to be a full-time parent and husband. I think I do fall between the two stools.'

By the time Edwards met up with Pospisil at Backley's home, Alison's mother had already had surgery on her brain tumour, which meant that each absence from home made him feel even more guilty. Yet his obsession with making the most of his athletic ability as his Christian commitment to God was a compelling reason for prioritizing his life. Edwards decided he would have to endure the loneliness of training away from home, temporarily sacrificing his family to concentrate on becoming the best athlete he could. There would be, of course, no room for excuses should he fail.

Thus it was that Edwards came to pass through immigration at Prague airport on 19 May 1999. Pospisil was present to meet him. So, too, was a Czech television crew and several newspaper reporters. Pospisil is deemed a celebrity at home. His association with Edwards was considered a news item important enough to entice the media to the airport. Typically, Edwards answered all their questions.

A mutual respect between Edwards and the Czech coach had been nourished by their time in Sierra Nevada, South Africa and London. Edwards was a convert to Pospisil's ideology on rhythm, balance and stretching. Although away from Alison and their sons, therefore, he was surprisingly light of heart when he checked in for a week at the Sportovni Centrum at Nymburk.

Once a symbol of the Communist ambition to rule world sport, nowadays the centre is a fading relic from an unlamented age. Edwards' room in a spartan, three-storey block was cramped and sparsely furnished. The cleaners had no detectable schedule. Fortunately, he had brought his own towels. His bed was rock hard. In the cavernous dining room, guests queued to be served watery soup and slabs of meat with macaroni or potatoes from giant urns. There were several types of sauerkraut. On the first day Edwards was admonished by the staff for not removing the cutlery when he returned his plate to a separate hatch. This was how you imagined boot camp to be.

Nonetheless, Edwards was an uncomplaining guest, living his own Bohemian rhapsody. He was enamoured with the facilities, not in the least disturbed by the lack of home comforts. He had come to sweat and learn on the road to Sydney, not write a travelogue. 'You need a change, especially as you get older,' he says. 'Each winter you set off up the mountain again and if you always use the same path, it's easy to become stale. If you approach it from a different angle, it becomes a different mountain.'

Pospisil introduced Edwards to an intensified pro-gramme of drills. He encouraged him to run with his arms in all manner of extravagant positions (to the amusement of those back home at the Gateshead gym) – over his head, behind his back, spread wide like a child impersonating a plane in flight. 'Pospa is very good at looking at patterns of movement,' he explains. 'His philosophy is based around the co-ordination of strength, speed and technique rather than simply looking at them in isolation.'

Under the terms of their agreement, Pospisil was receiving no payment in the first instance. 'Jonathan is my hobby!' exclaimed the avuncular 53-year-old Czech. 'I admit when he showed me his coaching diary I was surprised. So little information. Jonathan does not respect coaching law. He has broken the chain; his talent is from the gods.' As the most recognizable Christian in British athletics, Edwards has always understood the source of his gift – but that does not diminish his willingness to improve. 'The best part of Jonathan's potential is his co-ordination. That is wonderful.'

During that week in Nymburk, Edwards' envied speed and balance were unmissable. He trained with zeal. Pospisil had him running on an indoor track, strapped to a harness creating resistance to his movement. He had him standing upside down on his head. He had him doing other exercises quite clearly designed for an apprentice contortionist. He had him smiling. 'Jonathan is the only triple jumper to run down the track with the grace of a bird,' he said.

Later in the year, Pospisil drove from Prague to Paris to observe Edwards competing. He came to London to watch both Edwards and Backley, who had a torrid, best-forgotten summer. Then, of course, Pospisil was in Seville for the World Championships. He was a sad man after the triple jump had ended. 'He told me there were some people in the Czech Republic who were glad I failed, because they were jealous of his involvement with me,' says Edwards, shaking his head in disbelief at such pettiness.

The original plan had been for Edwards to work in block sessions at camps with Pospisil over the winter of 1999. After Seville, however, Edwards understood that he had to rearrange his priorities. His wife, watching her mother slowly die, had to be placed at the head of the agenda. His training could easily be conducted in Gateshead, as it had been so often in the past. After all, this was a regime that had worked with some phenomenal success leading into his world record-breaking triumph at the World Championships in Gothenburg. He determined that he would retain whatever contact he could with Pospisil, a man he holds in great respect, and he would continue to incorporate some of Pospisil's thinking into his training. That was all, though: Alison needed him at her side, not on the end of a telephone in some remote training camp.

Chapter 16

Citius, Altius, Fortius[1]

*If you can dream – and not make
your dreams your master.*

RUDYARD KIPLING

Almost six months after his failure in the World
Championships in Seville, Jonathan Edwards was a
man at peace. He had slotted gently into his winter training routine at Gateshead. He knew that in February 2000
retired American triple jumper Willie Banks was flying to
England from his home in California to work with him.
Banks is a charismatic figure. Knowledgeable, too.
Edwards looked forward optimistically to the American
addressing the technical flaws that he has been unable to
correct. Another session was pencilled in for them in the
spring, when they could share further time in Florida.
Banks just might turn out to be the keyholder to Edwards'
fortune.

In the weeks before Christmas 1999, however, Edwards
was simply revelling in being a home-based athlete. On

1 'Swifter, Higher, Stronger' – the motto of the Olympic Games.

Saturday mornings he often took his eldest son Sam to play football. With Alison, he attended the mid-week home study group run by friends from Holy Trinity Church. Edwards was gearing up, quietly, unfussily, for the job ahead. 'My last big year as an athlete,' he describes it. 'The story is nearing the end now. In the beginning there was excitement and expectation. The middle chapters were glorious, then quite traumatic. Now I'm looking to write a fitting finale. The challenge is stark, unconfusing. There will be no more chances.'

The Games in Sydney will be his fourth and final appearance at the Olympics. 'I just want to make sure I get there in the best possible shape.' Just because he is no longer driven by a selfish obsession to capture a gold medal, it does not mean that he has surrendered that ambition. 'I am completely committed to winning; and if I jump the way I know I can, probably the only man who can touch me is Kenny Harrison at his best.'

Edwards is no longer consumed by the notion that an Olympic gold medal is his destiny. That thought perished for ever on an unforgettable summer's evening in Seville. He smiles at the suggestion. 'It may not be my destiny – but I'm training as if it is!' His work in the earliest days of 2000, his last active year as an Olympic-bound athlete, was fulfilling and cheerful. He liked the point in his life at which he had arrived. 'I feel incredibly motivated. I haven't felt like this for a long time.'

His mood was in vivid contrast to how he had felt four years earlier, when he was being awarded the gold medal in every article that was written in the countdown to the Atlanta Games. All he had to do to find treasure in the sand in Atlanta was to turn up, or so it was widely imagined. 'I'm spending this winter out of the limelight, something I was unable to do in 1996.' That year, he opted to train in the warmth of Florida. Now, he was weathering the cold, inhospitable days of a British winter, but he was doing so in high spirits, balancing his professional ambition against the need to be with Alison and their sons. Alison's mother Anne was admitted to a hospice near her home at Musselburgh before Christmas. 'It's not been an easy time,' he says.

Nonetheless, he has been able to offer some support, as he had pledged, while gearing up his preparation for the fateful days ahead. 'The issue is not where I'm training, but how,' he says. 'I'm so enthused with the prospect of the Olympics, I could train in a lock-up garage in Gateshead. I'm not willing the Games to be here tomorrow, but they seem so close, so real, I can almost feel them. The people in the Northeast wish me good luck wherever I go. I sense a real warmth. They have watched me endure so much disappointment since 1995, and they realize that I'm coming towards the end of my career.'

The past 20 years, from the days when he was jumping into the sand on a windswept playing field at West Buckland School, have been a rehearsal for the Sydney Games. He can approach this autumn's challenge on the other side of the world in no other light. There is, however, a saying that Billie Jean King, the great tennis champion, is fond of repeating: 'Live in the now.' Edwards would recognize the wisdom of such advice. In the record books he may be the world record holder, but on the track he is just another athlete.

He suspects that part of his dilemma at the Atlanta Olympics was created by his record-breaking leap the previous summer. 'Mentally, I didn't leave myself anywhere to go,' he says. 'That caused a lot of my problems. You go to the top – but how do you go forward from there? On that night in Gothenburg, all my dreams – and some – were fulfilled. Now I go to Sydney knowing that I've won everything that's meaningful in my sport – except an Olympic gold. It's a motivating force.'

In the years since Gothenburg, Edwards has naturally matured. He has had to learn to deal with money, and that has sometimes proved an uncomfortable experience. He has had to examine the connection between his athletics and his faith, and there were times when that was an overwhelming task. His mistakes – and he has made mercifully few – have been played out in public.

In the course of this book, Edwards has been shown as vulnerable, at times naive and unworldly, but the commonly held belief that he is a man of decency, great integrity and honour has withstood all probing. When told that Edwards was willing to be subjected to the inquisition of a biographer, one colleague from the sportswriting benches smiled apologetically. 'That's one book where there won't be much sex, drugs and rock'n'roll, then!' He was right, of course.

Instead, there has been the portrait of a man who thinks about life and about sport in different terms. When asked to describe his emotional response to a specific achievement, clichés like 'over the moon' never once enter his vocabulary. Academically, Edwards might have applied himself to any profession or vocation of his choosing. Certainly, his schoolmasters never really believed he would make his living on the playing fields of the world. It was not that Edwards was not a talented young sportsman – in fact, he was sickeningly good at every game he played. No, what worked against him was his laziness.

In time, however, with the guidance of coaches like Carl Johnson, Norman Anderson and Peter Stanley, with the realization that his talent was world-class if properly harnessed, Edwards conquered the world. Then his real fight began – with himself. Edwards always suspected that success, much more than failure, would test his Christianity. He was not disappointed in this.

By succeeding in an event which – let's be honest – fell some way behind snooker as a television spectacle until he leapt into focus, Edwards is something of a phenomenon on the British sporting landscape. As Brendan Foster says, triple jumping is no more popular now than it ever was. 'It's Jonathan who's popular,' he explains. 'People down the pub don't talk about triple jumping; they talk about that nice lad who jumped out of the sandpit.'

Edwards won the BBC Sports Personality of the Year Award; he was asked to draw the Lottery; he was on the 'A list' of invitations. In November 1999, his stock advanced to an even greater cerebral level when he was a panellist on BBC's *Question Time*, that showcase for political debate. How many other sports stars can you imagine being invited onto the programme? Edwards shared the platform with politicians Mo Mowlam, David Willets and Malcolm Bruce, along with journalist Deborah Orr, and discussed topics such as the decommissioning of arms in Northern Ireland and the merit of the political philosophies of New Labour. 'Being on the programme was the scariest thing I've ever done,' he admitted later. He acquitted himself with sufficient aplomb, however, for *Question Time* host David Dimbleby to write him a personal note of congratulations after the show.

That programme, and his preparatory reading before the broadcast, caused Edwards to look harder at himself.

At heart, he is a conservative with a lower-case 'c'. He believes strongly in marriage and the family. He has republican leanings, though – humorously, he feels the royal family should be preserved in a museum. 'We could loan them out when required in the national interest.' As a Christian, he straddles the political divide. He feels strongly about social justice in society, which shifts him to the left. He is right-wing in his strident opinions about law and order, a man who feels that 'the human rights movement has moved the criminal justice system too far in favour of the criminal'.

Without being pretentious, Edwards feels that, when his days as an athlete are over, he may be drawn towards public life. 'I don't want to denigrate sport,' he says. 'It is important, to those who compete and to those who watch, but one day I would like to do something that materially impacts on people's lives – do something that might make a difference.'

Edwards has been candid in sharing his experiences and his emotions, in providing an insight into what makes him laugh, what makes him weep. If he appears to have shed a great deal of tears, do not suppose that he is unhappy. He is not. His wife and sons are the source of untold joy. To be at the dinner table when four-year-old Nathan offers grace is testimony to the values within the Edwards household. To see Sam and Nathan knocking one another over in pursuit of a ball 30 minutes later is to understand that Edwards' heartbeat has been transplanted to the boys. Alison, sometimes feisty, always thoughtful, binds the family together. She is his rock and his best friend, his true love.

What has happened to the Edwards family these past five years is a tale that Hollywood moguls would have rejected as being too implausible. When he does retire, we might confidently suppose that Edwards is unlikely to fade into the shadows. He will feel a need to contribute in some shape or form. Yet that is for tomorrow. For the time being, Edwards has to 'live in the now'. That means concentrating on getting to Sydney in the right condition to win an Olympic gold medal. His mind is set on accomplishing just that – but not at any price.

Defeat in Seville taught him much about himself. His faith is strong, his core values set in steel. Over recent years, we have spent much time together, in England, in the United States, in the Czech Republic and in Spain. He has talked for hours, profoundly and sensibly; he has stubbornly defended his ideology, he has unashamedly shown his vulnerability. One conundrum persists: where does the pursuit of a gold medal fit in the grand scale of Edwards' life?

To Jonathan Edwards, the meaning of life has always extended beyond jumping into a sandpit.

Chapter 17

Grief on the Gold Coast

*There is something both emotionally and
physically soothing about crying.*

THE LITTLE BOOK OF CALM, *PAUL WILSON*
(PENGUIN, 1997)

All roads in the year 2000 were leading to Sydney, but
that was not to deter Edwards from taking a diversion.
For his welfare as an athlete, and for his all-important
peace of mind as a husband and a father, he elected once
again to return to Tallahassee, Florida.

He is a fan of most things that Tallahassee has to offer;
the hospitable climate, born of the city's proximity to the
Gulf of Mexico; fast food; American four-wheel-drive cars;
and, most significantly, the group of friends he has
acquired from the congregation at Grace Church.
'Generally, though, I love the anonymity. A weight drops
off my shoulders as soon as I land in America. No one
knows who I am, what I do, and they probably don't care,'
he explains. 'I'm just another guy.'

Edwards was accompanied to Florida by Alison, Sam
and Nathan as he had no desire to be parted from them.

They live easily in America, with Edwards relishing the climate, the lifestyle and the freedom to be a professional athlete. He has talked earnestly with his wife about one day returning there to live. 'An example of my spontaneity,' he says, smiling. 'I think it is an endearing quality, though I am not sure Alison would agree!' But the serious point, the one not to be missed or underestimated, is that in Tallahassee Edwards feels he trains to his optimum levels. He happily crossed the Atlantic – and, remember, Alison is a poor flier – to sharpen himself for the coming months. To sharpen himself for two days in Sydney in late September.

Once in Tallahassee, Edwards again worked with Dennis Nobles, the jumps coach at Florida State University. Due to the excellence of his training, and his contentment in the community, he extended the length of his stay by two weeks and remained in Tallahassee for six weeks altogether. 'The trip was a big plus,' he insists. 'I realized I was as good as ever. My speed was excellent, my weightlifting really good. I thrive in the heat.' His optimism was easy to understand. All you needed was a look at the stopwatch in Nobles' hand. Edwards ran 100 metres in 10.5 seconds; that is seriously fast, even allowing for the minor discrepancies of a hand-held timing device against the dependable accuracy of an electronic one. 'And to be honest, I wasn't even flat out.' Over 60 metres, he was neck and neck with a young British athlete named Mark Lewis-Francis. In October 2000 the 18-year-old became world junior champion over 100 metres.

Edwards' sessions on the track, in the warmth of the sun, were to be the last real running he would do before the Olympic Games. The man is unorthodox in the extreme, as all his coaches will testify. Not that Edwards was specifically guilty of neglecting his track work. It was simply that, at home alone in the Northeast, with his old training partner John Hedley now away studying in Scotland, there was no one to compete with on a regular basis. Edwards had tried to rectify this after Seville by contacting Mark Byron, who had been his earliest sparring partner at Gateshead. 'Another of my spontaneous decisions!' says Edwards.

Byron, nowadays an actor whose credits include the BBC soap *EastEnders*, was unable to relocate himself from the Home Counties at such short notice. 'I would have loved to have helped,' he explains. 'We had good times training together all those years back. We'd be out there on the track at Gateshead in the cold and the wet. Mind, Jon used to hate running more than 100 metres. He was lazy. But he was also gifted ... so fast, so strong. He possessed what was needed, and when it mattered he became an incredibly good athlete.'

Edwards understood that it was impractical for Byron to join him; it was simply a measure of the man's need to find a trustworthy friend to offer some companionship on those chill mornings when, rather than face training, all you really wanted to do was to roll over and bury yourself under the duvet. Going to the gym at Gateshead, however, was never a problem. He had Norman Anderson to keep him motivated and the banter of the other Gym Irregulars to keep his feet earthbound.

'I was lifting considerably greater weights than ever,' he reports. He 'cleaned' 145 kilograms and was within a whisker of lifting 150 kilograms. 'He just didn't quite catch it, but it was still mightily impressive,' recalls Anderson. Edwards had broadened his knowledge in the weights room after going to Edinburgh to consult with American Mike Stone, and his wife Margaret. As Meg

Ritchie, she had established the British record for the discus, a record still standing at the dawn of the 21st century. 'I met Meg on the flight home from Seville,' says Edwards. 'We already knew one another and I knew that her husband, Mike, had a big reputation in weight conditioning. I arranged to see them in Scotland before Christmas. The meeting was educational.'

Yet it was Anderson who continued to be Edwards' rock in the timeworn gym deep inside Gateshead Stadium. Anderson, with his mobile phone that resolutely refused to ring, with his repertoire of risqué stories that had to be told out of Edwards' hearing, with his bandaged knees and blurred vision, still lifting himself. Anderson, the man cast in the role of extracting the last ounce of strength from Edwards. How through his unseeing eyes was he interpreting Edwards' preparation?

'Jon was quietly determined, working with a more steely edge than ever,' he explains. 'We both knew what he had to do. We both knew this was going to be his last chance. There was an unspoken bond. You didn't discuss the Olympics, you just knew they were all that mattered now. This was it … this was it.'

Against the background of this conditioning, Edwards flew to America in good heart. By the end of his stay his mood was brighter still. For he knew, just knew, from the quality of his training in America that those writing him off as being too old to win gold at the Games were suffering from premature speculation. 'Have you detected how ageist sport is?' he asks, rhetorically. 'They talk of people aged 30 as being over the hill or ready for retirement.' This was too rich to stomach for a man who celebrated his 34th birthday during his time in Tallahassee in May. 'In Florida, I began to appreciate that there is no reason for me to stop competing at the end of the Olympics,' he says. 'Age is not a factor. End of story.'

On that sun-drenched track at Florida State University, Edwards sensed he was primed to jump a long, long way. At this stage of his preparation, he was running to the board off a short run; 14 strides as opposed to the 18 he runs in competition. It is how he likes to wind up. 'I was jumping brilliantly and I would not have been surprised to have gone 17.80 metres.' Edwards concluded his stint in the United States, competing in a college meeting. In the event, he recorded 17.20 metres, disappointing considering the shape he felt he was in. Later, he would realize that the run-up problems that had so baffled him in Seville had resurfaced again at Florida State University.

On 27 June, Edwards made a quiet entrance into the athletics season at a small meeting in Bergen, Norway. He jumped 17.23 metres with his first-round leap, aware that he had become airborne a considerable distance behind the take-off board. His season had lift-off. Yet eight days later, Edwards fell to earth with a bump. In Rome on 30 June, meeting rivals like Charles Michael Friedek, Rostislav Dimitrov and Yoelbi Quesada for the first time in Olympic year, Edwards performed like a novice. Unusually, he participated in all six rounds, but could not jump any further than 16.83 metres. 'Basically, I never fully completed one of my jumps to satisfaction,' he moans. 'I was SHOCKED. I had expected to jump a metre further.' To those outside his immediate circle Edwards was perceived to be in a mental meltdown once again. Was he already buckling under the weight of expectation, some three months before his appointment in Sydney? You would have found a heavyweight consensus of critics prepared to place their tick in the box marked 'Yes'.

Edwards' search for a remedy was considered controversial in many quarters. He declared he would be unable to represent Britain in the European Cup in mid-July – a competition to be held at Gateshead – because he was going to fly to Israel to attend a warm-weather training camp. As far as it is possible to tell, no one went as far as calling him Judas; but the inference was clear. Edwards was damned for letting down Britain. 'I was accused of not being committed to my country, and for jumping only when I was getting paid,' he says. 'It's conveniently forgotten that I had competed in the previous seven European Cups. I simply needed to take a step back, to start again. I needed to be able to work on my technique in warm weather, not to perform under pressure. I pulled out of the European Cup with a fortnight's notice, but I was later lumped in with other athletes, like Steve Backley and Colin Jackson and Jason Gardener, who withdrew with niggling injuries only shortly before the competition. Surely, an athlete's wishes to look after himself at such a critical time should be respected? Besides, who remembers the European Cup now?'

In Israel, Edwards enjoyed the hospitality offered him at the Wingate Institute, effectively the Israeli team's Olympic headquarters, close to the Mediterranean resort of Netanya. If verbal flak was flying round Edwards' ears at home in Britain, the sound of gunfire at the Wingate Institute was at first disconcerting to the casual visitor until Edwards' friend, Rogel Nahum, explained that Israeli military students have their own fortified quarters alongside the athletes. Like the athletes, the students have to train; and in this volatile corner of the world that means firing weapons. Nahum, although a full-time triple jumper, remains an army reservist. His invitation was the principal reason for Edwards' choice of training location. 'Rogel's become like a brother,' he says.

Together, they trained in the merciless 35 °C heatwave settled over the eastern shores of the Mediterranean. 'I had to deliver myself from the wilderness into an athletic land of milk and honey,' says Edwards, laughing gently at his own biblical analogy. Shirtless in the sunshine, they competed against one another in the weightroom and on the field, throwing a cannonball-like shot two-handed out in front of them, or over their heads.

Edwards was both philosopher and realist on the night we dined in Netanya as the sun was vanishing into the Mediterranean. 'At the moment there is no great clamour to say that I am going to Sydney as a gold medal hope,' he said. 'But the truth is, if I don't win gold, I'll be hugely disappointed. I have no lasting scars from Seville nor from Rome. I know what's troubling me and it is a technical deficiency which can be corrected. With the talent I have been given, I should become Olympic champion. I am as fast as I was in 1996 and I am stronger. I am training at a new level. If anything, the speed I am achieving on the runway is working against me. I have discovered since Rome that my run-up was over 1.60 metres too short, a factor caused because my stride pattern is shortening as I am going so fast. I am here to rediscover my rhythm.'

His friendship with Nahum, as we have already learned, began at the Barcelona Games and, although the Israeli is no match for him in the competitive arena, Edwards finds him a strong motivating force. Nahum had already been nominated to carry Israel's flag at the opening ceremony in Sydney, a poignant assignment given that the Games are forever stained by the terrorist massacre of 11 Israeli team members at the Munich Olympics in 1972.

Edwards feels an empathy towards the Israelis through his religious convictions, but he also takes strength from secular men like Nahum. 'Israeli suffering through the ages has defined them,' says Edwards. 'I like the spirit and strength of community here.'

He terminated his two-week-long visit (with hindsight he wished he had stayed for just one week) by participating in the Israeli Championships which, with some predictability, he won. Unfortunately, he did not find some instant fix to his problems. In jumping 17.11 metres – 'There was no atmosphere and it felt little more than a glorified training session' – Edwards hurt his left ankle, which had already been operated on at the end of 1998. On his return home on 24 July, he placed an urgent call to Tudor Bidder, technical director for jumping disciplines. Twenty-four hours later he had a consultation with Dr Brian English and consultant radiologist Wayne Gibbens in Leeds. On the evidence of X-ray and ultra-sound scans, English administered a cortisone injection, the first Edwards had ever received. English was persuasive in his argument that there was no permanent damage, but for Edwards it was hard to accept that an injection, was the answer to his ailment. 'Believe it, Jonathan,' said his friend Nahum on the phone from Tel Aviv. 'It's like a miracle.'

As a precaution, Edwards opted to withdraw from his next scheduled competition in Stockholm to give himself more opportunity to perform with distinction at the Grand Prix event at Crystal Palace on 5 August. Yet Edwards confesses that the advent of the injury, as well as his struggling form, was weighing heavily on his mind. 'I felt uncommonly low,' he says. In the week before the star-spangled event in London, Alison had gone north to Scotland to be with her mother, now in a hospice at

Strathcarron. 'I used the time to do much praying and thinking,' says Edwards. He realized he had been focused too much on himself. 'I was self-absorbed.'

His mother Jill made a timely telephone call, which he only fully appreciated afterwards. 'Mum is a thoughtful, prayerful lady. She told me she did not think I was placing implicit trust in God. I was a bit defensive, but I continued to pray and think through how I was feeling, how I was behaving.' He came to accept his mother was only articulating what he knew to be an unarguable truth. That same week his friend Phil Wall came to stay from London. 'Phil came up with the same message.'

Edwards felt he had arrived at a vitally important spiritual watershed. 'God could have left me feeling worthless and crushed,' he says. 'But He was very gracious in disciplining me. He was gentle and loving. I handed over to the Lord my worries about competitions, about injuries, even my concerns about Alison's mother. I was going to trust in God.' Edwards went to London a different athlete; and, spiritually, an invigorated, new man.

'My relationship with God suddenly took on a new dynamic and a new vitality. Here I was, a Christian for most of my life, and I'd come face to face with the fact that I was trying to sort my life out on my own and had forgotten about trusting God. I think I'd lost that capacity in all the pressure I'd put myself under.' At Crystal Palace, Edwards' change of demeanour was not unnoticed by the media. 'I felt great – and everyone commented on that, including pressmen. My rhythm – and my smile – had returned.' He won the competition by leaping 17.34 metres, but says, 'It was a much better jump than that. My step phase collapsed because I landed on the long jump take-off board and that was a little loose.' But as with all athletes, Edwards is at continuous risk; and six days later he was confronted by the trauma of dealing with yet another injury.

Ironically, on the day of the competition in Zurich, Edwards had arranged to meet Dr Roland Biedert, the Swiss surgeon who had operated on his left ankle at the end of 1998. 'He looked at my ankle and told me it was fine,' recalls Edwards. 'He also reminded me how I had told him that I was not too bothered about being fit for the World Championships in Seville, how I had stressed that all that mattered was being right for Sydney.' The two men parted, smiling at the memory. By that evening, Edwards would have the smile wiped from his face.

He jumped 17.27 metres in the second round, following with 17.36 metres in the next round whilst landing almost upright. He sensed that his rivals were beginning to fear the worst. Not just here, but for Sydney. 'In 1995 when I was setting world records, you could tell that the other athletes had put me in a different league,' says Edwards, without a trace of boastfulness. He is merely reporting the facts. 'That was how they were talking on this night in Zurich. I felt I was ready to jump 18 metres again and they knew it.' Alas, in the fourth round he landed his 'hop' awkwardly and winced as the pain went through his body like an electric shock. Dr Biedert, the official medic at the meeting, was in immediate attendance. He placed a pad containing anti-inflammatories on the ankle and Edwards slept that night with his foot in the air. The next morning he returned for further consultation with the doctor. 'My ankle was black and blue,' says Edwards, who had been planning to compete 24 hours later in the AAA Championships, the Olympic trials, in Birmingham.

On Biedert's advice another scan was booked in England. And he was strongly warned against the wisdom of taking part in the AAA Championships. Historically, Edwards has not always supported the AAAs, but he had genuinely wanted to participate; not least because it would have provided a competition 48 hours after Zurich, replicating the gap between the qualifying round and the final at the Games in Sydney. He was also aware that the British number two triple jumper Larry Achike had missed the competition in Zurich through a slight hamstring strain, and called him to alert him that he would not be in Birmingham. This gave Achike the warning that he must participate, or put at risk his place on the plane to Sydney; he could have missed out as both Phillips Idowu and Julian Golley had the qualifying mark. 'Larry deserved to go the Olympics and I wanted to ensure he knew the situation,' says Edwards.

But, for some, Edwards' withdrawal seemed too much of a coincidence. Steve Smith, a successful British high jumper rehabilitating from injury in the TV commentary booth, criticized Edwards for missing the trials. David Powell, the athletics correspondent of *The Times*, was another to lambast the world record holder for failing to make it to Birmingham. 'Powell wrote a scathing article,' says Edwards. 'The essence of the piece was that I was governed by money. He wrote that of three competitions in Britain, I'd only taken part in one: the one where I was paid. It was just awful journalism, blatantly disregarding the facts. I was unable to jump in the AAAs because my ankle was black and blue. Full stop.'

His father, Reverend Andy Edwards, had been equally infuriated when he read Powell's article at his rectory on the outskirts of Whitehaven. 'Powell questioned Jonathan's integrity and honesty, and that was hard to take as his father,' says Reverend Edwards. 'He laid into Jonathan without foundation. Jonathan was injured, and here was a man virtually calling him a liar. It was little less than a character assassination; and what hurts is that what the papers say is gospel for some people.' Smith, incidentally, called Edwards to apologize once he appreciated the extent of his injury.

Edwards returned to Leeds, remarkably, in higher spirits even though his ankle looked as if it had been run over by a truck. His spiritual condition was in the rudest of health, and this was making all the difference to his mood and attitude. This latest scan, again conducted by Gibbens, provided uplifting news. 'There was no damage to the ligaments, just superficial bruising,' explains Edwards. 'I had nicked a blood vessel and that was responsible for the colouring of my ankle. It was surreal to be looking at my ankle, black and blue, and be told that there was nothing really wrong. I could have given him a kiss!' On 20 August in Leverkusen, Germany, Edwards achieved the longest triple jump witnessed in 2000 when he leapt 17.62 metres, the furthest he had leapt since having surgery on his ankle almost two years ago. He had tamed world champion Charles Michael Friedek in his own backyard.

Even so, Edwards remained critically aware of his injury and decided not to jump again after his second round success. 'I was in some pain and when I pulled out, Friedek's coach said he would get me some ice,' reports Edwards. 'In German, Charles shouted: "Don't help". The thing is with Charles you never know whether he is joking or not. It is amusing to watch him at times as he can rant and rave. Certainly, he was working himself into a frenzy trying to jump past me. He was swearing like mad; and then at the end, when he had gone no further than 17.20 metres, he told me: "You'll win the Olympics". Edwards left Germany being assured of only one fact – and it had nothing to do with Friedek's prediction. 'I knew I was going to spend the rest of the season having to live with the pain from my ankle,' he says.

The next day Edwards made a poignant visit to Scotland, to see his now frail mother-in-law Anne. He was accompanied by Alison and his two sons, suspecting that for him and the boys this would be the last time they would see her. 'At that stage, we felt there was a distinct possibility that Anne might die before I got on the plane to go to the Games.'

After the emotion of his trip north, Edwards returned to Gateshead to bid a fond farewell to his supporters by jumping 17.48 metres on a wet, cold afternoon. The Olympic final was less than a month away and the omens were good, at least athletically. He was uncertain whether to keep a scheduled appointment in Berlin five days hence. Why risk injury? Why not head for Japan, his final destination before Sydney, with his confidence high? Yet Edwards went to Germany, to experience the ignominy of three no-jumps and elimination from the event. Was this another manifestation of nerves overcoming Edwards before curtain-up on the big night? 'Not in the least,' he argues. 'I was not a bit distressed. I had gone to Berlin to try to jump well, and in the third round I was beautifully balanced and would have recorded a season-best but for nicking the plasticine on the take-off board.'

Given that this is a man capable of talking himself into depression after one poor performance, there was reason to believe he was not bluffing. He would go to Sydney strong, not withstanding the obviously depressing thought that Alison's mother was fast losing her long, courageous battle for life. 'Alison made it clear that I should leave as planned,' he says. 'Her father Ralph was just as supportive.' On 7 September, Edwards took his seat in first class on a British Airways 747 to Tokyo. The adventure was now entering the last phase, with Edwards unaware of the drama waiting to unfold after jumping in Yokohama.

He flew into Australia on Monday 11 September to be trapped in the epicentre of a storm that had blown across the world. He understood something was amiss when, on entering the Radisson Resort Palm Meadows Hotel, the splendid holding camp for British athletes organized by the British Olympic Association, he was greeted by a reception party including Max Jones, the team's performance director. Jones was not carrying a bouquet. Before Edwards had even checked in, shot-putter Mark Proctor mouthed at him across the lobby: 'You're dead meat.' To ensure Edwards assimilated the message, Proctor drew his index finger across his throat before walking off. 'I hadn't slept, I was disorientated,' says Edwards. 'I hadn't a clue what was going on.' He would wake soon enough.

Before leaving England, Edwards had signed a contract to co-operate with a Sky website. The first column, an interview, had arrived in Australia ahead of him. And the British swimmers, lodging in the same luxurious hotel as the athletes, were not about to award Edwards the Pulitzer Prize for literature. Rather they had the demeanour of a lynch mob, aggrieved to find themselves subject to Edwards' apparent criticism. In the article on the web, the swimmers had been unamused to find themselves labelled 'party animals' and informed that '90 per cent of them had no chance of winning medals'. In England,

Edwards' alleged comments had become newspaper head-line material and had led radio sports broadcasts. Edwards, the quiet evangelist, was now an outlaw.

'I felt like public enemy number one,' he admits. Suddenly, he was corralled into meeting Kevin Hickey, a top-ranking official of the BOA, and a significant figure in establishing the holding camp. 'It was all very unpleasant, with a dreadful atmosphere,' explains Edwards. Hastily, he penned a written apology for distribution to the entire swimming team. Then he was taken to meet Paul Palmer, captain of the swimming team, and Ian Turner and Brenda Bland from their management. Turner's fury at the damage to the team's integrity was unmistakable to Edwards. 'I can remember Kevin Hickey telling them that he had spoken to the Minister of Sport and had been assured that this was not going to affect their Lottery fund-ing,' says Edwards. 'I explained how there had been a des-perate misunderstanding, and that my words had been taken outrageously out of context.'

Palmer, a sensitive, intelligent man, who won Britain's only medal in the Olympic pool at the Atlanta Games four years earlier, recalls: 'I heard the rumours about the article before I read it. It was pretty damning and full of general-izations that were insulting to me, and to the team. Yet I couldn't imagine someone of Jonathan Edwards' maturity and experience saying those kind of things in that context. When we met, I was confident that he would have a rea-sonable explanation. I accepted his apology – but I have to say damage had already been done. Ian Turner was not prepared to simply accept an apology, he wanted to know what was going to be done to repair the damage.'

Edwards was flabbergasted by the hostility. He was sad-dened further when he discovered he had supposedly written off Colin Jackson's prospects as well. 'I saw Colin and he understood I would have said no such thing. Later, we had dinner with his coach Malcolm Arnold as a guest of Brendan Foster.' Edwards complained throughout that he was a victim, not a villain. 'Not only was I quoted utterly out of context, there was a clear breach of contract,' he says, explaining that the offending article should have been presented for the approval of his agent, Jonathan Marks, before it was posted on the website. Yet some of the swimmers seemed less than enamoured with him; and, in the circumstances, Edwards remained in his room until he saw from his window that the swimming squad had boarded a coach for Coolangatta Airport and their flight to Sydney. 'It was a case of discretion being the better part of valour,' he says. Palmer adds, significantly: 'Some of the team were young men, not so mature, and they were displeased in that kind of group mentality where things can get out of perspective.'

'But Jonathan made a smart move by being proactive. He put a stop to the trouble before it started. Luckily, it didn't affect his own preparations for the Games. At the end of the day, he became Olympic champion and that's what counts. No one will remember in two years time what he said. I was pleased he won the gold, just as I was pleased when he broke the world record in 1995.'

Edwards, through no fault of his own, had learned a painful lesson; some contracts can be more expensive than the income they generate. His entrance into Australia had been an appalling experience. Sadly, it was to get worse. After delivering his personal apology to the swimmers, Edwards spent the next morning conducting a round of media interviews to repair the damage at home. He did this with charm and a genuine desire to put the regrettable incident behind him. By the time we went for lunch, at a waterside restaurant at Surfer's Paradise, he was feeling considerably more at ease. But the mood was not destined to last.

The phone call Edwards dreaded, but was privately expecting, came a little before 2.00 p.m. on the Gold Coast, which was 4.00 a.m. in Britain. To be with him, it was not necessary to hear the tearful voice of his wife on the other end of his mobile telephone. His own reddening eyes told you that Alison was imparting the news that her mother had died. He searched for words of commiseration, words to comfort his grieving wife, but at this moment he was mute. 'I felt so impotent,' he would confide later, when the phone line between them had been disconnected. 'Emotionally I feel I am in the wrong place, away from all the people I love.' Due to the ten-hour time difference, Edwards had to wait several hours before he could call his home. 'I broke the news to the boys that Gran had died,' he says. 'I also tried to reach Alison at the hospice, but she had left. I spoke to her father, Ralph, and he reassured me that I was in the right place. He told me that they would all be all right in my absence. I felt very humbled.'

Twenty-four hours later, he was still distraught at being apart from the family at such a heartrending time. 'I've never missed Alison and the boys so much,' he explains. 'I was torn apart, I had few thoughts for the Olympics. I sobbed my heart out in my room. Had Alison asked me to come home, had I felt she desperately needed me, I would have flown back to be with her.' Four years before, you may recall, Edwards had been an emotional wreck on the morning of the Olympic final. On that occasion, Alison, distressed by her husband's anguish, had said then: 'Just come home.'

346

But this time there was a fortitude in Alison's voice on the other side of the world that Edwards could detect. 'I was encouraged by the fact that Alison sounded on an even keel,' he says. She had resolved before her husband left home that the family would manage, that she would draw strength from her faith, from her sisters, Margo and Lynsey, and her father. She was as good as her word.

Alison would explain later: 'We had seen Mum ill for so long, we had wished the suffering would be over for her. Yet as Jonathan went away she was a little stronger and I felt that she might survive for another three weeks. We had talked about what we would do should Mum die, and we felt it would be best for Jonathan to remain in Australia. Given the choice, I would have wanted him with me, but once he had left I knew it was too far for him to come back. Mum wouldn't have wanted him to come home on her account, so I knew that we would deal together as a family with whatever happened. When it matters, you know, I am someone who can cope.'

Anne died at around 2.00 a.m. with her husband and her daughter Margo at her bedside. Alison and her sister Lynsey had not long left her, to try to get some rest in another room at the hospice. 'In the end, Mum's death was very peaceful,' says Alison. 'We had all been with her not long before she died. Funny, isn't it – do you know what we did when we left her room? We drank tea together. You are in the midst of a tragedy and you find yourself drinking tea ... so British.'

The funeral was held on Friday 15 September, the day of the opening ceremony at the Games. Edwards' parents had travelled from Whitehaven to take care of Sam and Nathan. On the Gold Coast, Edwards was still struggling with his sleep pattern, still prone to moments of weepiness. 'But,' he says, 'there was also a feeling of relief that Anne's suffering was over. There was also a sense of release, that we had come to the end of a long, traumatic period in our lives. I felt that a chapter had closed, and a new one was beginning. Yet with Anne's death, I also felt that the Olympics had become an even bigger event in our lives. There would be an even bigger sense of loss if I failed.' Within a couple of days, news of her death had reached the assembled media in Australia and there was immediate speculation in the British newspapers as to how Edwards would react. Was another Olympic Games doomed to end in tears?

At this moment, however, Alison was uncomprehending of the Olympics. 'I'm glad Mum died when she did,' she says. 'The Briggs family had a chance to say our goodbyes, we had a lovely funeral service for her, and there was a sense that Mum had completed her race. To the newspapers, Jonathan Edwards may have lost his mother-in-law. But she was much more than that. She was my mum...'

Chapter 18

Mission Accomplished

Hopping and jumping all around,
I never stay long on the ground;
I may be gone for just a while,
but I'll be back and make you smile.

BEANIE BABY RABBIT

On Thursday 21 September, Edwards collected his bags, checked out of the Radisson Resort Palm Meadows Hotel on the Gold Coast and headed for the small airport at Coolangatta. His stay in the holding camp had not been as smooth as he might have wished, but he was leaving for Sydney healthy of body (as healthy as he could expect after years of wear and tear, anyway) and determined of spirit.

He knew the next time he unpacked his spiked shoes, he would be competing in the Olympic Games. The flight to Sydney took an hour and, once in the Olympic city, Edwards went straight to the Athletes' Village, a land-scaped conurbation built across the road from Stadium Australia. The Australians had promised that the athletes would be at the core of these Games and they were true to their word. The British quarters, chosen at the planning stage more than two years earlier, were self-contained with

349

inspiring views across the street to the stadium where dreams would be fulfilled or broken. In contrast to Atlanta four years before, there was not a word raised in criticism of the facilities at the Village. The rooms were spacious, the cafeteria cavernous. This was where someone like horse-woman Pippa Funnell, at her first Olympics for Britain, could share a coffee with rower Matthew Pinsent, a man seeking his third gold medal and fundamental to Steve Redgrave's aspiration to win a fifth gold. This is the charm of the Games, throwing men and women from wildly different circles into communion, no matter how briefly.

At his first Games in Seoul, Edwards had revelled in the camaraderie of the moment, the exhilaration of being in the midst of the greatest sporting show on earth. But times change, ambition swells. To Edwards, the Games had long since ceased to be a place to play. This was his office and he was chairman of the board, a man expected to deliver; sad, but true. Above all, he was a man answerable to his God.

As usual, Edwards' entrance to the Village had been delayed as late as possible to reduce the amount of distraction that cannot be avoided when you have thousands of athletes living together and working to independent agendas. Edwards was grateful that his roommate was Steve Backley, a same-generation athlete. He could rely on Backley to respect his space, just as the javelin man would have no worries about sharing a room with him.

The day after his arrival in Sydney, which was also the day before the qualifying rounds of the triple jump competition, Edwards' sponsors, Asics, arranged an informal media call not far from the Village. Also present to undergo scrutiny from the small assembly of newsmen was Larry Achike, the 25-year-old Commonwealth gold medallist aspiring to emulate Edwards' success one day. Achike, a tall, amiable Londoner who trains for half of the year in Australia, confessed to studying videos of Edwards in competition. 'You just look and try to learn,' he says. Edwards smiles. He has watched those same videos – and long since abandoned trying to recreate the double-arm shift that propelled him to such prodigious distances in 1995, when he leaped further than any man before or since. 'I am intuitive as an athlete, not that technical,' he explains. Of course, his event demands great technique, as well as placing the body under constant duress. 'You can be in fantastic shape, have a great sense of anticipation, but a small technical flaw can undermine your performance. There is so much to get right, you really are on a knife-edge. Let's be honest, a couple of months ago I was on a downward spiral. I had come back injured from my training camp in Israel and everything seemed to be falling apart. But now I feel very relaxed, and couldn't ask for any more: at 34 years old, I am in shape and have the opportunity to win a gold medal in the Millennium Games which promise to be the greatest ever.'

In contrast to Atlanta, Edwards was not an odds-on favourite in Sydney. But favourite he was none the less. 'Only Jonathan Edwards can beat Jonathan Edwards,' was the mantra Edwards had come to hear like a stuck recording from Andy Norman. In private reflective moments, Edwards accepted the truth of such a belief. But, publicly, he was more circumspect. He has always let others beat his drum. 'I have thought about both scenarios, and I am prepared for both winning and losing,' he admitted, his entry into the Games just over 24 hours distant. 'It's one thing to go through it in your head, another to have to deal with the reality.

'My prayer is that God gives me the strength to cope come what may. That in victory I don't glorify myself; in defeat I don't plumb the depths of despair.' In these moments, Edwards is speaking as the restrained, publicly modest Christian. But Edwards the competitive athlete also wishes to be heard on this warm, spring morning. 'Winning is everything to me,' says Edwards now. 'I haven't made so many sacrifices over the years and Alison, in particular, didn't give me her blessing to stay here for me to come second.'

But in the final analysis with Edwards there is always a sense of perspective. 'Whatever happens, the fundamentals of my life will not change no matter the result on Monday,' he said.

Edwards' sleep was uninterrupted and he awoke, not surprisingly focused on his qualifying rounds. His roommate Backley was consumed by his final that same day – and for a second consecutive Olympics he would win silver – and they were absently-mindedly watching television. Suddenly, Backley's coach John Trower burst into their room and changed the channel. And that is how they came to witness Steve Redgrave's row for gold, in company with Matthew Pinsent, Tim Foster and James Cracknell in the Coxless Fours. They shouted the Oarsome Foursome home in company with seven million viewers watching the BBC transmission at nearly 1.00 a.m. in Britain. 'In those final 100 metres, I was willing Steve not to get beaten,' says Edwards. 'He had given everything, and we just wanted him to get to the line. He was drained, empty. His record is beyond comprehension – he's an inspiration.'

That evening Edwards reported for Olympic duty, but

there were none of the usual misgivings or nervous butter-flies. Just a ridiculous calm. He was walking about greeting and shaking hands with the men who would be trying their utmost to deny him the gold. 'When it came time for me to jump, I was too relaxed,' he suggests. 'It was like, "This is in God's hands, what will be, will be" – and I forgot to jump. Those watching thought I was jumping at no more than 70 per cent capacity.' Those watching included Alison, who was mightily underwhelmed.

Never comfortable watching her husband compete, this was purgatory. 'I thought he looked like Andy Pandy out to play,' Alison commented, as she endured her husband's less than inspirational performance. 'What is wrong with him?' she asked. 'I couldn't believe it, this was the Olympic quali-fying and he didn't seem to be taking it seriously.'

Edwards actually qualified for the Olympic triple jump final as the third British competitor, behind Achike and Phillips Idowu. 'It was very strange, normally I am scared, very nervous, but I felt more relaxed than at any other competition in my life,' said Edwards. 'But Larry and Phillips were outstanding, both delivering personal best performances on an evening when they came in uncertain as to whether they could even make the final.'

Achike leapt an impressive 17.30 metres, while Idowu jumped 17.12 metres. In contrast, Edwards travelled just 17.08 metres. If, mentally, he was unexpectedly chilled out, Edwards was genuinely unconcerned. 'I'm not the least bothered,' he insisted. 'All qualifying does is get you a pass to play in the big game. I looked awful jumping under 17 metres in qualifying in Atlanta – but jumped 17.88 metres in the Olympic final.' He still felt he was the man to beat if you had the ambition of leaving Sydney with a gold medal in your luggage from the triple jump sandpit. 'The stadium is awesome, the atmosphere electric. Nothing has altered.'

On the telephone to her husband that evening Alison was slightly more demanding. She was to tell him: 'What are you playing at? If you want that medal, you are going to have to fight for it.' Alison came off the phone feeling better if not totally at ease, because that is something she can never attain when her husband is in competition.

Edwards spent much of the next day, his rest day, with Phil Wall, his friend from London who had pledged in the wake of his depressing performance in Seville in 1999 that he would join him in Australia. Wall put his life on hold for a week, accepted Edwards' offer of an air ticket and flew the 12,000 miles to join him on the Gold Coast. Wall is sounding board, philosopher and mate. Wall can talk to Edwards as someone without vested interest. He extends unconditional friendship – and Edwards listens. For much of the previous eight months, Wall and Edwards had been trying to put the Olympics into perspective. Their mantra was this: 'It's everything, and it's nothing.' In other words, says Wall: 'The Olympics may define Jon as an athlete, but as to defining him as a man and a father and husband, the Olympics are nothing.'

The dilemma, as Wall saw it on that rest day in Sydney after the unimpressive qualifying rounds, was that Edwards had taken the message to the extreme. 'I was concerned Jon had got to the point where the Olympics didn't matter.' So after attending church at the Shire Christian Centre, after lunch, Wall parked his borrowed car outside the entrance to the Olympic Village and engaged Edwards in intimate conversation for thirty minutes. 'I was strong with Jon,' he recalls. 'I told him, "We've been right to say the Games are everything and nothing, but, actually as an athlete, this IS absolutely everything. Your wife has paid a massive price for this, you can't go back home with a silver".

Edwards understood these sentiments, and in that car he had been close to tears when he said to Wall: 'A big part of this is that I just want to make Alison proud.' Wall feels that their conversation, deep and profound, acted as a 'wake-up' call. 'Jon is not a guy to respond to rah, rah, rah, up and at them, eye of the tiger nonsense,' he explains. 'That's not who he is. You have to hit different buttons and I felt a real sense of responsibility. It had been a long way to go for those minutes of conversation – but actually it was worth it. As I drove away I just hoped I hadn't been too harsh.'

He left Edwards with a small, symbolic gift. While at the Gold Coast holding camp, when they had shared prayers, and spent hours on the pool table where Edwards proved invincible, Wall listened hard. 'Jon told me that in a daydream moment, when he was standing on the station leaving home to become a professional athlete all those years ago, he felt like the small boy who came before Jesus with five loaves and two fish when there was such a massive need for food. He said to me: "Like the little boy, I was going to give Jesus my gift to make of it what he could".' Wall never forgot, and on the eve of the Olympic final he had planned to give Edwards a profound and symbolic parting shot.

'Well, getting caught up in traffic, time got away,' he says. 'So I bought Jon a can of sardines to symbolize the fish. There was something surreal about the moment in the intensity of that car. But I knew this was the last opportunity I had to speak with him before the final.' That evening Edwards sent Wall a text message to his mobile phone:

'God brought you here for today – I am ready.'

And when Edwards walked into Stadium Australia for the Olympic final, he had in his bag a rabbit Beanie Baby, a gift from Alison and the boys; and a can of sardines. Unbeknown to his family, the following apposite rhyme appeared on the Beanie Baby: 'Hopping and jumping all around, I never stay long on the ground; I may be gone for just a while, but I'll be back and make you smile.'

At home in Gosforth, breakfast on Monday 25 September was to prove a quiet, somewhat tense affair in the Edwards' household. After showering, Alison succumbed to her usual bout of nerves. 'I felt a bit weepy,' she says. Sam and Nathan had been granted a morning off school to watch their dad compete. Her father, Ralph, was also in the house, along with Edwards' parents, Andy and Jill, who had travelled from their Cumbrian parish to the Northeast to enable them all to be together on what, one way or the other, was going to be an unforgettable day. Breakfast was followed by prayers, with the competition scheduled to start at 10.00 a.m.

That, of course, was 8.00 p.m. in the evening for those of us in Sydney. Earlier, I had taken the unusual step of calling Edwards in the Village. We exchanged small talk for which he was grateful. 'I'm just counting the seconds, the minutes, the hours,' he said. 'At times like this it feels like the clock is going backwards.' We talked a little more, and during the conversation he came to understand that the triple jump would be taking place at the precise moment local heroine Cathy Freeman would be running in the 400 metres final. That would invite an avalanche of noise to descend on Stadium Australia. It was safe to predict that 110,000 people would rise as one voice, and the decibel pitch would make trying to compete in the triple jump like trying to run under the wings of a Boeing 747 as it is cleared for take-off. Edwards felt better armed for knowing the detail of the timetable, and he concluded the call in high spirits. 'It's going to be my day,' he said.

As the hour of destiny approached, Alison knew she could not bring herself to watch. 'I just had to get out of the house,' she explains. With her friend Linda for company, Alison went for a walk. The two women, Linda with her mobile phone for bulletins from Jill Edwards, aimlessly walked the streets of Jesmond.

Edwards, meantime, had entered the stadium with his rivals. He was wearing a dark blue fleece over his running vest, numbered 1792, and track pants. He had on a baseball cap and luminous lime-green spikes. He wore a faraway look, and busied himself marking out his run by placing one heel in front of the toe of his other foot, walking back from the take-off board. With the prospect of being out in the stadium for nearly two hours, the athletes were able to place discarded clothes on the side of the track at a Perspex hut, like those at rural bus stops. Appropriately, this was where the queue formed as athletes, one after another, waited turns to practise their stride pattern on the runway. Edwards never taxes himself. A few high steps, a short sprint, no more. Others like to explode and bound down the runway in final rehearsal. But Edwards prefers a more cerebral routine. He walks around, hands on hips, in silent contemplation. He prays. He absorbs himself in what must be done, alone in the moment. After a while, the time arrived for the stadium announcer to draw attention to the triple jump, on the far side of the track from the finish-line. The man on the public address ran through the list, then got to number

1792. 'With silver from the 1996 Olympic Games in Atlanta, from Great Britain, Jonathan Edwards.' He is used to more elaborate introductions, but he was prepared for a battle and this simply underscored that holding the world record counted for nothing on this evening.

The man to open the competition was Britain's Achike. With memories of his personal best from the qualifying still fresh in his mind, Achike cleared 17.29 metres to guarantee himself a place at the heart of the contest from the start. Yoel Garcia from Cuba, Australian Andrew Murphy and American Walter Davis followed in turn, before Edwards was invited to the start line. Edwards, you sensed, was keen to jump before Freeman took her blocks for the 400 metres that was to cause bedlam inside the stadium and, outside, paralyse the entire nation. Edwards managed 17.12 metres and returned to the 'bus shelter' to replace his tracksuit. Not what he had hoped for, but an improvement on the no-jump with which he began in Atlanta.

Across the track, Freeman was going to her blocks in a one-piece, hooded costume in green and gold. Pity poor Russian Denis Kapustin, now waiting on the triple jump runway. A wall of sound like thunder enveloped the stadium. Then, as the women were called to their marks, and these included Katharine Merry and Donna Fraser from Britain, there was silence. Library-like silence.

Bang! And the stadium exploded again. Freeman went past the triple jump pit to an accompaniment of thousands of flash bulbs, as spectators tried to capture the moment for posterity. Even Edwards' tunnel-vision was breached. Freeman was running for herself, for her country, but she was also burdened with running for the Aboriginal population, which had been so appallingly disenfranchised for generations. She was not remotely slowed by the expectation, until after she crossed the line in the gold medal position at the end of one of the most extraordinary foot races in Olympic history. And then she sat on the track, and she wept. She stared motionlessly at the giant screen. She breathed slowly, as though freezing the memory for old age. Eventually, she got to her feet shoe-less; and she took off on a lap of honour like no other lap these Games would witness. Freeman was draped in the Australian and Aboriginal flags as she passed the triple jump pit that was now as empty as a desert.

But, of course, for all the majesty of those precious moments the Games had to continue. And for Edwards that meant his second-round jump was going to coincide with Michael Johnson's appearance in the Men's 400 metres final. Edwards deliberately stripped his tracksuit slowly and Johnson was rounding the final bend, on the way to becoming the first-ever man to defend an Olympic 400 metres title, when he finally took off. The British athlete jumped cleanly, if behind the board, and when he looked back he saw he had recorded a distance of 17.37 metres. He showed no emotion, but he was now leading. Edwards' challenge was down.

Kapustin, the giant, bear-like Russian who had comprehensively beaten Edwards on his home turf, at Gateshead in 1999, responded with immediate effect. He assumed control with a jump of 17.46 metres. Meanwhile, for the reigning world champion Charles Friedek the competition was an ongoing nightmare. Edwards had heard a whisper on his way to Australia from Japan that Friedek was being troubled by a knee injury, and it seemed that after a second no-jump he was in the kind of trouble for which there is no remedy. Similarly Rostislav Dimitrov, the Bulgarian who won silver at the World Championships in Seville 13 months earlier, was not supplying any evidence to suggest he was going to be a factor. Friedek and Rostislav were duly eliminated at the halfway point, after three rounds.

The third round was to prove decisive for Edwards. On the runway he clasped his hands together as though in prayer. He placed them above his head, clapping and encouraging the crowd to form a noisy chorus. He rocked onto one heel a final time, then released himself down the runway. He held the jump together through willpower, not masterly technique. As he levered himself from the sand, he instinctively raised an arm aloft. He walked away with a fist clenched. He may not have flown like he had in Gothenburg – or in Atlanta for that matter – but he could tell instinctively that this was the jump they would have to beat. A roar accompanied the numbers being posted on the board at the side of the track: 17.71 metres. This was the furthest he had jumped all year, the furthest anyone had jumped. His timing may not have been perfect in execution, but his timing was nevertheless perfect.

Edwards had one hand on the gold, but you would not know from studying his demeanour. He was unsmiling and just walking around, unaware that 12,000 miles away at home his wife was doing precisely the same. 'We got a phone call telling us Jonathan had jumped 17.37 in the second round,' recalls Alison. 'But it seemed an eternity before we got the next one informing us about his 17.71 metres.' She asked Linda to stop, and they sat on a bench overlooking allotments in Gosforth. 'I felt faint and needed a drink of water.' On the track, Edwards was also taking a slug of water, his face almost as grey as the hair at his temples. He could not let himself get a step ahead. He had to stay in the moment, so he kept pacing around, willing himself to concentrate. Again, there was a further distraction elsewhere in the stadium, on this night of all nights of athletics. This time the rolling thunderclap of support was reserved for an Australian pole-vaulter, the gorgeously named, gorgeously proportioned Tatiana Grigorieva, who was challenging America's Stacy Dragila for gold. Ms Grigorieva would ultimately settle for silver, while in the triple jump the fourth round passed without event. The medal places remained unchanged. Once again, the focus of the stadium was to fall on Freeman as she returned for her medal ceremony. The largest choir assembled under one roof joined with her in singing the National Anthem, 'Advance, Australia Fair'.

But these fabulous cameos of colour and noise were not the reason Edwards opted to pass on the fifth round. Those who know him, like Alison, like his father, like Andy Norman, like coach Peter Stanley, all expected him to conserve himself for a last push in the final round, if required. Edwards was now one jump away from gold. One jump from placing himself in Olympic history. One jump from fulfilling a dream that had taken shape on a windswept school playing field in Devon. One jump…

Edwards kept walking. He would watch and he would wait. For Achike, the final round was to be heartbreaking. With his last jump of 17.37 metres, Cuban Yoelbi Quesada was to put the British athlete out of the running for the bronze medal. And then Kapustin was to be the victim of more heartache as another Cuban, Garcia, dug within himself to jump one centimetre past the Russian, with 17.47 metres. When the Russian was unable to improve with his sixth and last attempt, he knew he had to console himself with the bronze.

And for Edwards there was the sudden, wonderful realization that he was the Olympic Champion for 2000. Tears began to gather in his eyes. Several thousand British fans, mostly assembled in the seats on the first corner, began waving Union flags in celebration. He went to the start of his run-up, spread his arms wide and signalled that he wished the crowd to clap him down the runway. Dutifully, they obliged. Edwards, unfortunately, registered a no-jump, but he cared not. He emerged from the pit, took a flag as a cloak and wiped a tear with the corner. He found Israeli Rogel Nahum in the crowd and gave him a hug, then Kelly Holmes, running courageously to a bronze medal in the 800 metres after a catalogue of serious injuries, stopped her own celebratory march to kiss Edwards. Young Idowu hugged him, Achike whispered heartfelt congratulations in his ear, before Garcia and Kapustin dispensed their own handshakes. Edwards was smiling like a child at Christmas, innocent and bewildered at the magnitude of the gifts he was unwrapping. Slowly, he walked back round the track with the Union flag as his suit of honour. When he reached the bank of British supporters they waved their flags and cheered in a synchronized display of affection. Edwards stopped and stared, caught momentarily in the glare of his own achievement. A voice he recognized broke the spell. Shouting loudest was Linford Christie, the 1992 Olympic 100 metres champion. 'Linford was delighted for me – he also wanted me to throw my shoes into the crowd.' Edwards duly complied, just as Maurice Greene had done after he won the Men's 100 metres title. Astonishingly, also in the stands on this utterly unforgettable evening was Val

Davison, the woman who gave him his first (and only) job as a scientific officer in the cytogenetics laboratory at the Royal Victoria Infirmary in Newcastle back in 1988, which set Edwards on his way. More remarkably still, she and her husband, Kelsey, were seated next to Phil Wall.

Finally, Edwards completed his walk of honour and made it to the mixed zone, the area where the media can grab a soundbite from the athletes. 'What a dog fight!' he confided. 'I was just overwhelmed. I was on the point of crying on a number of occasions and had to choke back the tears. I couldn't believe what was happening – this awesome arena, the Olympic Games, and I was the champion. It was almost too much.'

He walked past a long line of television networks, offering each of them his scrambled thoughts. And then on a chair at the rear of the mixed zone he borrowed his coach Peter Stanley's mobile telephone and called Alison. It can be disclosed that, although she had made it home in time for the climax of the competition, she had taken refuge upstairs in her bedroom when the fifth round was taking place, too nervous to watch. 'When Linda rushed up the stairs and said, "He's done it", I just burst into tears.'

Sam and Nathan, by now, were itching for life to return to normal, to make the most of this present of what had become a full day off school. 'Who wants to play football?' asked one. 'What's for lunch?' enquired the other. Outside, a group of reporters were politely waiting on the Edwards' doorstep. Andy Edwards good-naturedly answered most of the questions. Edwards himself was subjected to gentle interrogation from those athletics writers who, in truth, were never quite certain he had the head or the heart to match his undoubted gifts. But there was to be no shortage of tributes for Edwards as the next morning his triumphant story began on most front pages of the British newspapers, before spilling over into the sports sections.

'Only once in the course of winning Britain's second athletics gold medal of the Games yesterday did the triple jumper Jonathan Edwards give a glimpse of the interior fire required of Olympic champions,' wrote Mike Rowbottom in the *Independent* (26 September 2000). 'Scrambling to his feet after a third-round effort of 17.71 metres, the furthest achieved in the world this year, the man who had once remarked that all he did was jump into a sandpit betrayed another attitude to his vocation. His right fist pumped the air. His eyes burned. Could this possibly be the nice Mr Edwards who had agonized over the years about whether God wanted him to jump on Sundays, or to own a Mercedes? One and the same. And what he achieved in the packed, 110,000 capacity Olympic stadium here at the age of 34 offered conclusive evidence that he is one of British athletics' greatest competitors.'

Edwards had talked self-deprecatingly of being on this night only 'a side show', and with Freeman, Johnson and Haile Gebreselassie (10,000 metres) all strutting their stuff, this was a plausible point of view; but Edwards' accomplishment was a stunning triumph for a man who never lost faith in his ability, and who kept that faith in tandem with his faith in God. 'An athlete, whoever he is, cannot be considered among the greatest until he wins the Olympics,' said Donovan Bailey, the 1996 100 metres Olympic champion.

By my watch it was 11.22 p.m. when Edwards re-entered the stadium to receive his gold medal from Craig Reedie, chairman of the British Olympic Committee and an IOC member. He watched as they ran a replay of his jump on the large screen, and he fought again with the emotions twisting his gut like a corkscrew. He was over-come by the poignancy of hearing himself declared Olympic champion, first in French, then in English. As the Union flag started its slow, ceremonial journey to the top of the flagpole, Edwards found himself involuntarily, some might say ironically, singing along with the National Anthem. 'If I hadn't I would have cried!' Beside him Garcia and Kapustin seemed equally satisfied; as though they knew that with Edwards in the competition they had only ever been competing for the minor medals.

'I have had a lot of disappointments in the last few years and I didn't want the family to have to face another together,' Edwards would explain. 'I wanted to go back to Alison, to my boys, to show them a gold medal.'

Yet as Edwards had pledged in the countdown to the Games, he would not allow a gold bauble to affect him dramatically. 'It was everything for me to win the gold medal, and it was nothing,' he says. 'I am not defined by the fact I am Olympic champion. I am defined by God's love for me and my love for Him; and my love for my family and their love for me. But as a Christian athlete I felt I had a debt of duty to give my all in pursuit of Olympic gold.'

And so Edwards finally found his weary way back to the Village, where he went with Kelly Holmes in search of sus-tenance. Kelly settled for a bag of McDonald's fries, but Edwards could not satisfy his craving for a Magnum lolly. His roommate Steve Backley, a silver medallist for the second Games in succession, was snoring, so Edwards' momentous day ended with him taking a couple of sleep-ing pills to get some rest. Beside him as he went to sleep was his gold medal. 'It seems absurd now, but it was the most natural thing at that moment.'

The next morning was another whirlwind tour of the media, with his friends Phil Wall and Mark Byron both joining him when he met Brendan Foster and a BBC crew at an Asics conference on the harbourside. Foster was ebullient, thrilled that an athlete trained and living in the Northeast had finally won an Olympic gold. Foster, offering Edwards a glass of champagne, said to me: 'You remember a year ago, when you first interviewed me for your book on Jonathan, you asked: "When did the British public fall in love with the triple jump?" Well, the answer is last night!'

Edwards went from microphone to notebook, and when he took a taxi to the Main Press Centre at the Olympic Stadium, the driver politely asked to handle his gold medal. 'Can I kiss it?' he enquired, and he invited Edwards to sign his crumpled street guide to Sydney to ensure that his mates at the taxi depot believed his story when he next met them. Oh the power of an Olympic gold!

All Edwards wanted now, of course, was to fly home to Newcastle, through London. On board was Colin Jackson, again having to live with the spectre of Olympic failure. 'I felt for Colin because I knew how difficult it would have been for me if the tables had been turned.'

The ground crew of British Airways at Sydney ensured Edwards was upgraded to first class, and the cabin crew assured him a memorable journey home. To minimize the fuss in Newcastle, Alison and the boys waited for him at home while he was chauffeured from the apron of the airport to his front door.

Later, the Edwards family went to the boys' school, Ascham House, and his gold medal was passed from little hand to little hand. 'Everyone was so kind and excited,' says Alison. Of course, Edwards took the medal with him when he met Norman Anderson to drive them both to the gym at Gateshead Stadium a couple of days after he got home. 'The guy cutting the grass in the middle of the stadium stopped to come over and inspect the medal,' says Anderson. 'You know, I've seen all colours except gold. I was disappointed in Bren's medal (Foster won a bronze at Montreal in 1976). It didn't look of special value. Jonathan's gold looked the part, though. Everyone wanted to touch it, you know, even some of the real hard men that we get in here.

'For me, there was just a sense of relief of a job well done. World records get beaten, but once you are an Olympic gold medallist you are that for life. Relief, yes, that's what it was.'

Edwards, not surprisingly, was feted wherever he went. At Holy Trinity Church, Jesmond, they organized a party in his honour. 'I never appreciated how much people followed me,' he says. 'There was an overwhelming sense of happiness for me that I had won. It's exceedingly humbling. I just think God has been so incredibly gracious to us.

'Only by winning can you begin to realize what it would have meant to have lost again.' For days, make that weeks, Edwards was in a daze trying to make sense of what being Olympic champion meant. Alison confessed to a sense of anti-climax, her emotions a maelstrom of joy for her husband while still overcome by the grief of her mother's death. 'You have worked towards this for so long and now it's happened it is wonderful, don't get me wrong,' she says. 'But now it's over, now what? I admit to feeling a little numb.' In contrast, it is perhaps understandable that Edwards feels somewhat different. 'There is no sense of anti-climax, just a quiet and private sense of fulfilment.'

There were other more obvious side effects to Edwards' success, as his agent Jonathan Marks explains: 'We worked through what is right for Jonathan, in terms of commercial contracts. If he wanted, he could conceivably turn the gold medal into a million-pound payday. For instance, Jonathan would command £10,000 an appearance on the motivational speech-making circuit. Jonathan is a tremendous speaker, but his motivation is his faith, so at the moment he is not comfortable where that sits in the corporate market place. He is definitely not milking the dollar – 80 per cent of offers are politely dismissed. But I sense there is a greater acceptance for Jonathan as an individual than ever. He has invoked more passion since his accomplishment in Sydney.' One successful contract with Energizer Batteries was in position before the Games, but a gold medal undeniably increased the ante. He also agreed to a picture shoot and interview with *Hello!* magazine, the anodyne glossy so beloved by minor royals and aristocracy.

In the main, though, Edwards remains difficult to entice from his home in the Northeast, and on his return from Sydney the family moved into a five-bedroom, detached house that they had fallen in love with at the end of the summer. In spite of the central heating being condemned within 24 hours of their move, Edwards says: 'We love the space and the character of the house.' With the trauma of the house move, Edwards declined invitations to appear on *The Des O'Connor Show* and *Call My Bluff*, although he did an Olympics' special of *A Question of Sport* with Steve Redgrave, Matthew Pinsent and gold medal winning boxer Audley Harrison. He was also unable to make an appointment at Buckingham Palace in mid-November, an invitation extended to the entire British Olympic team with medallists being granted an introduction to the Queen.

On Friday 24 November, Edwards was honoured to be made a Freeman of the Borough of Gateshead, reporting that there have been only 25 others granted that distinction since 1873. Mayor Pitch Wilson sent his own official limousine to collect the Edwards family from home, with a second car despatched to chauffeur Reverend Andy Edwards, his wife Jill, and Ralph Briggs. At the Civic Centre, they were greeted by the Mayor, council officers and councillors. Employees had assembled to form a friendly guard of honour as the Edwards family were ushered to their seats in the council chamber, walking behind a lone Northumberland Piper. The Bishop of Durham, Michael Turnbull, offered prayers before Councillor George Gill proposed the motion to make Edwards a Freeman of Gateshead, drawing a unanimous response from the chamber. Edwards then signed a register and accepted a framed scroll and a specially commissioned piece of art, depicting him jumping. 'It was an overwhelming experience, a ceremony of unexpected gravitas,' said Edwards. 'There was a great solemnity to proceedings, but there was also an unmissable warmth to the celebration. It meant a huge amount to me – more than I anticipated – and it was especially moving to imagine that I was the first to be granted this honour in over twenty years. The Mayor suggested this would be the highlight of his year's office.' Edwards, who spoke with his customary humility in response, never did get to sample the buffet. He was too busily engaged in talking and signing autographs. 'It was wonderful to have such public acceptance.'

Edwards carried a secret with him to the civic ceremony, as his post the day before had included a letter from 10 Downing Street. Edwards, already an MBE, was informed that he had been recommended to the Queen to become a Commander of the British Empire in the New Year's Honours. 'Another huge honour,' said Edwards. 'I wrote a letter to convey my gratitude to Prime Minister Tony Blair.'

That same weekend, Edwards was named by the Athletics Writers' Association as Athlete of the Year, in company with heptathlon gold medallist Denise Lewis. On the horizon were further ceremonies; he was to receive the Freedom of Newcastle on the same occasion as Newcastle and England striker, Alan Shearer; and he was to be given an honorary degree from Newcastle University, a Doctorate of Civil Law. Edwards and his wife were pictured constantly in their local newspapers, almost to the point of embarrassment. 'We were in danger of becoming the Posh and Becks of the Northeast!' he said, self-mockingly.

There was also a weekend at EuroDisney in Paris – for his sons, of course! – when the Edwards family were feted guests along with the Redgrave family, entertainer Jonathan Ross and his family, retired international footballer Ian Wright and his family, actress Leslie Ash and her husband, retired footballer Lee Chapman, and GMTV journalists Fiona Phillips and Martin Frizzel, all with their children.

Through the upheaval of his life being turned upside down and his family being transplanted to the other side of Gosforth High Street, Edwards has resumed training in the gym at Gateshead. He is planning to compete in the indoor season at the beginning of 2001, as well as entering a couple of events in South Africa. 'I feel I could go on for another ten years,' he says, and while this is an obvious exaggeration it is indicative of his mindset. Edwards is an athlete with no immediate designs on retirement.

Indeed, returning to training at Gateshead has proved therapeutic. Inside that worn but warm gymnasium, he is able to switch onto autopilot as he lifts weights, or steps hurdles, or throws a medicine ball, or simply stretches. Edwards welcomes this almost non-thinking state. Within his own euphoria, his sense of accomplishment, is the realization that not one, but several chapters in his life have been closed. He has shown that what happened on a summer's night in Gothenburg in 1995 was not a fleeting flame of chance, that being world record holder was not to be the summit of his achievement. He has proved that after failure in Atlanta, when he was at the peak of his athletic powers, he had the resilience to survive another exhausting four-year cycle to become the Olympic champion in Sydney. And after two years' anguish, especially for Alison who had to endure her mum's illness and slow death, he feels this is a new beginning, in a new home with the future a wonderful, unpredictable adventure.

Edwards will jump on, not only exploiting his gold medal, but because he is wise enough to appreciate that an athlete is a long time retired. He is an Olympic champion moved by his triumph, stirred by the emotions evoked, but, mostly, humbled by the entire experience. He remains also articled to the ambition to spread God's word through his gift.

For the foreseeable future, he can envisage no better landscape to deliver that gospel than to continue running round the playing fields of the world and jumping into a sandpit. After Sydney, this makes more sense to him than ever.

Appendix

The Sunday Question

Jonathan Edwards writes:

Towards the end of 1992, I wrote an article for the quarterly magazine of the Christians in Sport organization, articulating a radical change of heart in my intention to compete on Sundays. Towards the end of 1999, reviewing that piece is instructive: even as I changed my decision about Sunday jumping, I perceive myself a much changed man from the one who penned those words seven years ago.

If I were sitting down today to write that same piece for the first time, it would appear quite different. It would be more reasoned, explaining my freedom to compete on a Sunday from my understanding of the Bible. It would be more objective, balancing the pragmatic reasons for my decision with the more subjective call of God.

These differences are both an encouragement and a rebuke to me. I am encouraged because I believe that my faith is on a firmer foundation than it was back in 1992, but I am challenged by the simplicity of the former article and, in particular, the immediacy of God that I express there. I am reminded of some of Jesus' words to his disciples: 'He called a little child and had him stand among them. And he said: "I tell you the truth, unless you change and become like little children, you will never enter the kingdom of heaven. Therefore, whoever humbles himself like this child is the greatest in the kingdom of heaven"' (Matthew 18:2–4).

Those who know me well will recognize that this is no defence of 'blind faith', that refuses to interact seriously with the ever-present challenges of marrying the reality of life with the Christian faith. But the call back to a more childlike belief is nonetheless very real.

The purpose of this piece, however, is not primarily introspective! I intend to outline more fully than before my understanding of the Sunday issue. I am acutely aware that many Christians were saddened by my change of heart and, judging by the letters I still receive, Sunday sport is yet a live debate. My aim is not to try to convert anyone to my way of thinking, but to be as transparent as possible about the processes that brought about my decision. In doing so, I hope that those who feel I have 'let the side down' might be reassured of my commitment to serve God.

It is indeed ironic that I first gained renown as an athlete through my *lack* of performance. Looking back, I still cannot believe the level of media attention that my decision to miss the 1988 Olympic trials caused. I was one of four triple jumpers fighting for three places, without any of us having a realistic chance of medalling – not exactly high-profile stuff. Yet cause a stir it did, and I was launched as 'the athlete who didn't jump on Sundays'.

The reality, however, was that I had never played sport on a Sunday, initially through my parents' insistence, but latterly out of my own personal conviction. The fast did not end there: it included all 'work', specifically academic work in my situation. If I had an exam on the Monday, Sunday revision was a nonstarter. This might all sound rather restrictive (and it did have its moments in my earlier years), but in fact, quite the opposite was true. Sunday was a great day and a very positive factor in my life, because I never felt under any compulsion to work. From the point of view of my studies, it was tremendously liberating. I could have a whole day off without feeling guilty! As Jesus said, 'The Sabbath was made for man, not man for the Sabbath' (Mark 2:27).

If Sunday was such a good thing, then, why the change? The context within which I made the decision was clear enough in my earlier article, namely, the desire to serve God more effectively as an athlete. The basis for the step was not so clear – in fact, it was non-existent. That is what I want to elucidate now. If the basis of my decision is faulty and does not stand up to biblical criticism, then I have, at best, made a terrible mistake and, at worst, I am a fraud.

Perhaps the most important stage in the development of my faith in recent years has been in the manner that I approach the Bible. It is not that my view of its truth has changed in any way, but when I sit down to read the Scriptures now, I have an interpretive framework within which to work. It is a frame of reference that takes account of the historical nature of the Bible and, in particular, recognizes the distinct stages in the outworking of God's purposes on earth, often termed 'dispensations'. I believe such parameters are vital for clear biblical interpretation and I have found such an approach instrumental in helping me better to understand and apply the Bible to my life. Certainly, it is an approach that helps to unravel the 'Sunday' debate.

Exodus 20:8–10a says, 'Remember the Sabbath day by keeping it holy. Six days you shall labour and do all your work, but the seventh day is a Sabbath to the LORD your God. On it you shall not do any work.' Our present-day 'Sunday' finds its origin in this commandment, the fourth of the Ten Commandments, and an examination of it is foundational to our subject. I would make the following observations.

Sunday is *not* the Sabbath. At first glance, this might seem churlish, but it proves to be a significant point. In the Sermon on the Mount, Jesus said these words in reference to the Jewish Law of which this command is a part: 'I tell you the truth, until heaven and earth disappear, not the smallest letter, not the least stroke of a pen, will by any means disappear from the Law until everything is accomplished' (Matthew 5:18). The Sabbath to which the Exodus verse refers is indisputably from sundown on Friday until sunset on Saturday. As I understand it, Sunday has become the 'Christian Sabbath' because this is the day on which Christ rose from the dead and the day on which the first-century Church congregated. There is, however, no biblical justification for this change. Moreover, if we take Jesus' words seriously, quite the opposite is true.

The next point closely relates to the first. The Sabbath commandment is not found in isolation. In its immediate context, it is part of the Ten Commandments. More widely, it is part of the entire Jewish Law, the Mosaic Law. This code covered the whole of Israel's national life – moral, ceremonial and civil. In his epistle, James, the half-brother of Jesus, makes the following comments with respect to this group of commandments: 'For whoever keeps the whole law and yet stumbles at just one point is guilty of breaking all of it. For he who said, "Do not commit adultery," also said, "Do not murder." If you do not commit adultery but do commit murder, you have become a law-breaker' (James 2:10–11). The essence of what James says is that the Law is a unity; we do not have the freedom simply to pick and choose which commands we will obey and which we will disregard.

From considering the fourth Commandment in light of the teaching of Jesus and the apostle James quoted above, we have a problem. If we believe that we have a mandate to keep the Sabbath on the basis of Exodus 20:8–10a, then it would appear that not only have we got the day wrong, but we are also ignoring a large number of commandments. Consistent interpretation demands that we follow the entire Mosaic Law to the letter – something that I do not think any Christian actually believes. Therefore, the question we need to answer is this: What is the applicability of Old Testament Law to contemporary believers?

It is here that a dispensational framework proves its value. Writing to Timothy, Paul says, 'Do your best to present yourself to God as one approved, a workman who does not need to be ashamed and who *correctly handles* the word of truth' (2 Timothy 2:15, emphasis mine). A dispensational approach to the Bible helps us to do just that, by delineating the various and distinct stages in God's purposes and thus guiding our interpretation and application. I see the following points ensuing from such an approach.

The Mosaic Law was exclusively given to the nation of Israel as part of the covenant that God made with her after he had delivered her from the Egyptian captivity. Sabbath observance was a sign of that arrangement (see Exodus 31:12–17).

The testimony of many New Testament passages is that this covenant is now finished (Galatians 3:19ff, for example). The Law stood for the whole covenantal agreement that God made with Israel, which has now clearly been superseded by the new covenant in Christ. If the old covenant is over, then the jurisdiction of the Law, which was an integral part of the agreement, is surely over as well. This fact strikes at the heart of the Sabbath command, since it was the sign of the covenant relationship between God and Israel.

If we look more closely at the New Testament and consider further the writings of the apostles, the group to which Christ entrusted the work of establishing the Church, to which present-day Christians belong, we find the Sabbath directly addressed. Paul, who had to fight a constant battle against the 'Judiazers', a group who challenged his teaching that followers of Christ were free from the Law and specifically circumcision, writes these words: 'Therefore do not let anyone judge you by what you eat or drink, or with regard to a religious festival, a New Moon celebration or a Sabbath day...' (Colossians 2:16). He also said, 'One man considers one day more sacred than another; another man considers every day alike. Each one should be fully convinced in his own mind' (Romans 14:5). The clear implication from these observations is that contemporary Christians are under no compulsion to observe a communal Sabbath based on Old Testament Law.

The original question concerned the applicability of Old Testament Law and I hope I have answered that, and shown its ramifications for the fourth Commandment.

(I do wish to say here that I am not antinomian – i.e. against law – and that is an issue I address at the end of this piece.) There is, however, another argument for Sabbath observance that pre-dates Jewish Law and is universal in its scope, not simply limited to the Hebrew nation.

We read the following in Genesis 2:1–3: 'Thus the heavens and the earth were completed in all their vast array. By the seventh day God had finished the work he had been doing; so on the seventh day he rested from all his work. And God blessed the seventh day and made it holy, because on it he rested from all the work of creating that he had done.' Here, surely, is a more powerful line of reasoning for a mandatory and common day of rest; one that is written into the very fabric of the created order.

I would preface the following analysis by saying that this is a standpoint with which I have much sympathy. Nevertheless, I do not believe it does provide a basis for a compulsory Sabbath. If this is a so-called 'creation ordinance', it does not appear to be mandatory. The verses only make reference to what God did and make no mention of our responsibility. There is no command here. The fact that there is no record of Sabbath observance from Adam until Moses supports this view.

Compare this passage with Genesis 2:18–25, which records the institution of marriage. This is also a 'creation ordinance', but no one would argue that it is obligatory to all. In the New Testament, celibacy and singleness are considered equally valid options (see Matthew 19:10–12) and even superior (see 1 Corinthians 7:1,7).

The New Testament treats the Genesis passage about the seventh day symbolically and eschatologically, not as a creation imperative. In the book of Hebrews it is interpreted in terms of the salvation rest that is available through Christ and the believer's future heavenly rest.

These points are alluded to in Genesis 5, in association with a reference to Noah: 'He named him Noah and said, "He will comfort us [some translations say "bring us relief" or "give us rest"] in the labour and painful toil of our hands caused by the ground the LORD has cursed"' (v. 29). I think it is a valid view that Lamech, who spoke these words, thought that Noah was God's promised Saviour (see Genesis 3:15). Of course, he was in one sense – God chose him to preserve life through the Flood – but he was not *the* Saviour. The 'comfort' or 'rest' referred to here is the removal of God's curse that arose from Adam's disobedience.

My conclusion, then, is that God's rest, recorded in Genesis 2, is more symbolic than prescriptive. It is representative of the inherent goodness and harmony in his creation – a 'rest' that was shattered by the Fall, and the restoration of which God is now working towards, with Christ crucified and resurrected as the foundation.

I do, though, see a clear principle of rest in these verses which fundamentally challenges the rhythm and pace of Western culture. Many have commented wisely not only on the benefits of regular rest, but of regular *communal* rest. Theoretically, my leanings are still on the side of a shared 'Sabbath'. Quite how that could work in practice is another matter altogether – which brings us back to the kind of society we have created. Despite my theoretical leanings, however, I am convinced that, whether on the basis of created order or Old Testament Law, there is no biblical imperative for contemporary believers to observe the Sabbath or Sunday as a day of rest.

Once I did not compete on Sunday because of my

commitment to serve Christ. Now I compete out of an equally deep commitment, based on the full conviction that I have the freedom to do so.

Nevertheless, there is a very real paradox in my present position, one which I have already touched upon. In practice, my Sundays are not much different from the way they were. I only competed on Sunday on three occasions during 1999 and the status of Sunday as a family day, a day of relaxation and communal worship at church, remains largely unchanged. It is something I cherish as much now as I did prior to my change of heart. I am no doubt more relaxed about what I will or will not do – for example, I am writing these words in a few quiet moments before we all head off to church – but I am as committed as ever to the principle of rest and the necessity of regular Christian fellowship.

This last point is vital. If, in regarding 'every day alike', a believer is starved of meeting with other believers, I think very serious consideration needs to be given as to the wisdom of such a course of action. Of course, Christian fellowship is not limited to Sunday services. One could argue quite accurately that Sunday services only scratch the surface of true Christian community. But I hope the point is well made. Elsewhere in this book, there is testimony to the spiritual effect of isolation in my own life. As believers we cannot afford to neglect regular, close Christian contact if we hope to serve God effectively.

As something of a postscript, I am very much aware that what I have written has probably posed as many questions as it has supplied answers. Therefore, I want to take a few lines to address what I perceive to be a couple of the principal queries or objections.

First, I am not dismissing the Old Testament Law as

irrelevant. I would be on a collision course with
2 Timothy 3:16 if I did. The Mosaic Law is a treasure trove
of wisdom that teaches us many things about the character
of God and his dealings with humanity. Take these exam-
ples: the Jewish feasts and sacrificial system, which beautifully portray the life and ministry of Jesus; the seemingly
pointless purification laws, which surely speak volumes
about the absolute holiness of God; the principle of
jubilee, mirrored in the present-day campaign called
Jubilee 2000, that seeks to relieve the burden of un-
payable debt crippling so many Third World countries.
Saying that the Law does not have jurisdiction over us
does not infer that it is of no value to us.

Second, the question is one that Paul himself raises with
reference to the same debate, i.e. the application of Old
Testament Law: 'For sin shall not be your master, because you
are not under law, but under grace. What then? Shall we sin
because we are not under law but under grace? By no
means!' (Romans 6:14–15). I agree. Asserting that the Jewish
Law does not bind believers now does not mean that we are
free to live how we choose – or, more accurately, to indulge
our sinful natures. Jeremiah 31 speaks of a new covenant that
God will make with Israel, one that still awaits future fulfilment, I believe. Nevertheless, as believers today, I do think
that we enjoy one of the benefits of this covenant: God's Law
written on our hearts. In one sense, there is no need for an
external moral code for Christians, since we are new crea-
tions in Christ, indwelt by God's Spirit. There is a part of us
that naturally does the things of God. But the principle of sin
is still at work, a reality to which we can all testify.

What about that? If we look at the various epistles
which the apostles wrote, we see that they are actually
full of commands on how to live. They were under no

illusions about the Christian's continuing capacity for wrongdoing. Therefore, although the Mosaic Law is redundant as a rule of life for believers today, we are not without a thoroughly rigorous set of guidelines by which to live. (Dispensational theology refers to it as 'the law of Christ', from Galatians 6:2.)

As a final comment on the 'Sunday question', it is instructive to note that the Sabbath command is the only one from the Ten Commandments that is *not* repeated after Pentecost, the time when the Church began.

The Career of Jonathan Edwards

The following lists do not contain every single competition Jonathan Edwards has taken part in, but do include all of his most significant performances.

Key to abbreviations

AAA	Amateur Athletic Association	Q	Qualification round
dnq	did not qualify/overall placing in competition	s	semi-final
		w	wind-assisted (greater than two metres per second following, so illegal for record purposes)
ht	heat		
i	indoor		
IAC	International Athletes Club	WR	world record
m	metres	x	no-jump
NR	national record	-	pass
pb	personal best		

Personal Bests

Event	Mark	Wind	Venue	Date
50m	5.9i		Gateshead	14 Jan 1993
			Gateshead	15 Jan 1998
60m	6.73i		Tampere	4 Feb 1998
100m	10.48	1.2	Tallahassee	11 May 1996
200m	22.2		Cudworth	5 Aug 1989
Long Jump	7.45w	2.4	Belfast	31 Aug 1992
	7.41		Rotherham	22 Aug 1992
Triple Jump	18.43w	2.4	Lille (Villeneuve d'Ascq)	25 Jun 1995
	18.29	1.3	Gothenburg	7 Aug 1995

A TIME TO JUMP

Major Championship placings (at Triple Jump)

Gold
1995 World Championships
1998 European Indoor Championships
1998 European Championships
2000 Olympic Games

Silver
1990 Commonwealth Games
1994 Commonwealth Games
1996 Olympic Games
1997 World Championships

Bronze
1993 World Championships
1999 World Championships

6th
1993 World Indoor Championships
1994 European Championships

9th
1987 World Student Games

Non-qualifier
1988 Olympic Games
1992 Olympic Games

Other major events (at Triple Jump)

World Cup winner 1992 and 3rd 1989
European Cup winner 1995, 1996, 1997, 1998; 2nd 1993 and 1999; 4th 1994
AAA Champion 1989, 1994, 1998 and 2nd 1990
United Kingdom Champion 1989, 1992 and 2nd 1990, 1993
English Schools Champion 1984

* International Athletic Foundation Athlete of the Year 1995
* BBC Sports Personality of 1995
* 'L'Equipe' Champion of Champions 1995
* 22 successive wins at triple jump between 11 June 1995 and 27 July 1996

Annual progression

	Triple Jump	Long Jump	60m	100m	British Caps	17m+ Competitions
1981	12.65	5.47	-	-	-	-
1982	12.75	-	-	-	-	-
1983	13.84	-	-	-	-	-
1984	15.01w/14.87	6.64	-	-	-	-
1985	15.09	-	-	-	-	-
1986	16.05	6.95	-	-	-	-

	Triple Jump	Long Jump	60m	100m	British Caps	17m+ Competitions
1987	16.35	-	-	11.0	-	-
1988	16.74	6.97	-	-	1 + 1 England	-
1989	17.28	7.23	-	10.8/10.6w	4 + 1 England	2
1990	16.93w/16.51	-	-	10.6w/10.63w/10.97	1 + 2 England	-
1991	17.43	7.28	-	10.8	2	4
1992	17.34	7.45w/ 7.41	-	10.6w/10.7/10.80	3	5
1993	17.70w/17.44	-	6.77i	10.69w/10.8/10.92	7	9
1994	17.39	7.27	6.95i	-	5 + 1 England	5
1995	18.43w/18.29	-	-	10.7	3	15
1996	17.88	-	-	10.48	3	16
1997	17.74	-	-	-	2	7
1998	18.01	-	6.73i	-	3	18
1999	17.71w/17.52	-	-	-	3	11
2000	17.71	-	-	-	1	11
Totals					38 + 5 England	103

Records set at Triple Jump

World [3]

17.98	1.8	Salamanca	18 Jul 1995
18.16	1.3	Gothenburg	7 Aug 1995
18.29	1.3	Gothenburg	7 Aug 1995

British [7]

17.58	1.2	Loughborough	11 Jun 1995
17.72	0.5	Lille (Villeneuve d'Ascq)	25 Jun 1995
17.72	1.1	Gateshead	2 Jul 1995
17.74	1.7	Gateshead	2 Jul 1995
17.98	1.8	Salamanca	18 Jul 1995
18.16	1.3	Gothenburg	7 Aug 1995
18.29	1.3	Gothenburg	7 Aug 1995

British indoor [1]

17.64i		Birmingham	15 Feb 1998

Best Series of Triple Jumps

(Includes all 17.90m+ series, and all those with four or more 17m jumps)

					1	2	3	4	5	6
18.43w	European Cup	Lille (Villeneuve d'Ascq)	25 Jun 1995		17.90w	18.43w	17.72	18.39w	-	-
18.29	World Championships	Gothenburg	Aug 1995		18.16	18.29	-	-	17.49	-
18.08w	BUPA International	Sheffield	23 Jul 1995		17.81w	x	-	17.45	-	18.08w
18.03w	BUPA Gateshead Games	Gateshead	2 Jul 1995		14.21	17.60	18.03w	17.72	-	17.74
18.01	Bislett Games	Oslo	9 Jul 1998		17.33	16.77	15.78	17.46	-	18.01
18.00	McDonald's Games	Crystal Palace	27 Aug 1995		17.42	17.42	-	x	-	18.00
17.99	European Championships	Budapest	23 Aug 1998		17.84w	17.53	-	-	-	17.99
17.98	Diputacion de Salamanca	Salamanca	18 Jul 1995		17.39	17.98	-	13.43w	-	-
17.79	Weltklasse	Zürich	14 Aug 1996		17.17	17.40	x	17.15	-	17.79
17.71	Olympic Games	Sydney	25 Sep 2000		17.12	17.37	17.71	17.06	-	x
17.69	Internationales Stadionfest	Berlin	30 Aug 1996		17.13	15.82	17.26	17.16	17.69	-
17.67	Meeting del internazionale Sestriere	Sestriere	7 Aug 1996		17.11w	17.22w	17.26w	x	17.28	17.67
17.69	World Championships	Athens	8 Aug 1997		17.33	x	16.80	17.66	17.57	17.69

Career record

* denotes the best legal jump within a series where the furthest mark had illegal wind assistance

Mark	Event	Place (Cap)	Meeting	Venue	Date
5.47	Long Jump	5	Devon Schools Championships (Intermediate Boys)	Plymouth	13 Jun 1981
12.65	Triple Jump	2	Devon Schools Championships (Intermediate Boys)	Plymouth	13 Jun 1981

Mark	Event	Place (Cap)	Meeting	Venue	Date
12.75 pb		Triple Jump 4	South West Schools Championships (Intermediate Boys)	Yeovil	19 Jun 1982
13.84 pb		Triple Jump 9	English Schools Championships	Plymouth	8 Jul 1983
14.52 pb		Triple Jump 1	North Devon Schools Championships	Bideford	16 May 1984
6.64 pb		Long Jump 1	Devon Schools Championships	Plymouth	9 Jun 1984
14.87 pb		Triple Jump 1	Devon Schools Championships	Plymouth	9 Jun 1984
14.75		Triple Jump 1	South West Schools Championships	Bideford	16 Jun 1984
14.65		Triple Jump 1	Southern League	Brighton	30 Jun 1984
15.01w pb	4.0	Triple Jump 1	English Schools Championships	Thurrock	14 Jul 1984
14.74		Triple Jump 3	South v Loughborough v Civil Service	Crystal Palace	24 Apr 1985
14.99 pb		Triple Jump 2	British Universities Championships	Crystal Palace	6 May 1985
15.09 pb	1.2	Triple Jump 1	Scottish Championships	Edinburgh	22 Jun 1985
14.75		Triple Jump 1	Southern League	Ealing	17 Aug 1985
14.94		Triple Jump 1	Southern League	Yeovil	31 Aug 1985
16.05 pb	1.9	Triple Jump 1	British Universities Championships	Derby	5 May 1986
6.95 pb		Long Jump 1	Northern League	Gateshead	10 May 1986
15.26		Triple Jump 1	Northern League	Gateshead	10 May 1986
15.73w	>2.0	Triple Jump 1	Northern Championships	Gateshead	7 Jun 1986
14.37		Triple Jump 4	Loughborough v AAA	Loughborough	14 Jun 1986
15.33w	>2.0	Triple Jump Q	AAA Championships	Crystal Palace	21 Jun 1986
		Triple Jump Fouled out	AAA Championships	Crystal Palace	21 Jun 1986
15.41		Triple Jump 1	British Universities Championships	Edinburgh	2 May 1987
16.35 pb		Triple Jump 1	Northern League	Derby	9 May 1987
16.22	1.3	Triple Jump 2	Scottish Championships	Edinburgh	20 Jun 1987
16.27		Triple Jump 1	Northern Championships	Wigan	27 Jun 1987
16.18	0.0	Triple Jump Q	World Student Games	Zagreb	15 Jul 1987
15.96	1.3	Triple Jump 9	World Student Games	Zagreb	18 Jul 1987
14.50		Triple Jump 1	Northern League	Kirkby	25 Jul 1987
15.81		Triple Jump 5	Dairy Crest Games	Crystal Palace	22 Aug 1987
15.86		Triple Jump 1	British League Qualifier	Stoke	5 Sep 1987
14.88		Triple Jump 1	Northern League Cup Final	Gateshead	12 Sep 1987
15.84i		Triple Jump 2	Scottish Indoor Championships	Glasgow	16 Jan 1988
16.37i pb		Triple Jump 4(1)	England v USA	Cosford	12 Mar 1988
6.97 pb		Long Jump 1	Northern League	Gateshead	7 May 1988
14.20		Triple Jump 1	Northern League	Gateshead	7 May 1988

Mark		Event Place (Cap)		Meeting	Venue	Date
16.38 pb		Triple Jump	4	Kodak Classic	Gateshead	16 Jul 1988
16.74 pb		Triple Jump	1	Northern League Cup	Newcastle	23 Jul 1988
16.53w	2.8	Triple Jump	2	Miller Lite IAC International	Edinburgh	29 Jul 1988
16.47		Triple Jump	*		Edinburgh	29 Jul 1988
14.87		Triple Jump	1	Northern League	Kirkby	13 Aug 1988
15.88	0.0	Triple Jump	(2) dnq/23	Olympic Games	Seoul	23 Sep 1988
15.71i		Triple Jump	1	Scottish Indoor Championships	Glasgow	14 Jan 1989
16.13i		Triple Jump	2(3)	Great Britain v West Germany	Glasgow	28 Jan 1989
15.83i		Triple Jump	2	AAA Indoor Championships	Cosford	3 Feb 1989
15.94i		Triple Jump	6(4)	Great Britain v USA v USSR	Glasgow	10 Mar 1989
10.6w pb	>2.0	100m	1	Northern League	Carlisle	13 May 1989
7.02 pb		Long Jump	1	Northern League	Carlisle	13 May 1989
15.31		Triple Jump	1	Northern League	Carlisle	13 May 1989
10.8 pb	1.6	100m	2	North East Championships	Jarrow	20 May 1989
16.06	0.9	Triple Jump	1	North East Championships	Jarrow	20 May 1989
16.07	1.1	Triple Jump	1	Midlands v North v Wales	Birmingham	24 May 1989
16.63	1.5	Triple Jump	1	Inter-Counties Championships	Corby	29 May 1989
16.54w	2.7	Triple Jump	1	United Kingdom Championships	Jarrow	4 Jun 1989
16.72	-0.7	Triple Jump	1		Helsinki	9 Jun 1989
16.92w pb	4.7	Triple Jump	3(5)	Great Britain v USSR v USA v West Germany	Birmingham	24 Jun 1989
16.86 pb	1.0	Triple Jump	*		Birmingham	24 Jun 1989
17.07w pb	3.4	Triple Jump	2	Gran Premio Ciudad de Vigo	Vigo	30 Jun 1989
15.87	1.8	Triple Jump	*		Vigo	30 Jun 1989
10.8 pb		100m	1	Northern League	Carlisle	15 Jul 1989
7.23 pb		Long Jump	1	Northern League	Carlisle	15 Jul 1989
11.2		100m	1	Copeland v Tyneside v Cumbria	Whitehaven	22 Jul 1989
16.46		Triple Jump	1	Copeland v Tyneside v Cumbria	Whitehaven	22 Jul 1989
11.0		100m	1	Northern League Cup	Gateshead	29 Jul 1989
16.53		Triple Jump	1	Northern League Cup	Gateshead	29 Jul 1989
10.9		100m	1	Northern League	Cudworth	5 Aug 1989
22.2 pb		200m	1	Northern League	Cudworth	5 Aug 1989
16.53	0.5	Triple Jump	1	AAA Championships	Birmingham	11 Aug 1989
16.72	0.4	Triple Jump	4	Internationales Stadionfest	West Berlin	18 Aug 1989
16.91 pb	-0.2	Triple Jump	1(6)	England v Oceania v Italy	Gateshead	28 Aug 1989
17.28 pb	1.1	Triple Jump	3(7)	IAAF World Cup	Barcelona	9 Sep 1989

The Career of Jonathan Edwards

Mark		Event	Place (Cap)	Meeting	Venue	Date
16.83w	2.2	Triple Jump	1	McVities Challenge Invitation	Crystal Palace	15 Sep 1989
16.67	2.0	Triple Jump	*		Crystal Palace	15 Sep 1989
10.6w pb	2.3	100m	3		Sydney	9 Jan 1990
16.19		Triple Jump	1		Sydney	13 Jan 1990
10.63w pb	5.0	100m	6		Hamilton	17 Jan 1990
15.61	-0.8	Triple Jump	3		Auckland	20 Jan 1990
16.19	-0.1	Triple Jump	1		North Shore City (NZL)	23 Jan 1990
16.50w	2.3	Triple Jump	Q(8)	Commonwealth Games	Auckland	2 Feb 1990
16.93w	2.5	Triple Jump	2	Commonwealth Games	Auckland	3 Feb 1990
11.1		100m	3	Tyneside League	Gateshead	2 May 1990
10.97 pb		100m	1	North East Championships	Gateshead	19 May 1990
15.49	-0.1	Triple Jump	2	United Kingdom Championships	Cardiff	2 Jun 1990
16.41	1.0	Triple Jump	13	Grand Prix Slovakia	Bratislava	20 Jun 1990
16.84w	2.6	Triple Jump	2(9)	Great Britain v GDR v Canada	Gateshead	29 Jun 1990
16.42	1.8	Triple Jump	*		Gateshead	29 Jun 1990
16.14	-0.3	Triple Jump	6	Compaq IAC Grand Prix	Edinburgh	6 Jul 1990
		Triple Jump Fouled out		Athletissima	Lausanne	14 Jul 1990
15.79	-0.1	Triple Jump	8	Royal Mail Parcels Games	Crystal Palace	20 Jul 1990
16.51	0.7	Triple Jump	2	AAA Championships	Birmingham	4 Aug 1990
15.91	0.2	Triple Jump	Q	AAA Championships	Birmingham	4 Aug 1990
16.61w	3.0	Triple Jump	5	IDAG Galan	Malmö	7 Aug 1990
15.89	1.2	Triple Jump	5		Stockholm	13 Aug 1990
15.99		Triple Jump	8	Weltklasse	Zürich	15 Aug 1990
16.15	-0.3	Triple Jump	2(10)	England v Commonwealth	Gateshead	17 Aug 1990
11.0		100m	1	Tyneside League	Gateshead	1 May 1991
10.8 pb		100m	1	Gateshead Open	Gateshead	25 May 1991
17.21	-1.4	Triple Jump	1		Dijon	15 Jun 1991
17.36	2.0	Triple Jump	2(11)	Great Britain v Germany	Crystal Palace	19 Jun 1991
11.0		100m	2	Northern League	Carlisle	22 Jun 1991
7.28 pb		Long Jump	1	Northern League	Carlisle	22 Jun 1991
17.43 pb		Triple Jump	1	Northern League	Carlisle	22 Jun 1991
16.96	-0.5	Triple Jump	4	DN Galan	Stockholm	3 Jul 1991
17.11w	2.4	Triple Jump	1	Palio Citta Della Quercia	Rovereto	13 Jul 1991
16.12	0.2	Triple Jump	*		Rovereto	13 Jul 1991
16.52	1.5	Triple Jump	3(12)	Great Britain v USSR	Edinburgh	19 Jul 1991
16.50	0.7	Triple Jump	2	AAA Championships	Birmingham	26 Jul 1991
16.49	0.9	Triple Jump	8	IDAG Galan	Malmö	5 Aug 1991
16.57	-1.3	Triple Jump	1	Pearl Assurance Invitation	Gateshead	9 Aug 1991
10.6w pb	>2.0	100m	1	North East Championships	Gateshead	16 May 1992
10.9		100m	1	Gateshead Open	Gateshead	23 May 1992
16.94		Triple Jump	3	Olympicscher Tag	Jena	28 May 1992
17.18	0.7	Triple Jump	1	Slovnaft	Bratislava	1 Jun 1992
17.26	0.8	Triple Jump	1(13)	Great Britain v Italy v Hungary	Sheffield	5 Jun 1992

Mark		Event	Place [Cap]	Meeting	Venue	Date
16.51	0.5	Triple Jump	1	United Kingdom Championships	Sheffield	6 Jun 1992
10.80 pb	-0.1	100m	5h1	AAA Championships	Birmingham	27 Jun 1992
16.79	0.0	Triple Jump	6	Athletissima	Lausanne	8 Jul 1992
17.22	0.8	Triple Jump	1	TSB Grand Prix	Crystal Palace	10 Jul 1992
16.70	0.3	Triple Jump	5	Nikaia	Nice	15 Jul 1992
17.09	-0.3	Triple Jump	1	Vauxhall Invitation	Gateshead	17 Jul 1992
15.76	0.9	Triple Jump	dnq/ 35(14)	Olympic Games	Barcelona	1 Aug 1992
10.7 pb		100m	1	Northern League Cup	Leeds	15 Aug 1992
7.37 pb		Long Jump	1	Northern League Cup	Leeds	15 Aug 1992
16.40		Triple Jump	1 – guest	Northern League Cup	Leeds	15 Aug 1992
16.33	0.0	Triple Jump	10	Weltklasse	Zürich	19 Aug 1992
11.1		100m	2	Northern League	Rotherham	22 Aug 1992
7.41 pb		Long Jump	1	Northern League	Rotherham	22 Aug 1992
16.25		Triple Jump	1	Northern League	Rotherham	22 Aug 1992
15.68w	2.1	Triple Jump	5	Palio Citta Della Quercia	Rovereto	26 Aug 1992
15.63	1.2	Triple Jump	*		Rovereto	26 Aug 1992
7.45w pb	2.4	Long Jump	4	Les Jones Memorial	Belfast	31 Aug 1992
7.39	1.0	Long Jump	*		Belfast	31 Aug 1992
16.48	0.2	Triple Jump	8	IAAF Grand Prix Final	Turin	4 Sep 1992
17.34	1.7	Triple Jump	1(15)	IAAF World Cup	Havana	26 Sep 1992
5.9i pb		50m	1	Winter Standards Meeting	Gateshead	14 Jan 1993
16.24i		Triple Jump	1	Winter Standards Meeting	Gateshead	14 Jan 1993
16.80i		Triple Jump	2(16)	Great Britain v Russia	Glasgow	30 Jan 1993
16.45i		Triple Jump	3(17)	Great Britain v USA	Birmingham	13 Feb 1993
17.16i pb		Triple Jump	1	TSB International	Birmingham	20 Feb 1993
6.79i		60m	1h4	AAA Indoor Championships	Birmingham	27 Feb 1993
6.77i		60m	5s1	AAA Indoor Championships	Birmingham	27 Feb 1993
16.58i		Triple Jump	Q(18)	IAAF World Indoor Championships	Toronto	12 Mar 1993
16.76i		Triple Jump	6	IAAF World Indoor Championships	Toronto	13 Mar 1993
16.79w	2.1	Triple Jump	2(19)	Great Britain v Italy v Hungary	Portsmouth	5 Jun 1993
16.61	1.1	Triple Jump	*		Portsmouth	5 Jun 1993
17.18w	2.3	Triple Jump	2	United Kingdom Championships	Crystal Palace	12 Jun 1993
16.67	1.9	Triple Jump	*		Crystal Palace	12 Jun 1993
17.28	0.5	Triple Jump	1	Pearl Belfast Games	Belfast	19 Jun 1993
17.27	-1.0	Triple Jump	2(20)	European Cup (his first competition on a Sunday)	Rome	27 Jun 1993
17.70w pb	2.9	Triple Jump	1(21)	Great Britain v USA	Edinburgh	2 Jul 1993
16.66	1.0	Triple Jump	*		Edinburgh	2 Jul 1993
17.14w	3.3	Triple Jump	1	Bislett Games	Oslo	10 Jul 1993

The Career of Jonathan Edwards

Mark		Event	Place (Cap)	Meeting	Venue	Date
17.07	1.4	Triple Jump	*		Oslo	10 Jul 1993
10.69w	3.8	100m	5h3	AAA Championships	Birmingham	16 Jul 1993
16.94w	3.5	Triple Jump	2	TSB Games	Crystal Palace	23 Jul 1993
16.77	1.1	Triple Jump	*		Crystal Palace	23 Jul 1993
17.22	0.8	Triple Jump	1	Vauxhall Invitational	Gateshead	30 Jul 1993
10.8		100m	1	Northern League	Blackpool	7 Aug 1993
16.56		Triple Jump	1	Northern League	Blackpool	7 Aug 1993
16.98	0.7	Triple Jump	QQ(22)	IAAF World Championships	Stuttgart	15 Aug 1993
17.44 pb	0.1	Triple Jump	3	IAAF World Championships	Stuttgart	16 Aug 1993
17.27w	2.2	Triple Jump	1	McDonald's Games	Sheffield	29 Aug 1993
16.94	2.0	Triple Jump	*		Sheffield	29 Aug 1993
10.92	-0.5	100m	7	IAAF Grand Prix Final	Crystal Palace	10 Sep 1993
16.65i		Triple Jump	3(23)	Great Britain v Russia	Glasgow	29 Jan 1994
16.83i		Triple Jump	2	Sparkassen Cup	Stuttgart	6 Feb 1994
6.95i		60m	7	Great Britain v USA (Invitation race)	Glasgow	12 Feb 1994
16.71i		Triple Jump	2(24)	Great Britain v USA	Glasgow	12 Feb 1994
16.11i		Triple Jump	7	TSB International	Birmingham	26 Feb 1994
10.85		100m	2	North East Championships	Gateshead	14 May 1994
7.27		Long Jump	1	North East Championships	Gateshead	15 May 1994
17.02w	3.9	Triple Jump	4	Slovnaft	Bratislava	1 Jun 1994
16.83	0.7	Triple Jump	*		Bratislava	1 Jun 1994
16.97w	5.6	Triple Jump	5	Gran Premio Diputacion	Seville	5 Jun 1994
16.73	2.0	Triple Jump	*		Seville	5 Jun 1994
17.39	1.9	Triple Jump	1	AAA Championships	Sheffield	12 Jun 1994
16.88	0.8	Triple Jump	4(25)	European Cup	Birmingham	26 Jun 1994
17.05	1.2	Triple Jump	2	BUPA Gateshead Games	Gateshead	1 Jul 1994
16.88	0.5	Triple Jump	1	TSB Challenge	Edinburgh	8 Jul 1994
16.73w	2.6	Triple Jump	6	DN Galan	Stockholm	12 Jul 1994
16.20	-0.1	Triple Jump	*		Stockholm	12 Jul 1994
16.71	0.5	Triple Jump	3	TSB Invitational	Crystal Palace	15 Jul 1994
16.80	-0.1	Triple Jump	1(26)	Great Britain v USA	Gateshead	20 Jul 1994
16.57		Triple Jump	7	Goodwill Games	St Petersburg	29 Jul 1994
17.06	0.0	Triple Jump	3	Herculis Grand Prix	Monaco	2 Aug 1994
16.72	0.1	Triple Jump	Q(27)	European Championships	Helsinki	11 Aug 1994
16.85	0.5	Triple Jump	6	European Championships	Helsinki	13 Aug 1994
16.52	0.9	Triple Jump	Q(28)	Commonwealth Games	Victoria	27 Aug 1994
17.00	1.6	Triple Jump	2	Commonwealth Games	Victoria	28 Aug 1994
15.81	0.3	Triple Jump	8	IAAF Grand Prix Final	Paris	3 Sep 1994
15.85w	2.1	Triple Jump	7	McDonald's Games	Sheffield	4 Sep 1994
10.7		100m	1	Northern League	Jarrow	6 May 1995
17.58 NR	1.2	Triple Jump	1	Loughborough Students v England British Students v British Juniors	Loughborough	11 Jun 1995
17.46	-0.3	Triple Jump	1	Meeting Vittel du Pas de Calais	Lille (Villeneuve d'Ascq)	17 Jun 1995

Mark		Event	Place (Cap)	Meeting	Venue	Date
18.43w pb	2.4	Triple Jump	1(29)	European Cup	Lille (Villeneuve d'Ascq)	25 Jun 1995
17.72 NR	0.5	Triple Jump	*		Lille (Villeneuve d'Ascq)	25 Jun 1995
18.03w	2.9	Triple Jump	1	BUPA Gateshead Games	Gateshead	2 Jul 1995
17.74 NR	1.7	Triple Jump	*		Gateshead	2 Jul 1995
17.69	0.5	Triple Jump	1	KP Games	Crystal Palace	7 Jul 1995
17.98 WR	1.8	Triple Jump	1	Diputacion de Salamanca	Salamanca	18 Jul 1995
18.08w	2.5	Triple Jump	1	BUPA International	Sheffield	23 Jul 1995
17.45	1.0	Triple Jump	*		Sheffield	23 Jul 1995
17.58w	3.3	Triple Jump	1	Meeting internazionale del Sestriere	Sestriere	29 Jul 1995
17.46	1.4	Triple Jump	Q(30)	IAAF World Championships	Gothenburg	5 Aug 1995
18.29 WR	1.3	Triple Jump	1	IAAF World Championships	Gothenburg	7 Aug 1995
17.49	0.4	Triple Jump	1(31)	Great Britain v USA	Gateshead	21 Aug 1995
17.60	0.3	Triple Jump	1	Van Damme Memorial	Brussels	25 Aug 1995
18.00	1.3	Triple Jump	1	McDonald's Games	Crystal Palace	27 Aug 1995
17.35	0.8	Triple Jump	1	Internationales Stadionfest	Berlin	1 Sep 1995
17.29	1.6	Triple Jump	1	Rieti '95	Rieti	5 Sep 1995
2.97i		Standing Long Jump	2	BBC TV Sports Review of 1995	London (Westminster)	10 Dec 1995
10.48 pb	1.2	100m	2	Seminole Twilight Meeting	Tallahassee	11 May 1996
17.59w	3.7	Triple Jump	1	Atlanta Grand Prix	Atlanta	18 May 1996
17.45	1.4	Triple Jump	*		Atlanta	18 May 1996
17.79w	3.3	Triple Jump	1(32)	European Cup	Madrid	2 Jun 1996
17.55	0.0	Triple Jump	1	Golden Gala	Rome	5 Jun 1996
17.82	1.6	Triple Jump	1	World Games	Helsinki	25 Jun 1996
17.02	1.0	Triple Jump	1	BUPA Games	Gateshead	30 Jun 1996
17.68	-1.6	Triple Jump	1	Bislett Games	Oslo	5 Jul 1996
17.29	0.3	Triple Jump	1	DN Galan	Stockholm	8 Jul 1996
17.52	1.4	Triple Jump	1	Securicor Games	Crystal Palace	12 Jul 1996
16.96	0.0	Triple Jump	Q(33)	Olympic Games	Atlanta	26 Jul 1996
17.88	0.9	Triple Jump	2	Olympic Games	Atlanta	27 Jul 1996
17.67	1.1	Triple Jump	1	Meeting internazionale del Sestriere	Sestriere	7 Aug 1996
16.93	0.3	Triple Jump	1	Performance Games	Crystal Palace	11 Aug 1996
17.79	-0.7	Triple Jump	1	Weltklasse	Zürich	14 Aug 1996
17.38	-0.5	Triple Jump	1(34)	Great Britain v International Select	Gateshead	19 Aug 1996
17.50	0.0	Triple Jump	1	Van Damme Memorial	Brussels	23 Aug 1996
16.90	1.1	Triple Jump	1	McDonald's Games	Sheffield	25 Aug 1996
17.69	-0.5	Triple Jump	1	Internationales Stadionfest	Berlin	30 Aug 1996
17.59	1.3	Triple Jump	1	IAAF Grand Prix Final	Milan	7 Sep 1996
17.38	1.2	Triple Jump	2	Super TOTO Meeting	Tokyo	15 Sep 1996
17.21	1.8	Triple Jump	1	Riga – 97	Riga	30 May 1997
17.35	-0.2	Triple Jump	2	Slovnaft	Bratislava	10 Jun 1997
16.94	-0.6	Triple Jump	1	Tallinn – 97	Tallinn	13 Jun 1997

The Career of Jonathan Edwards

Mark		Event Place (Cap)	Meeting	Venue	Date
17.74	0.9	Triple Jump 1(35)	European Cup	Munich	22 Jun 1997
17.54	0.6	Triple Jump 1	Securicor Grand Prix	Sheffield	29 Jun 1997
17.28	0.4	Triple Jump Q(36)	IAAF World Championships	Athens	6 Aug 1997
17.69	0.3	Triple Jump 2	IAAF World Championships	Athens	8 Aug 1997
16.74	-0.5	Triple Jump 8	Weltklasse	Zürich	13 Aug 1997
16.84	-0.2	Triple Jump 2	Spar British Challenge	Crystal Palace	17 Aug 1997
17.38	-0.5	Triple Jump 1	Lahti Games	Lahti	20 Aug 1997
16.59	0.4	Triple Jump 2	BUPA Series Final	Gateshead	7 Sep 1997
1:38.36		4x200m Relay 4 (leg 1)	BUPA Series Final	Gateshead	7 Sep 1997
5.9i pb		50m 1	Winter Standards Meeting	Gateshead	15 Jan 1998
6.85i		60m 1h	Telenor Indoor Games	Stange	24 Jan 1998
17.26i		Triple Jump 1	Telenor Indoor Games	Stange	24 Jan 1998
6.73i		60m 4	Meet of the Stars	Tampere	4 Feb 1998
17.23i		Triple Jump 1	Meet of the Stars	Tampere	4 Feb 1998
6.81i		60m 2h4	AAA Indoor Championships	Birmingham	7 Feb 1998
17.64i NR		Triple Jump 1	BUPA Indoor Grand Prix	Birmingham	15 Feb 1998
17.15i		Triple Jump Q(37)	European Indoor Championships	Valencia	27 Feb 1998
17.43i		Triple Jump 1	European Indoor Championships	Valencia	1 Mar 1998
16.22i		Triple Jump 2	Gunma International	Maebashi	7 Mar 1998
17.37	0.6	Triple Jump 1	Engen Series	Pietersburg	11 Mar 1998
16.96w	2.2	Triple Jump 1	Leeds International	Leeds	7 Jun 1998
17.04	-0.3	Triple Jump 1	World Games	Helsinki	13 Jun 1998
17.22	0.4	Triple Jump 1	Tallinn – 98	Tallinn	19 Jun 1998
17.29	1.7	Triple Jump 1(38)	European Cup	St Petersburg	28 Jun 1998
18.01	0.4	Triple Jump 1	Bislett Games	Oslo	9 Jul 1998
17.60	0.0	Triple Jump 1	Golden Gala	Rome	14 Jul 1998
17.18	1.3	Triple Jump 1	BUPA Games	Gateshead	19 Jul 1998
17.65	1.8	Triple Jump 1	Goodwill Games	Uniondale	21 Jul 1998
17.12	-1.6	Triple Jump 1	AAA Championships	Birmingham	26 Jul 1998
17.14	1.6	Triple Jump 1	British Grand Prix	Sheffield	2 Aug 1998
16.99	0.7	Triple Jump 1	DN Galan	Stockholm	5 Aug 1998
		Triple Jump Fouled out	Herculis Grand Prix	Monaco	8 Aug 1998
17.75	-0.2	Triple Jump 1	Welklasse	Zürich	12 Aug 1998
16.97	0.1	Triple Jump Q(39)	European Championships	Budapest	22 Aug 1998
17.99	0.5	Triple Jump 1	European Championships	Budapest	23 Aug 1998
17.00	1.6	Triple Jump 2	Athletissima	Lausanne	25 Aug 1998
16.98	0.6	Triple Jump 1	Engen Grand Prix	Pietersburg	13 Mar 1999
17.01	-0.3	Triple Jump 1	All Africa Meeting	Roodepoort	19 Mar 1999
17.30w	4.1	Triple Jump 1	Engen Summer Series	Cape Town	26 Mar 1999
16.72	0.4	Triple Jump *		Cape Town	26 Mar 1999
17.43	0.2	Triple Jump 1	Live 1999	Nuremburg	13 Jun 1999
17.24	0.7	Triple Jump 2(40)	European Cup	Paris	20 Jun 1999

Mark		Event	Place (Cap)	Meeting	Venue	Date
16.98	0.0	Triple Jump	2	CGU Classic	Gateshead	27 Jun 1999
17.34	0.5	Triple Jump	1	Athletissima	Lausanne	2 Jul 1999
17.71w	3.4	Triple Jump	1	Diputacion de Salamanca	Salamanca	15 Jul 1999
17.52	0.4	Triple Jump	1	Lahti Games	Lahti	28 Jul 1999
17.06	-0.5	Triple Jump	1	CGU British Grand Prix	London	7 Aug 1999
17.28	-0.3	Triple Jump	Q(41)	IAAF World Championships	Seville	23 Aug 1999
17.48	0.4	Triple Jump	3	IAAF World Championships	Seville	25 Aug 1999
17.07	1.1	Triple Jump	1(42)	Great Britain v USA	Glasgow	4 Sep 1999
17.20	1.8	Triple Jump	1	Seminole Twilight Meeting	Tallahassee	13 May 2000
17.23	1.5	Triple Jump	1	Bergen Grand Prix	Bergen	27 Jun 2000
16.81	-0.6	Triple Jump	4	Golden Gala	Rome	30 Jun 2000
17.11	0.0	Triple Jump	1	Israeli Championships	Tel Aviv	23 Jul 2000
17.34	0.2	Triple Jump	1	Norwich Union British Grand Prix	London	5 Aug 2000
17.36	0.2	Triple Jump	1	Weltklasse	Zurich	11 Aug 2000
17.62	1.4	Triple Jump	1	Bayer Meeting	Leverkusen	20 Aug 2000
17.48	0.6	Triple Jump	1	Norwich Union Classic	Gateshead	28 Aug 2000
		Triple Jump	fouled out	Internationales Stadionfest	Berlin	1 Sep 2000
17.32	1.2	Triple Jump	1	Super Meeting	Yokohama	-9 Sep 2000
17.08	0.7	Triple Jump	Q(43)	Olympic Games	Sydney	23 Sep 2000
17.71	0.2	Triple Jump	1	Olympic Games	Sydney	25 Sep 2000
17.12	0.9	Triple Jump	1	IAAF Grand Prix Final	Doha	5 Oct 2000

Compiled by Mark Butler and Tom Hurst, with thanks to Ian Hodge, Peter Matthews, Robert Clarke, Jan Phillips, Barnstaple Library and members of the Association of Track and Field Statisticians and National Union of Track Statisticians.